BEYOND SNOWDEN

BEYOND SNOWDEN

Privacy, Mass Surveillance,
and the Struggle to Reform the NSA

TIMOTHY H. EDGAR

BROOKINGS INSTITUTION PRESS
Washington, D.C.

The Brookings Institution is a private nonprofit organization devoted to research, education, and publication on important issues of domestic and foreign policy. Its principal purpose is to bring the highest quality independent research and analysis to bear on current and emerging policy problems. Interpretations or conclusions in Brookings publications should be understood to be solely those of the authors.

Library of Congress Cataloging-in-Publication data are available.

ISBN 978-0-8157-3063-7 (cloth : alk. paper)
ISBN 978-0-8157-2970-9 (ebook)

9 8 7 6 5 4 3 2

Typeset in Sabon and Trade Gothic

Composition by Elliott Beard

To Anna
who believes in impossible things

CONTENTS

BEYOND SNOWDEN

1

INTRODUCTION: MAKING A DIFFERENCE

AROUND THE TIME EDWARD SNOWDEN BEGAN WORKING FOR THE CENTRAL INTEL-ligence Agency in 2006, I decided to leave my position as a lawyer for the American Civil Liberties Union in the hope I could make a difference by going inside America's growing surveillance state.[1] Surprisingly, senior intelligence officials took a chance on hiring me in a unique new office safeguarding civil liberties and privacy. My job was to advise the director of national intelligence, who oversees the seventeen agencies of the U.S. intelligence community.

Before I joined the government, I had testified before Congress as an ACLU lawyer, arguing against expanded surveillance in the "war on terror." Since information on national security surveillance was secret, my arguments were based on hypothetical scenarios about how intelligence agencies might use their new powers.[2] After joining the government I learned the truth—about bulk collection of data, the weakening of internet security, and other intrusive surveillance activities. The imaginative ways intelligence agencies were using their legal authorities exceeded the most alarming visions I had conjured up in my years as a privacy and civil liberties activist. The government was collecting immense volumes of data both inside and outside the United States, including data pertaining to Americans, creating serious privacy risks.

For the next seven years, I worked with a growing team of internal privacy watchdogs inside the intelligence community. We reviewed the U.S. government's most secret surveillance programs. Our job was to ensure these programs had a firm basis in law and included safeguards to protect privacy and civil liberties. As surprised as I had been by the breadth of surveillance, I was just as surprised by how seriously everyone inside the government took the rules that governed it. We brought the legally questionable surveillance policies of the Bush administration under the supervision of Congress and the judiciary, and devised new oversight mechanisms to ensure compliance with the rules. Our efforts put the U.S. government's mass surveillance programs on a stronger legal basis, helping the intelligence community weather the storm when these programs became public in 2013.

While I am proud of the work I did to keep intelligence agencies in bounds, it is fair to say my success in protecting privacy as an insider was limited. In retrospect, my focus on ensuring that the intelligence agencies were true to the complex and sometimes arbitrary legal rules that govern surveillance caused me to miss the broader impact of the U.S. government's programs on the privacy of all the world's data, and what this meant for the privacy of Americans. The rules that guided my work were designed to prevent "spying on Americans." They were mostly written in the 1970s. They depended on geography and borders in a way that the internet and globalization had made largely obsolete. The digital data, communications, and personal lives of Americans now transcended national boundaries. Compounding the problem, the rules were based on analog technology. They made distinctions that no longer made much sense between types of data, offering inadequate protection in an age of digital surveillance. Inside the intelligence community, these problems were well understood, and many shared my concerns. Our efforts to start a meaningful public dialogue about privacy were largely frustrated by the decisions of top officials to keep modern programs of mass surveillance a secret.

In 2009 I was detailed to the White House national security staff to serve a stint as its first-ever director of privacy and civil liberties. Barack Obama had won election as president with a promise to review the surveillance programs initiated by President George W. Bush after the events of September 11, 2001. I had high hopes that Obama's fresh approach would force needed reforms that would protect privacy. But after Obama took office, he continued and even expanded mass surveillance programs. Despite my lofty White House perch, my broader hopes for reform proved elusive. Obama's top aides showed little interest in reforming mass surveillance until after I left, when Edward Snowden forced them to confront the issue.

In 2013 I left government to pursue research and teaching. As my work to provide privacy and civil liberties safeguards for mass surveillance programs had been highly classified, I expected I would never speak or write publicly about it. Instead, much to my surprise, I found myself thrust into a global conversation about privacy and mass surveillance. Only a few days after my formal resignation in June, the first stories based on secret documents leaked by Snowden appeared in the press. They described surveillance programs on which I had worked. That summer the Obama administration confirmed these programs and declassified details about the rules that governed them, including some of the safeguards I had helped devise.

The Snowden revelations concerned the operations of the largest of the secret "three-letter" intelligence agencies, the National Security Agency. The NSA collects "signals intelligence," which means it scoops up the world's communications, processes them into intelligible form, and turns them into intelligence reports. NSA operations are essential to national security and to international stability, but it is a challenge to reconcile them with the values of a free society. The Snowden revelations forced the NSA to take painful steps to open up. Before Snowden, basic information such as the number of targets affected by court-ordered surveillance was a closely guarded secret, obscuring important facts such as how much surveillance could be authorized by a single court order. Today the head of the intelligence community publishes an annual transparency report, revealing that one such order authorized surveillance of more than 100,000 foreign targets, and that data about Americans collected under that order were queried more than 30,000 times, among other details.[3]

This new transparency would not have happened without Snowden. "Where you're in positions of privileged access," Snowden said, "you see things that may be disturbing." During this interview from a hotel in Hong Kong, Snowden revealed himself to the world as the source of ongoing leaks of classified information. "This is something that's not our place to decide," Snowden said, explaining his decision. "The public needs to decide if these programs and policies are right or wrong."[4] Without a basic level of transparency about mass surveillance programs, the NSA's operations lack democratic legitimacy. The most secret of the government's secret agencies will never be a model of transparency. Still, it has never been more transparent than it is today.

Thanks to Snowden, the government has also been forced to become more accountable for mass surveillance. Before Snowden, the NSA used a secret interpretation of the Patriot Act, the antiterrorism law passed in 2001, to amass a nationwide database of telephone records from American companies of calls to, from, and within the United States. In 2015 a federal appeals court declared this program of bulk collection unlawful.[5] Less than a month later Congress passed the Freedom Act, which replaced this program with an alternative one that leaves the data with the telephone companies.[6] Before passage of the Freedom Act, the secret court that authorizes intelligence surveillance almost never heard more than the government's side of the argument. Now, outside lawyers routinely appear to argue the case for privacy.[7]

More fundamentally, the Snowden revelations have enlarged the way the U.S. government thinks about privacy. Before Snowden, there was no written order, directive, or policy that gave any consideration to the privacy of foreign citizens who live outside the borders of the United States. When intelligence officials asked lawyers like me about privacy, it went without saying that we were talking about American citizens and residents. In 2014 President Obama signed a directive reforming signals intelligence collection, requiring that some privacy protections apply to the personal information that agencies collect about foreigners outside the United States. By 2015 all agencies had issued new procedures, or revised existing procedures, to fulfill this requirement.[8] Today, for the first time in history, it is the policy of the United States that the privacy and civil liberties of everyone in the world must be taken into account when agencies collect signals intelligence.

The Snowden revelations have also helped the public better understand how the NSA's programs targeting foreigners affect the privacy of Americans. At the end of the Bush administration, Congress gave the government broad power to compel American companies to assist in surveillance of foreign targets with a secret court order. Section 702 of the Foreign Intelligence Surveillance Act (FISA) allows collection of data inside the United States belonging to foreign citizens outside the United States. While the law itself was no secret, Snowden leaked the existence of two programs authorized by section 702, the Prism program and "upstream collection." Prism, also known as "downstream collection," allows the NSA to obtain stored e-mails and other communications from American technology companies. Upstream collection gives the NSA access to data in transit across the internet backbone facilities of American telecommunications companies.[9] Both programs permit what critics call a backdoor search: routine queries by other agencies about Americans who may be in contact with the NSA's foreign targets or who may be mentioned in e-mails or other communications. This practice has now been limited, although critics would like stricter limits, including warrants.[10] Such privacy issues used to be known only to people like me: those privileged to attend classified briefings or to participate in the secret proceedings of the Foreign Intelligence Surveillance Court.

In short, the Snowden revelations have made the NSA more transparent, more accountable, and more protective of privacy. Surprisingly, the reforms have also made the NSA more effective. Jack Goldsmith, a former Justice Department official in the George W. Bush administration, marveled in June 2016 that "the intelligence community, and especially the NSA, have emerged in astonishingly good shape" in the aftermath of the Snowden revelations.[11] For example, the system Congress created to end the NSA's bulk collection of telephone records from American companies actually gave NSA analysts access to a broader volume of data than before. This allowed the agency to collect more than 151 million records in 2016, without the NSA having the responsibility for storing the billions of records it used to collect each day under the old program.[12]

Former attorney general Eric Holder has offered warm words for Snowden. "We can certainly argue about the way in which Snowden did what he did, but I think that he actually performed a public service by raising the debate that we engaged in and by the changes that we made," he said in May 2016.[13] Holder's praise raised eyebrows. After all, he was the attorney general when Snowden was charged with serious felonies, including theft of government property and disclosure of classified communications intelligence. I found Holder's views less surprising than many did. I had heard similar views expressed privately by several of my colleagues in the national security community.

WHEN I JOINED THE INTELLIGENCE community, I wondered if I would be able to make a difference. My hope was that my position of privileged access would allow me to argue for privacy in a way I never could have done as an outside advocate. The post-Snowden reforms described in this book are more significant than any my colleagues and I achieved during my time in public service. That it took a Snowden to force these changes made me question whether I had done the right thing by working within the system. While I kept my promise not to spill the government's secrets, Snowden's strategy proved more effective than mine. Snowden explained his decision to leak classified information as an act of self-sacrifice, motivated by patriotism. Many do not believe Snowden's claims about why he did what he did, regarding him as an attention-seeking opportunist. Some even speculate (without much evidence, it should be said) that he acted in concert with Russian or other foreign intelligence services.[14] Whatever Snowden's true motives, it is undeniable that he made a difference. Snowden has said that his greatest fear when he decided to give his purloined documents to journalists was not that he would be imprisoned but that no one would care, and "nothing will change."[15] That fear has not been realized. The post-Snowden reforms represent the first real step toward addressing the privacy issues posed by mass surveillance.

Of course, Snowden's strategy also resulted in substantial costs—to Snowden himself and to American national security. Snowden not only told the world about the NSA's impact on global privacy, he also compromised many legitimate programs focused on China and other potential adversaries of the United States, and in some cases compromising these programs lacked any obvious privacy or civil liberties benefits, even for foreign citizens.[16] Many of these revelations caused the NSA relatively little embarrassment but did result in damage to national security. They received little attention, at least in the American press, but were carefully noted by foreign governments. For reasons involving national security—but also because of excessive secrecy and bureaucratic inertia—it has been difficult for officials to make this case in public in a compelling way, but that does not make the damage from Snowden's disclosures less real.

Was the damage worth it? Geoffrey Stone, a law professor at the University of Chicago and a former colleague of President Obama, served on a review group Obama appointed in 2013 to scrutinize NSA programs and recommend reforms. "To say I was skeptical about the NSA is, in truth, an understatement," he told the NSA in a speech to its employees after the review was complete. To his surprise he found, as I had, that the NSA "operates with a high degree of integrity and a deep commitment to the rule of law." The NSA was doing what it had been told to do: the agency's employees were being "demonized" unfairly for decisions made "not by them, but by Presidents, the Congress, and the courts."[17] These decisions, Stone and his colleagues found, had resulted in unacceptable privacy risks, requiring significant reforms.

The fact that a series of massively damaging leaks was needed to achieve such sensible reforms can only be described as a failure of leadership. For me, that failure is at least in part a personal one. As a privacy and civil liberties official inside the intelligence community and later at the White House, I was supposed to provide top officials with confidential advice about how to ensure that intelligence programs protected our liberties. In essence, I was to be an authorized whistleblower for classified programs—a sort of official Snowden. In performing that role, I tried to make just the kind of arguments about privacy and NSA surveillance that many have said Snowden should have raised internally instead of compromising classified information. Unlike Snowden, I had direct access to the officials who could have made surveillance reform a reality—and who did so, after the Snowden leaks forced their hand. I can say from experience that there is simply no way that Snowden, a junior NSA contractor, could have accomplished more to reform mass surveillance by working inside the system.

"MASS SURVEILLANCE" IS A TERM that rankles my old colleagues in the intelligence community, and for good reason. Many object to its imprecision, arguing that it lumps together programs in which the NSA collects all the data traveling across a communications channel, a form of surveillance known as bulk collection, with more targeted forms of signals intelligence that nevertheless involve surveillance of many, many targets without prior, individual judicial review. These distinctions matter both in the law and in the privacy implications of particular signals intelligence programs. The indiscriminate use of a term like mass surveillance may elide these distinctions and confuse the debate, as has happened at times in discussions between American and European officials about privacy.

A more fundamental objection is that describing the NSA's programs as mass surveillance is simply unfair. The NSA is not interested in ordinary people but in finding terrorists and other valid intelligence targets, and it collects masses of information only in order to find those targets. The term *mass surveillance* conjures up visions of totalitarianism. Intelligence officials prefer to describe the NSA's vast surveillance operations as *signals intelligence*, a term associated with battles against totalitarianism, evoking American and British successes in reading enemy communications in World War II and later conflicts.

Perhaps the most effective organization to engage in mass surveillance for social control in history was the Ministry for State Security of the German Democratic Republic—the feared Stasi of East Germany. With German thoroughness, the Stasi ran a far more pervasive surveillance apparatus in defense of a Communist dictatorship than the Soviet Union did. The Stasi amassed 6 million files during its history, a figure amounting to more than one-third of the East German population. At its height, it employed one secret policeman for every 166 East German citizens, a ratio that shrinks to one informer for every 6.5 citizens when part-time agents are included. About 2,000 Stasi officers were used to tap 100,000 telephone lines in West Germany and West Berlin.[18]

These numbers seemed alarming when East Germany collapsed and the secrets of the Stasi were revealed. They seem almost quaint in the age of Snowden. The NSA collects far more data about ordinary people than the Stasi ever did, using far more sophisticated technology. Given the amount of digital data that the NSA obtains on a daily basis without anything like a search warrant, I believe that to describe what the NSA does as mass surveillance is simply a statement of fact, and that to insist on euphemisms like "collection of signals intelligence" is to deny this inconvenient truth. Nevertheless, the debate over the NSA's mass surveillance programs merely begins and does not end with this acknowledgment. While the idea of mass surveillance vividly captures the risks involved in what the NSA does, the NSA is nothing like the Stasi, an agency that amassed private information on perceived enemies of a totalitarian state as a weapon to defend a closed society.[19] The NSA serves the most diverse, complex, and free society the world has ever known, operating under a variety of imperfect, outdated, and often inadequate rules, struggling to do its best to provide intelligence to its democratically elected officials and to keep people safe not only in the United States but around the world.

In his polemical account of his role in the Snowden affair, Glenn Greenwald argues that the NSA's true objective is not to provide intelligence that can stop international terrorism and achieve other worthy objectives but to induce social control by destroying privacy. "The US government had built a system that has as its goal the complete elimination of electronic privacy worldwide," he claims.[20] If Greenwald is right, the answer is easy. End mass surveillance—which is to say, most of what the NSA does. Those of us who believe that the NSA's far-flung operations are essential to national security and global stability have the harder task of keeping the agency's mass surveillance capabilities under control.

Keeping intelligence agencies under control has rarely been more urgent. Presidents have abused surveillance powers in the past. During the 2016 presidential campaign, Donald Trump gave a vague but alarming answer to a reporter's question: "Do we need warrantless searches of Muslims?" In an answer that almost went unnoticed, Trump replied in the affirmative, saying, "We're going to have to do things that we never did before," dismissively noting that "some people are going to be upset about it."[21] President Trump's unusually fraught relationship with his own intelligence community could also result in abusive surveillance in an effort to ferret out leakers or other perceived enemies within. While the United States has a robust system of intelligence oversight—arguably the strongest in the world—it still largely depends on the good faith of intelligence officials and those who oversee them. It is a delusion to believe that the NSA or other intelligence agencies are now tyrant-proof. In Snowden's first interview, he warned against "turnkey tyranny." He worried the NSA was building an "architecture of oppression" with its mass surveillance programs. One day, he said, "a new leader will be elected" and "they'll flip the switch."[22] It is important that this warning not be proved prophetic. Despite the surveillance reforms of the past four years, it is not nearly hard enough for a would-be tyrant to turn the key.

It is time to move beyond Snowden. He deserves our thanks for this round of surveillance reform, but while his strategy is effective, it is not sustainable. The public should not have to rely on employees of the NSA and other agencies to leak information about the government's most sensitive programs in order to forestall abuse. One way to judge success in the struggle to reform the NSA and other intelligence agencies is to ask what a friend might tell a future Edward Snowden, if he were to ask that friend whether he should reveal the government's deepest surveillance secrets in order to launch a new conversation on privacy, at great personal cost and despite serious risks to national security. If surveillance reform is a success, the friend could tell him with confidence that such a course of action was simply not necessary. Surveillance agencies are following the rules at least most of the time. They are adapting when those rules become obsolete. Checks and balances are working.

We are not there yet—not by a long shot. There is much more to do.

THE PAGES THAT FOLLOW TRACE my part in the struggle over privacy and mass surveillance, first as a civil liberties lawyer, then as a privacy official inside intelligence agencies and later at the White House, and finally as an academic and commentator. While others have played a more central role in many of the battles I describe, this journey has offered me a unique vantage point from which to see the larger struggle to ensure that the NSA and other American surveillance agencies collect the intelligence they need while respecting privacy, civil liberties, and human rights.

My journey unfolds in three stages, reflected in the organization of the book. Part I, "Into the Shadows," covers the period from 2001 to 2013. The story begins with the passage of the Patriot Act, the antiterrorism law rushed through Congress in the aftermath of the terrorist attacks of September 11, and the civil liberties debate that followed—a debate that was seriously distorted by secrecy. It continues with the NSA's development of its transnational mass surveillance programs, along with the secret checks and balances that apply to them. When Barack Obama took office, there were hopes for a fresh start on issues of privacy and civil liberties. Yet for five years the Obama administration missed an opportunity to further reform surveillance, remaining content to build on the approach of the late Bush administration.

Part II, "Out of the Shadows," addresses the Snowden revelations that began in June 2013. The intelligence community faced a severe crisis in public confidence and reacted with a transparency drive to put revelations in perspective. Congress also faced tough questions about its decisions on multiple occasions to reauthorize the Patriot Act, a provision of which had enabled the program of bulk collection that Snowden revealed. In 2015 Congress chose to reform that provision with the enactment of the Freedom Act. Finally, the new transparency turned a harsh spotlight on the FISA court, showing that while its judges were far from the rubber stamps that critics claimed, they were certainly friendly to the government and had not kept up with changes in law and technology.

In Part III, "The Struggle for Reform," the narrative shifts to consider more fundamental changes that may be on the horizon, beginning with the promise that advanced technology may enable the NSA and other agencies to collect information with greater privacy assurances. The journey continues with stops in London, Brussels, and Berlin to explore how the global movement to reform mass surveillance has fared among some of the closest allies of the United States. The struggle returns to Washington, D.C., to consider the implications for privacy and civil liberties of Donald Trump as president.

The story concludes with a call for privacy and civil liberties advocates and the national security community to recognize their common values in the face of a world that seemingly is turning its back on liberal democracy and human rights, and offers some practical ideas for reform.

Part I

INTO THE SHADOWS

2

PHANTOMS OF LOST LIBERTY

IT WAS A BEAUTIFUL FALL DAY—OCTOBER 12, 2001, A MONTH AFTER THE TERROR-
ist attacks of September 11. The nation had just gone to war in Af-
ghanistan. Along with the rest of the staff of the Washington office
of the American Civil Liberties Union, I was standing on a sidewalk
next to Independence Avenue, just south of the U.S. Capitol. A bill to
give the government's intelligence and law enforcement agencies more
power in the name of fighting terrorism, the Patriot Act, was on the
floor of the House of Representatives. Together with my fellow lawyers and activists, I was searching for stray members as they walked
from their offices on the other side of the street to cast their votes
in the House chamber. We were armed with copies of the ACLU's
letter opposing the bill and explaining why it posed a danger to civil
liberties.[1]

A month earlier, on the morning of 9/11, I had been evacuated
by Capitol police from a Senate office building, where I was meeting
another activist to prepare for a visit with Senator Edward Kennedy
to discuss his immigration reform bill. Within hours of the attacks,

the ACLU was inundated with calls asking what the nation's oldest and largest civil liberties organization was planning to do to protect liberty in a time of crisis. The fear of another terrorist attack was palpable. For many Americans, it was soon colored by another fear. Wild rumors spread about Muslims.[2] There was a rash of hate crimes against anyone who appeared Muslim or Arab, or simply foreign. On September 12 my legislative assistant and I put away the files on immigration reform. We were now playing defense, I told her.

In the days after the attacks, Senate staff shared with the ACLU a draft of antiterrorism legislation they had just received from the Justice Department. It featured a host of new powers for the government. The staffers wanted the ACLU's view as to just how draconian they were. After reading the bill, I knew civil liberties were in trouble. The initial flurry of phone calls to the ACLU soon resulted in a broad coalition "in defense of freedom," composed of more than 150 organizations. They included not only the ACLU and other progressive groups but also several organizations on the right of the political spectrum, among them Gun Owners of America and Americans for Tax Reform, headed by the influential conservative activist Grover Norquist. At a press conference announcing the coalition on September 20, Norquist explained that he had just personally written every member of Congress with a simple request: Do not vote for "legislation you have not actually read."[3]

Norquist's pleas were in vain. Except for a handful of key staffers, few in Congress read and even fewer understood the draft bill. (Michael Moore, in his provocative documentary *Fahrenheit 9/11*, later satirized the point by driving around the U.S. Capitol in an ice cream truck and reading the Patriot Act through a loudspeaker.) The Patriot Act's language is dense and highly technical. The law makes dozens of changes to the complex federal laws that constrain intelligence agencies. Its most important provisions amend the Foreign Intelligence Surveillance Act of 1978 (FISA). At the time, few members of Congress outside the intelligence and judiciary committees had even heard of FISA, and those few had only the vaguest notion why the law was important.

At a meeting shortly after 9/11, I met a veteran civil liberties activist and national security expert who explained to me just how vital FISA was to preventing civil liberties abuses. Mort Halperin had worked for the ACLU for many years and had been a national security official during the Clinton administration. Mort also had personal experience with abusive warrantless surveillance. As a young staffer on the National Security Council in the Nixon White House, Halperin had been a victim of one of seventeen FBI wiretaps directed at White House staff and reporters in an unsuccessful effort by a suspicious president to control news leaks.[4]

At the time, the FBI engaged in wiretapping for national security purposes without any review by judges. The government had long argued that surveillance for national security purposes was an exception to the Fourth Amendment's warrant requirement, so long as the surveillance was not "unreasonable." (The Fourth Amendment protects the "right of the people to be secure in their persons, houses, papers, and effects, against unreasonable searches and seizures," and states that "no warrants shall issue, but upon probable cause, supported by oath or affirmation, and particularly describing the place to be searched, and the person or things to be seized.") In 1973 the Supreme Court decided that national security wiretapping required a warrant if the purpose was to uncover threats from domestic groups, but it did not rule on whether a warrant was required for surveillance of targets the government thought might be acting for a foreign power. In the mid-1970s, a committee led by Senator Frank Church uncovered widespread abuses of national security wiretapping, including the FBI's wiretapping of Dr. Martin Luther King Jr. and other Americans involved in the civil rights, antiwar, and other protest movements—and even White House staffers like Mort Halperin. In 1978 Congress passed FISA. The law set out detailed rules for surveillance involving foreign powers and put surveillance under the authority of a court for the first time. In passing FISA, Congress weighed in on the question the Supreme Court had left unresolved, balancing the needs of the government for surveillance of foreign threats and the risks to civil liberties such surveillance could pose.[5]

FISA was a grand bargain, a delicate compromise over constitutional power between Congress and the executive branch. Halperin told me he was deeply concerned that the Patriot Act would undermine the constitutional compromise that FISA embodied. The Patriot Act's most controversial provisions made surgical changes to FISA. By changing a single word, the bill did away with the so-called wall between ordinary criminal investigations and the more secret and wide-ranging investigations that make use of the government's foreign intelligence surveillance powers.[6] Keeping the two kinds of investigations separate had for decades been regarded by lawyers inside and outside the government as one of FISA's more important civil liberties safeguards. Another key provision, section 215, broadened the government's little noticed power to obtain "certain business records" in intelligence investigations with an order from the FISA court. Such business records orders included a secrecy requirement forbidding a recipient from disclosing the existence of the order. Before the Patriot Act, these secret demands applied only to a few types of records, such as hotel and car rental records, that might be generated by an international terrorist or other "agent of a foreign power." The government was allowed to issue demands for these records only if there was individual suspicion connecting them to an agent of a foreign power. When the bill passed, the government became able to order any person to provide any "tangible things," including whatever "books, records, papers, documents and other items" the government believed would be helpful in a national security investigation. FISA's requirement of individual suspicion was gone.[7]

Our urgent warnings about unraveling FISA's grand bargain fell on deaf ears. The divisiveness of the previous year's election campaign had given way to a spirit of national unity in the face of the deadliest attack on American soil since the Civil War. By the first week of October, the battle was lost. Even some of the ACLU's closest allies were telling us they would vote for the bill. Congress was not going to reject new surveillance powers just because of the "ghosts of the past," one lawyer for the Bush administration told me. On October 11 the Senate approved the bill by a vote of 96-1, with only Senator Russ Feingold of Wisconsin heeding the ACLU's calls to vote no.[8] At the ACLU's small building across the street from the Supreme Court, I listened as the director of the office, Laura Murphy, expressed her fears that the United States was on the cusp of becoming a "surveillance society."

The next day the House would be voting. Laura knew we had no chance, but she still rallied me and the rest of her staff to buttonhole members as they crossed the street to vote. It was hopeless, but at least we were doing something, I thought. Laura spotted Representative John Conyers of Michigan, the senior Democrat on the House

Judiciary Committee, coming down the steps of the Capitol. Ordinarily, Conyers was a steadfast supporter of the ACLU. In the heated atmosphere after 9/11, he had been wavering. Laura gathered her staff around him. Conyers told Laura he had just voted no, and we thanked him. It was a very minor victory. The vote was overwhelming: 337-79.[9] There would have to be another vote after the House and Senate reconciled competing versions, but the outcome was a foregone conclusion. The final bill passed the House by the even wider margin of 357-66.[10] President Bush signed it into law on October 26.

It was largely because of our work that there had been any debate at all, even a deeply flawed one that took only six weeks. President Bush's attorney general, John Ashcroft, had demanded that Congress pass the administration's proposal without any changes only a few days after the attacks. The chairs of the judiciary committees in the House and Senate—Representative Jim Sensenbrenner of Wisconsin, a Republican, and Senator Patrick Leahy, a Democrat—pleaded for more time. After Ashcroft hinted they would be to blame if there were further attacks, they buckled. Leahy's staff came up with a clever name for the Senate version of the surveillance bill: the Uniting and Strengthening America Act, or the "USA Act." Sensenbrenner's staff spent time inventing a more extravagantly Orwellian acronym for the House version: the Providing Appropriate Tools Required to Intercept and Obstruct Terrorism Act, or the "PATRIOT Act." At least in this respect, the law's official name reflects a compromise. It is the "USA PATRIOT Act."

We never had much hope that we could defeat it. Our goal had been to get a few changes in the draft, or at least to force members to consider the gravity of the changes they were making to surveillance law. One outcome of our work during those six weeks was a sunset clause, a provision that the Patriot Act's enhanced surveillance powers would expire in four years.[11] In 2005 Congress would have to extend them, change them, or let them lapse. The sunset clause proved to be our most important achievement, prompting multiple reviews and reforms as Congress renewed the Patriot Act's expiring provisions for additional periods while resisting calls to make the entire law permanent. The most significant of these reforms did not take place until 2015, with the passage of the USA FREEDOM Act—two years after Edward Snowden revealed a top-secret court order to Verizon Business Services showing how the Patriot Act's business records provision was being used for the bulk collection of telephone records.

Although we did not then realize that efforts to reform the Patriot Act would span more than a decade and two administrations, we knew we were in for a long-term campaign. Over the next several months the ACLU conducted focus groups, hired new field organizers, and held countless strategy sessions. Any successful effort would require a diverse array of grassroots activists that went well beyond the largely Washington, D.C.–based coalition we had hastily organized in the days after 9/11. Somewhat to my surprise, section 215 of the Patriot Act became a central focus of our campaign. Although this provision had not even been mentioned in our letter opposing the Patriot Act,[12] it soon became clear that its potential impact was quite broad. Because the government could use the provision to obtain "any tangible things," it affected anyone who cared about the confidentiality of records or data. The law has long understood the term "tangible things" to include any type of record, including records held only in electronic form.[13]

The breadth of section 215 of the Patriot Act provided the ACLU with a host of potential allies. Whether a particular interest group was concerned with the privacy of medical records, gun purchase records, financial records, or student records did not matter. All were fair game under section 215. One of the many organizations that echoed the ACLU's concerns about the Patriot Act was the American Library Association.

Why librarians, I wondered.

My boss at the time, Greg Nojeim, was a veteran ACLU activist. He told me all about the long-standing advocacy of librarians at the local, state, and national levels regarding free speech and other civil liberties issues, and also shed some light on the librarians' concerns about privacy. The Patriot Act's association with library records has puzzled government officials, members of Congress, and journalists for years, so it is worth explaining in some detail the story of how section 215 became known as the "library records" provision.

Greg recalled that in the late 1980s the ACLU had worked with librarians against an FBI intelligence effort called the Library Awareness Program. Although Greg was not at the ACLU at the time, he was diligent in keeping meticulous files on how the ACLU had handled past controversies. The files were immensely useful after 9/11. In those files, I discovered a statement that Mort Halperin, then the director of the ACLU's Washington office, had written in 1988 in support of the librarians. Librarians in New York were approached by the FBI to report on library users from potentially hostile countries, including the Soviet Union. "Hostile intelligence has had some success working the campuses and libraries," a deputy assistant director of the FBI's New York field office said at the time.[14] Librarians said they were willing to cooperate with law enforcement in cases where the government obtained a subpoena or court order, or under other extraordinary circumstances. However, they were alarmed by the effort to enlist them in a broader program of intelligence gathering, even one ostensibly limited to foreign citizens. Librarians regarded what they knew about the reading habits of library patrons as something akin to a sacred trust. As a result of the work of the ACLU and the American Library Association, the Library Awareness Program was over almost before it began. It had netted no spies. Its main impact was to increase librarians' awareness of their role in safeguarding civil liberties.

Ever since, librarians had been working with the ACLU to strengthen laws at the state level to protect the privacy of library records. Along with other state and federal laws that protected particular types of sensitive records, the Patriot Act overrode state laws that protected the privacy of library users. The librarians wanted to preserve those state laws, but the Justice Department was never willing to consider amending the Patriot Act to do this. I never fully understood why the Justice Department was so unwilling to budge on this point, given that library records never proved to be of much importance in a counterterrorism case. When I discussed the issue with Justice Department lawyers, their biggest concern was that if they agreed to accommodate the librarians' concerns, they would have to negotiate similar accommodations for other sensitive records.

Our new field organizers were eager for us to work with the librarians again, this time against the Patriot Act. Together with the American Library Association, we decided to make the privacy of library records an important part of our campaign. Librarians became part of our effort to get cities, towns, and other local governments to pass resolutions opposing the Patriot Act. The organizers told me and other lawyers at the ACLU that raising the specter of the government monitoring the reading habits of library patrons was a perfect opportunity to raise awareness about the Patriot Act among ordinary people. Librarians had already begun to post notices warning patrons that their library records could be obtained by federal agents and that they were prohibited from saying anything about it.

In one of our earlier strategy meetings, one organizer expressed concern that librarians might face an avalanche of questions about the notices. The government should be answering the questions, I argued, not the librarians. At my suggestion, the text we were recommending for library notices included a pointed disclaimer. "Questions about this policy should be directed to Attorney General John Ashcroft, Department of Justice, Washington, D.C. 20530."[15]

Soon, even more libraries around the country were putting up signs. The Justice Department was furious.

JOHN ASHCROFT HAD A MESSAGE for the ACLU and other critics. "Your tactics only aid terrorists—for they erode our national unity and diminish our resolve," he growled in testimony before the Senate Judiciary Committee on December 6, 2001. He accused us of trying to "scare peace-loving people with phantoms of lost liberty."[16]

Ashcroft was the perfect villain for the ACLU's campaign. The ex-senator from Missouri and former member of the Senate Judiciary Committee had been a divisive choice for attorney general. His strident views on any number of social issues—abortion, civil rights, even adult pornography (he famously demanded that a nude statue in the Great Hall of the Department of Justice building called *Spirit of Justice* be covered for modesty)—had galvanized opponents of the Bush administration. When Ashcroft argued that those who questioned the Patriot Act were unpatriotic, he gave the ACLU another golden opportunity to wax eloquent in defense of the Constitution. Still, there was some truth to Ashcroft's complaint about phantoms of lost liberty. Neither I nor anyone else at the ACLU had any idea whether the government was using the Patriot Act to obtain library records. Everything about the government's use of its surveillance authorities was classified—including whether they had been used at all.

Of course, prying information out of the government about how it was using its surveillance powers was part of the point. Our goal was to convince Congress that the government should not be able to obtain the records of just anyone in an effort to prevent terrorism, as section 215 allowed, at least not without showing facts to a judge that met a standard of reasonable suspicion. Since we did not know what was actually happening, we had little choice but to describe a myriad of hypothetical ways that the government might abuse its powers. If it came out that the government actually was engaging in sweeping surveillance, as we said the law allowed, our argument for reform was stronger. Yet if the government could show its surveillance was targeted only at suspicious people, this did not weaken our case. If the law really was being used sparingly, why not raise the legal standard to reasonable suspicion?

In September 2003 Ashcroft walked right into our trap. He decided he had enough of our "public distortion and misinformation" (as he called it) about the Patriot Act. Ashcroft declassified a surprising fact: the "number of times Section 215 has been used to date is zero (0)."[17] The government had not been using the Patriot Act to get library records, or any other kind of records. Ashcroft seemed to think this revelation would embarrass his critics. Instead, he faced new questions from Congress about why he had insisted that this provision of the Patriot Act was so essential it had to be enacted immediately, without hearings or much debate, insofar as it had still not been used after nearly two years.

In 2005 Congress began considering whether to renew the now infamous "library records" provision, along with other sections of the Patriot Act that were set to expire at the end of the year. The Justice Department declassified updated figures. By March 2005, the government disclosed, it had used section 215 a total of thirty-five times to get various business records in national security investigations. There still had been no orders issued to libraries.[18] Still, the Justice Department said it was willing to work with Congress to resolve whatever concerns Congress might have about ambiguities in the hastily drafted law.

Perhaps the most obvious problem was that there simply was no legal standard for when the government could demand records under the Patriot Act. While Congress had eliminated the requirement of reasonable suspicion for business records by enacting section 215, it had failed to include any other standard to replace it. The law said only that the records must be "sought for" an authorized investigation.[19] The government's lawyers argued that in the absence of more specific language, the standard for obtaining records under the Patriot Act was relevance—the lowest standard in the law, but a standard nonetheless. The law's failure to specify this had simply been an oversight. Justice Department lawyers urged Congress to include language to make clear that it could obtain only "relevant" records. The ACLU argued that this was not good enough: at a minimum, the reasonable suspicion standard should be restored. This was not a terribly high bar. Legal standards for investigations require less certainty than the standards of proof that the government must meet when a case goes to trial. Probable cause, required for search warrants and wiretap orders, is the highest standard, but, in fact, this standard is a fairly low one. According to the Supreme Court, probable cause requires only "a practical, common sense decision" that "there is a fair probability that contraband or evidence of a crime will be found"— or, in the case of foreign intelligence, that the target is an agent of a foreign power. Relevance, required for grand jury subpoenas, is an exceptionally broad standard: it permits the government to demand "all information that might possibly bear" on whether a crime has been committed. Reasonable suspicion offers a middle ground between probable cause and relevance. Reasonable suspicion requires more than a hunch, but less than the probable cause required for a search, a wiretap, or an arrest. It is the legal standard police are supposed to use for a brief "stop and frisk" when patrolling the streets.[20]

By July 2005 it was clear the ACLU and its civil libertarian allies were losing again. Both the House and the Senate had passed competing bills renewing the expiring provisions of the Patriot Act, including section 215. As the year wore on and time ran short, House and Senate staff met to reconcile the different versions. My colleagues at the ACLU and I still had hope we might make at least some modest improvements. Staff for Senator Leahy and Representative Sensenbrenner told us there was no support for raising the standard for records demands under section 215 to reasonable suspicion. However, they hoped our coalition might have suggestions for language to give the relevance standard additional teeth. If the Justice Department's lawyers could live with it, they would push to include the new language in the conference report, the final version of the bill.

I did not see much point in the exercise. The problem with the Patriot Act was not sloppy draftsmanship. The problem was the low standard for obtaining records. Intelligence investigations were not like other kinds of investigations. Intelligence was about preventing attacks, not solving crimes that had already taken place. Just about anything might be "relevant" to prevention, even the library or any other records of someone the FBI just had a hunch might be a danger. The low standard could not be fixed by making it clearer; the failure to require a standard of reasonable suspicion was why the ACLU had opposed the Patriot Act in the first place.

A colleague from another civil liberties organization, Kate Martin, thought language that reinforced the relevance standard might not be so useless after all. Without it, she argued, the government could use the Patriot Act to demand entire databases in order to mine them for potential terrorists. She did not use the term "bulk collection," but that is what she meant. Kate argued that if we could tighten up the relevance standard, we could prevent the use of section 215 for bulk collection. Although the government might still use the law to go on fishing expeditions, at least it would be limited to fishing for the records of particular people.

As Kate and I discussed the issue in the fall of 2005, she reminded me of a controversial Defense Department program that had been launched after 9/11. In 2002 the Pentagon had hired retired admiral John Poindexter to head a new research office, focused on surveillance and information technology. The goal of Poindexter's "Total Information Awareness" program had been to develop computer algorithms that could uncover previously unknown suspects whose data left a trail of suspicious behavior. The ACLU worked with Senator Ron Wyden of Oregon to raise a stink about it over privacy, and Kate had worked with me and other ACLU lawyers to raise the obvious problems posed by such an effort.[21] Poindexter protested that his efforts had been misconstrued—his office was interested in research, not operational intelligence activities, and that included research into data mining techniques that might be protective of privacy. This time the ACLU and its allies prevailed. Congress shut down the office in 2003. Poindexter retired. Still, there were persistent rumors that the program lived on in some classified research office somewhere in the intelligence community.[22]

As I worked late in my office at the ACLU in early December 2005, Kate called me with what she said was good news. The Justice Department lawyers had agreed to new language suggested by lawyers on the staff of the Senate Judiciary Committee. The revised section 215 now required a "statement of facts showing that there are reasonable grounds to believe" that records are "relevant" to an investigation to prevent terrorism. The language also said that records were "presumed" to be relevant in only three specific circumstances, all involving agents of foreign powers. If the records did not involve a suspected terrorist or other foreign agent, the government could still try to make the case to the FISA court that the records were relevant, but it would not have the benefit of one of the presumptions.[23] Kate believed it was an important victory. By requiring such a "statement of facts" and by listing the three presumptions, she was confident the FISA court would reject a proposal to use the Patriot Act to obtain entire databases. In other words, it would ban bulk collection.

I was annoyed. I had (and have) great respect for Kate. She is an extraordinary advocate—experienced, tenacious, and with a deep knowledge of national security issues. Still, I thought that Senate staff had just played her. What had really happened was that our "friends" in Congress had agreed to renew the Patriot Act without fixing it. They hoped they could distract her and other civil libertarians by banning something that was never going to happen. After all, Total Information Awareness was over. It had never been more than a research program anyway. The idea that the FISA court would allow the Patriot Act to be used to obtain massive quantities of data, for data mining or anything else, was in my mind even more unlikely than the idea that the government was using the law to monitor the reading habits of library users. I thought that Kate had started to believe in the phantoms we had invented to illustrate our fears of lost liberty. I was sure that whatever the Patriot Act's problems might be, they had nothing to do with mass surveillance.

In fact, Kate and I both turned out to be wrong. I was wrong to dismiss Kate's concerns about bulk collection. The government, I would learn in just a few months, had begun using the Patriot Act to obtain entire databases, just as she had feared. Kate was also wrong. The language about a "statement of facts" that Kate had thought would prevent this proved no obstacle to bulk collection. Starting in 2006, the government began to issue secret court orders under section 215 to require major American telephone companies to turn over all of their customer records. The FISA court went along with the government's argument that the NSA needed all the records in its efforts to find terrorists, and that this satisfied the law's relevance standard. At the same time, bulk collection of telephone records had not started with the Patriot Act. Instead, it had started without any court review at all, under an aggressive theory of presidential power in the "war on terror." The government was using the Patriot Act not to obtain new data but to provide safeguards, including new limits, oversight, and judicial review, to govern how it could use the data it was already collecting.

Laura Murphy, the director of the ACLU's Washington office, had been right—up to a point. The United States was becoming not only a surveillance society but a mass surveillance society. It was doing so in a peculiarly American fashion, involving detailed rules administered by legions of lawyers. The trouble was that these checks and balances were based on outdated laws, drafted in another age, and they operated entirely in secret. Those of us on the outside were left fighting shadows.

3

TRANSNATIONAL SURVEILLANCE

SHORTLY AFTER MY LATE-NIGHT CONVERSATION WITH KATE MARTIN ABOUT whether intelligence agencies were using the Patriot Act for bulk collection, I went to CIA headquarters for a job interview. As I passed through the security gates of the heavily guarded compound in Langley, Virginia, I felt out of place but also intrigued. I was being recruited to become the "deputy for civil liberties" in a new office advising the director of national intelligence. If I got the job, I would no longer be fighting shadows. Instead, I would be reviewing classified programs in the National Security Agency, the CIA, the FBI, the Department of Homeland Security, and a dozen other intelligence agencies, offering advice about how these programs could be reformed to include stronger safeguards for privacy and civil liberties.

The creation of the director of national intelligence was the principal recommendation of the 9/11 Commission. Previously the head of the intelligence community was the head of the CIA. Running the CIA left little room for coordinating the work of sixteen different federal intelligence agencies scattered across seven federal departments. A new full-time cabinet official devoted entirely to making the agencies share information and work together could help prevent the next terrorist attack. The idea was a bipartisan one. It had been supported not only by President Bush but also by his opponent in the 2004 election, Senator John Kerry of Massachusetts.

At the time, I had not been so sure about the wisdom of creating a director of national intelligence. In testimony for the American Civil Liberties Union in the summer of 2004, I warned members of the House intelligence committee that a director of national intelligence who "centralize[d] power over both foreign and domestic surveillance" could create real risks for privacy and civil liberties. "When a democratic society puts the very citizens from which it derives its legitimacy under surveillance," I said, abuses were bound to result.[1] To ensure the new director's independence from any agency and from the White House, Congress created a new agency to support the director, the Office of the Director of National Intelligence (ODNI). After considerable internal debate, the ACLU chose to take no position on the creation of the director or the ODNI but instead to use the debate to push for new oversight of intelligence agencies. In a rare victory for the civil liberties community, the law that created both the director of national intelligence and the ODNI also included an independent privacy and civil liberties board and a "civil liberties protection officer" reporting directly to the head of the intelligence community. It was a first in the history of American intelligence. Now there would be someone charged by law with "the protection of civil liberties and privacy" in the "policies and procedures" of the very agencies conducting the world's biggest surveillance programs.[2]

During my work on intelligence reform for the ACLU, I had received invaluable advice from Suzanne Spaulding, a former CIA lawyer. She told me that many inside the government shared the ACLU's concerns about the impact of the "war on terror" on civil liberties. After the ODNI became a reality, Suzanne told me that the man who had been named its first "civil liberties protection officer," Alex Joel, wanted a deputy with strong civil liberties credentials.

It was Alex who had asked me to come to CIA headquarters for my first interview. Alex had been a judge advocate general—a military lawyer—and then a lawyer in the private sector, handling privacy issues for Marriott. After 9/11 he had joined the CIA's Office of General Counsel. As the ODNI did not yet have its own building, Alex was still working in his old office. He met me in the lobby. Etched on the wall are stars (in place of names) to memorialize those CIA officers who had lost their lives for their country. Also on the wall is a verse from the Bible: "And ye shall know the truth and the truth shall make you free." At the time, it seemed more ominous than inspiring. Did I really want to know the truth about what the intelligence agencies were doing with their post-9/11 powers? It was an unsettling moment.

Even more unsettling was the lead story in the *New York Times* that day, December 16, 2005, by James Risen and Eric Lichtblau. I had spoken with Eric on several occasions about the ACLU's objections to the Patriot Act, including our view that the law made it much too easy for the government to get court orders for records in intelligence investigations, and that its provisions for wider sharing of information garnered from intelligence surveillance might be abused. Eric had been looking for a more dramatic story, and it seemed he had found one. The article described a secret Bush administration surveillance program that dispensed with court orders altogether, illegally bypassing the special surveillance court established by federal law. "Bush Lets U.S. Spy on Callers without Courts," the headline read.[3]

Alex was plainly caught off guard by the story. Despite his proximity to the head of the intelligence community, he had not been "read in" to the program, code-named Stellar Wind—nor, I learned later, had almost everyone else in the ODNI, not even the general counsel.[4] Still, Alex was determined to make his new privacy and civil liberties office a success. He had read my testimony. He shared my vision for his position. The law gave him significant powers, and he intended to use them to ask tough questions. Alex's evident sincerity more than made up for my distrust. Alex and I would be able to take our concerns straight to the top. Alex's boss was the director of national intelligence, John Negroponte. His boss's boss was the president of the United States. Despite our lofty status, our resources would be few. If I got the job, Alex explained, I would immediately double the size of his office.

Most of my colleagues in the civil liberties community were skeptical I could do much good. The growing controversy over what was now being called Bush's "warrantless wiretapping" program did not inspire confidence. A few suggested my best hope to make a difference would be to become a whistleblower, saying they would support me if I felt the need to leak classified information about questionable spying programs. I resolved that I would honor my secrecy agreement, even if officials disagreed with our advice. Somehow, Alex had convinced the leadership of the intelligence community that an ACLU lawyer could be trusted to review the most secret surveillance programs in government. It was a chance to speak truth to power, even if that truth would have to remain secret. Alex was taking a chance by hiring me, and I did not want to betray his trust.

MY JOB REQUIRED NOT ONLY a top-secret clearance but also access to "sensitive compartmented information"—the kinds of programs with code names like the one Alex was busy asking about. Alex pulled strings to have my background investigation expedited. It included a polygraph. In the spring of 2006, I found myself in a windowless room on a military base in southeast Washington, D.C., strapped to a chair measuring my autonomous responses for signs of deception. After a few preliminaries—what was my name, was I comfortable, and so forth—the man conducting the test got down to business.

"Have you ever had any contact with a member of a foreign terrorist organization?"

"Yes, I may have," I replied.

It was not the answer he expected. I explained that my work with the ACLU had involved a few meetings with Sami Al-Arian, a Florida professor born in Kuwait to parents who were Palestinian refugees. The ACLU had challenged the use of secret evidence in the deportation case of his brother-in-law, evidence that the government said showed links to terrorism. Sami Al-Arian had taken up his brother-in-law's cause and had become a civil liberties activist. The government was now saying Al-Arian himself was involved in terrorism. It was accusing him of raising money for Palestinian terrorists, and it had evidence of his guilt because of FBI intelligence wiretaps. The Patriot Act had made it easier to share such intelligence with criminal

prosecutors. In 2003 Al-Arian was indicted. (After years of controversy, Al-Arian pled guilty and served several years in prison. He was
deported to Turkey in 2015.)[5]

When I told Alex about my experience with the polygraph, he said
there was no need to worry. It was just the sort of thing the polygraph
operators were hoping to uncover. I had probably made the man's
day. As long as I had been truthful and my contact with Al-Arian had
been related to my ACLU work, there should be no problem. Alex
was right. In June 2006 I received my blue badge, indicating that I
was now a full member of the intelligence community with access to
its facilities, its computer systems, and its secrets.

The top-secret computer networks on which I worked every day
did little to restrict access to insiders. Employees are not routinely
searched for secret files or documents when they leave, and it would
be wildly impractical to do so. The summer I began work, Julian
Assange was putting the finishing touches on a new website providing a secure portal for whistleblowers to upload embarrassing secret
files. WikiLeaks would post its first document by the end of the year.
Leaking information required no special skills. As long as you had a
blue badge, security was a matter of trust.

At around the same time as I received mine, Edward Snowden
received his.

OVER THE NEXT FEW YEARS, Alex and I made repeated visits to the headquarters of the NSA in Fort Meade, Maryland. Our meetings invariably took place in OPS 2B, a dark glass office building built in the
Reagan years, surrounded by barbed wire and acres of parking lots.
OPS 2B is shielded in copper to prevent emanations from electronic
equipment from leaking information to Soviet spies. It has been less
effective in preventing leaks to the press.

At our first meeting, senior NSA officials briefed us on the agency's sprawling surveillance operations. A dizzying volume and variety
of data were ingested daily through collection sites all over the world.
Some sites are run in cooperation with the "Five Eyes"—the NSA's
partner agencies in the United Kingdom, Canada, Australia, and
New Zealand. Although the arrangement had been publicly known

for years, I was told not to discuss the existence of the Five Eyes. The original agreement was finally declassified in 2010.[6] The NSA's cooperation with a host of other governments, known as "third parties," is now a matter of widespread public debate in those countries but remains officially secret.

The technological challenges were immense. Like Google, Facebook, and other technology companies, the NSA had to use sophisticated methods to keep up with what it called the "tsunami" of data generated by the internet. Unlike the giants of Silicon Valley, it also had to preserve its ability to read the decades-old analog communications still in use by smaller militaries and insurgent groups. The NSA's most precious resource was not its surveillance technology but its personnel—its hackers, technicians, analysts, and translators. NSA officials explained how the agency's operations were constrained by the Constitution, federal laws, executive orders, and internal regulations, policies, and directives. They stressed to the point of defensiveness that the NSA's job was not to spy on Americans. Foreigners were fair game, as long as they were outside the United States and the surveillance was for valid intelligence purposes.

"We don't spy on Americans" is a simple message, but it has never been accurate. Since the NSA's founding by top-secret directive in 1952, its mission has been to intercept "foreign communications," but these were defined by even earlier directives to include not only purely foreign communications but also international communications between the United States and another country.[7] As a result, the NSA has always collected the communications of Americans. Some collection is inadvertent—the NSA is collecting a broad stream of communications in bulk for later analysis, and some of those communications belong to Americans. Some collection is incidental—an American is in communication with a foreigner outside the United States whose communications the NSA has intentionally selected for collection. It is important to understand that neither "inadvertent" nor "incidental" is the same thing as "accidental." The NSA is not making a mistake when it collects the communications of Americans; such collection is simply a by-product of how its surveillance programs work.

The NSA officials I met were steeped in the agency's history, including the times when the agency had overstepped its mandate. When Congress investigated abuses by the intelligence community in the mid-1970s, the committee, led by Senator Frank Church, directed most of its attention at other agencies. This included the FBI warrantless wiretap that had ensnared Mort Halperin and others. Yet after the Church Committee got around to looking at the NSA, it uncovered two programs that involved spying on Americans. The first NSA program, Shamrock, was an illegal program of bulk collection of international telegrams, which the Church Committee described at the time as "probably the largest governmental interception program affecting Americans ever undertaken."[8] In the second program, Minaret, the NSA searched the international communications it was collecting against a "watch list" of Americans. The list came to include civil rights leaders, among them Dr. Martin Luther King Jr.; prominent activists; journalists; and even elected officials. According to an internal NSA history, declassified in the fall of 2013, NSA officials themselves believed Minaret to be "disreputable if not outright illegal." The history also revealed that Senator Frank Church himself had been a Minaret target, though he never knew this. "I suspect Senator Church never had any idea the NSA was tapping his phone," said Matthew Aid, one of the historians who obtained the history through the Freedom of Information Act.[9]

In the Foreign Intelligence Surveillance Act of 1978 (FISA), Congress set a boundary between foreign and domestic surveillance for national security purposes. Congress did not want to subject the NSA's major programs to judicial review, but it did want to make sure the NSA would no longer be able to collect wire communications in bulk inside the United States, as it had done in Shamrock, or use its global surveillance capabilities to intentionally spy on Americans without a warrant, as it had done in Minaret. To accomplish this goal, the law contains a complex definition of the activities Congress intended the new court to cover. The definition is based on the analog communications technology of the time. Satellites were the dominant form of international communication in the late 1970s. FISA allows the NSA to intercept these signals carried by communications satellites from U.S.-based listening stations so long as the agency is not intentionally targeting a "particular, known" person who is inside the United States.[10] Congress made clear that this comparatively lax standard was adopted deliberately, in order "to exempt from the procedures of the bill certain signals intelligence activities of the National Security Agency."[11]

By contrast, Congress adopted a much more restrictive rule for domestic collection of data from a wire. It prohibits interception if there is any possibility the communications might include a party who is inside the United States, regardless of whether the NSA is intentionally targeting that person. Because the NSA cannot usually predict in advance of collection whether someone overseas will or will not communicate with a person inside the United States, as a practical matter, the definition of electronic surveillance often forecloses collection of data or communications from a wire or switch inside the United States without a court order, even for communications between two foreign citizens outside the United States.[12]

FISA was written to draw a firm line between foreign and domestic surveillance, yet that line has never really been a neat one, requiring a host of exceptions and qualifications. The terminology itself is confusing. "Foreign intelligence surveillance" normally means domestic surveillance of suspected foreign agents or international terrorists who are located inside the United States, including Americans. Truly foreign surveillance, in which the NSA uses its foreign or satellite collection programs against targets who are located outside the United States, is not called surveillance at all but "signals intelligence." If you talk about "surveillance" in the NSA's Fort Meade headquarters, people will assume you mean some activity that has a domestic connection, requiring the approval of the FISA court.

The NSA's foreign and satellite surveillance have never been authorized by any federal statute and require no court review. They are governed instead by a decades-old executive order, Executive Order 12,333, signed by President Reagan in 1981. After 2013 the NSA's activities under it were sometimes wrongly described as another "program" of collection. Instead, the order is the source of legal authority for most of what the NSA and other intelligence agencies do.[13] Executive Order 12,333 requires the NSA and other intelligence agencies to have rules that protect the privacy of "United States persons"—American citizens and permanent residents, along with U.S. corporations and organizations composed substantially of U.S. persons. The NSA's detailed privacy rules are contained in United States Signals Intelligence Directive 18. While the full rules are classified, the agency has periodically released redacted versions of USSID 18.[14] A central requirement is that whatever information the NSA collects "to, from or about" U.S. persons must be removed before NSA analysts provide their reports to other agencies. Typically, NSA reports will replace the identities of U.S. persons with generic terms. A report might describe the conversation of a named foreign target with "a U.S. person." Recipients of these reports may ask that U.S. person identities be "unmasked." The NSA will agree if an official with the right approval authority believes the identity of the U.S. person is "necessary to understand the foreign intelligence information or assess its importance."[15]

The NSA is a military organization dominated by engineers, combining two kinds of people who love rules. Most of the NSA employees I met could cite the key parts of USSID 18 from memory. NSA training emphasizes that compliance with USSID 18 is essential to ensuring that the NSA's programs under Executive Order 12,333 do not violate the constitutional rights of Americans. Intelligence officials argue that the NSA's surveillance is constitutional because it focuses on foreign targets and uses procedures to protect the privacy of "United States persons." This argument is heavily influenced by concepts of intelligence law and oversight—so much so that government lawyers sometimes fail to remember that while this theory on targeting and incidental collection has been embraced by the FISA court and some other federal courts, it has never been upheld by the Supreme Court. It remains controversial with constitutional scholars, even among some conservatives who are usually friendly to the government. One of them, Orin Kerr, has criticized the theory as "surprisingly weak," saying, "There is no 'targeting' doctrine in Fourth Amendment law": the idea of a "foreign target" is primarily an intelligence collection concept, not a constitutional one.[16] Significant doubts remain about the constitutionality of NSA collection that may involve incidental communications of U.S. persons or persons in the United States—which is to say, much of what the NSA does.

"WHEN WILL I GET A briefing on the TSP?" I asked Alex, some months after our first visit to Fort Meade. Alex looked surprised. He was working on it, he said—he had only recently been "read in" to the program himself. President Bush had confirmed one part of the NSA's warrantless Stellar Wind program in a radio address in December 2005. The NSA's domestic collection of the contents of international telephone calls in which one party to the call was a suspected terrorist was now called the Terrorist Surveillance Program, the TSP. Alex had misunderstood my question. I wasn't asking about the Terrorist Surveillance Program. The initials for the NSA's program—at least the part that had been confirmed, involving the collection of content—overlapped with those of another government program in which I had a more personal interest. I wanted information about the Thrift Savings Plan, the retirement account system for federal employees.

In retrospect, both TSPs were on shaky ground at the end of 2006. While my retirement account eventually recovered from the market collapse that was just around the corner, the NSA's experiment in circumventing court approval for surveillance activities inside the United States came to an end in early 2007, shortly after Alex finally managed to have me cleared for access to the program. (Alex's own clearance had been delayed for almost as long as a result of White House intransigence, even though Director Negroponte supported it.) The surveillance, however, did not end. Instead, Stellar Wind was being replaced by a series of successor programs authorized by secret court orders. The first news story published as a result of Edward Snowden's disclosures was based on a court order associated with one of these successor programs. It was a replacement for a part of the Stellar Wind program that Bush had kept secret: the NSA's collection in bulk of metadata, such as call detail records, including both international and purely domestic calls, like those kept by American telephone companies.[17] (Metadata are data about communications, including telephone numbers, e-mail addresses, routing information, the date, time, and length of communications and similar information, but not the contents of messages or calls.)

Bush had kept bulk collection of metadata officially secret even though this part of Stellar Wind had also leaked. In May 2006 a front-page headline in *USA Today* proclaimed, "NSA Has Massive Database of Americans' Phone Calls." In response, the NSA simply issued a terse statement saying "We have no information to provide."[18] It was understood that we should not discuss anything about Stellar Wind that had not been disclosed by Bush in his radio address, which had focused exclusively on the NSA's interception of the content of international telephone calls of suspected terrorists. This meant avoiding public discussion of internet surveillance and keeping mum about bulk collection of both internet metadata and telephone records.

It is still a mystery why the *USA Today* leak provoked so little response at the time. A national security reporter for a major newspaper told me years later, somewhat chagrined, that he had been on the verge of piecing together the NSA's bulk collection program before Edward Snowden leaked the order to Verizon—a document the government almost immediately confirmed—but had simply forgotten about the *USA Today* story. In any event, Congress's attention in 2006 was absorbed in the debate over those NSA activities Bush had confirmed in his radio address in December 2005. Members who had been fully briefed on Stellar Wind kept quiet about bulk collection. Those who had not been briefed either did not understand that the *USA Today* story contained a major new revelation about NSA surveillance or did not press the issue publicly. With no new statement from the NSA, no pressure from Congress, and no new leaks, there simply was no news.

AS I LEARNED WHEN I was finally briefed on Stellar Wind, the NSA's access to domestic data went well beyond the limited surveillance of international telephone calls described by President Bush in his 2005 radio address. Stellar Wind began shortly after 9/11, when General Michael Hayden, the NSA director, urged broader access to data and communications inside the United States after Vice President Dick Cheney had pressed the issue of whether the NSA was doing everything it could to prevent another terrorist attack. Hayden's concern was driven in part by changes in technology. By the turn of the millennium most of the world's communications (telephone and internet) were no longer carried by satellite. Instead they traveled as digital packets, usually carried by fiber-optic underseas cable. Communications that the NSA had been accustomed to collect from satellites were now traversing switches, servers, and other digital equipment inside the United States. FISA's rule for domestic collection of data from a wire meant that a court order was required to monitor these communications, even if the NSA's target was a foreign terrorist in Yemen who was using a U.S.-based e-mail service to communicate with a foreign terrorist in Pakistan, along with others whose location is unknown. If the NSA could not be sure ahead of time that all parties to the communication were located abroad, it could acquire the communication only with an individual order, based on probable cause—a standard the intelligence community has always argued should be reserved for domestic national security surveillance. The world had entered the digital age, but the definition of electronic surveillance in FISA remained unchanged, stuck in the analog era.[19]

The result of sticking with analog-era FISA rules included a missed opportunity to prevent the 9/11 attacks, or so intelligence officials sincerely believed. The story was repeated over and over in classified briefings I attended. It has now been made public. In early 2000 the NSA intercepted several telephone calls from someone named "Khalid" to an al-Qaeda safe house in Yemen. The NSA did not know where Khalid was. In accordance with the law, the NSA was monitoring the safe house only from its collection sites overseas. Because of this, the metadata associated with the call were incomplete: the NSA had only the telephone number associated with the foreign end. NSA analysts did not know the number that Khalid was calling from. If they had, they would have learned that Khalid was calling from a number in San Diego, and they could have passed that information to the FBI for investigation. "Khalid" turned out to be Khalid al-Mihdhar, a member of the team that hijacked American Airlines Flight 77 on September 11 and crashed it into the Pentagon. The "Khalid" story has now become part of the standard defense of the NSA's post-9/11 surveillance activities involving data collected inside the United States.[20]

Although many intelligence mistakes contributed to the events of

9/11, this one haunted the NSA. There was little debate among senior intelligence officials that the NSA needed to get its hands dirty with domestic data if it was to avoid dropping the ball again. The question was whether ignoring FISA was the right way to do it. The decision to bypass Congress stemmed in part from the NSA's penchant for secrecy—the agency did not want to reveal just how much foreign data was inside the United States—but it also served Dick Cheney's agenda of expanding executive power at the expense of Congress and the courts. Cheney was refighting a very old battle. Ever since he served as chief of staff in the Ford administration, Cheney had opposed court review of national security surveillance. He regarded the 1978 FISA as one in a series of obnoxious and unwarranted post-Watergate encroachments on executive power.[21] The failure of surveillance laws to adapt to the digital age gave Cheney his opening to attack FISA. It was the NSA's excessive secrecy that allowed Cheney to succeed for as long as he did.

Stellar Wind allowed the NSA to collect two kinds of data inside the United States without authority from Congress and without the court orders required by law. First, the NSA was collecting the content of international communications in which the target was a suspected member of al-Qaeda, including both telephone calls and e-mail. At the insistence of General Hayden, the NSA did not use Stellar Wind to collect the content of purely domestic communications, although it did sometimes acquire such content by mistake. Second, the NSA was collecting metadata, and it was collecting it all, without filtering this data based on its targets. The NSA obtained telephony metadata, such as the call detail records kept by telephone companies. It obtained internet metadata by harvesting the data from the internet backbone facilities of telecommunications providers.[22]

The legal theory for the program was devised by John Yoo, the same Justice Department official who wrote the infamous "torture memos" allowing waterboarding and other "enhanced interrogation" methods for al-Qaeda detainees. At the time, Yoo argued that warrantless surveillance was part of the president's powers over war and foreign affairs under Article II of the Constitution. However, Congress had made clear that FISA was the "exclusive means" for conducting electronic surveillance. Yoo argued that if this provision of FISA meant what it said, FISA "would be an unconstitutional infringement on the President's Article II authorities."[23] Yoo's conclusion was an audacious claim, upsetting a decades-old compromise between the executive and legislative branches, and it was made in secret. (Later, the Justice Department made a slightly different defense of the program, based on Congress's authorization of the use of military force.)[24] When I learned of Yoo's reasoning, I saw it as both a weak argument and profoundly undemocratic. I also took it somewhat personally. I had just spent the past five years of my life participating in a broad national debate about surveillance under the Patriot Act, which is all about changes to FISA. What was the point of that debate if following that law was optional?

My concerns, I learned to my surprise, were shared by more than a few of my new colleagues in the intelligence community, whose views on civil liberties were rarely in alignment with the ACLU. Intelligence officials were much more concerned with collecting intelligence than they were with questions of executive power. From the NSA's perspective, Stellar Wind had a host of negative aspects. If Yoo's legal theories were wrong, NSA officials were breaking the law, and their partners—the telecommunications companies—would face millions in civil liability for allowing illegal wiretaps. Many career intelligence officials were deeply uncomfortable with ignoring a federal statute, regardless of memos from John Yoo or other Justice Department officials or the supportive arguments offered by Cheney and his lawyer, David Addington, about the president's power to do so indefinitely in the "war on terror." Intentional violation of federal wiretapping laws, including FISA, is a crime. While prosecutions seemed unlikely, Stellar Wind was a serious threat to the NSA's rules-based culture. Many saw ignoring FISA in the war on terror as a slippery slope. Doubts about Stellar Wind's legality contributed to the decisions of NSA employee Russell Tice and Justice Department lawyer Thomas Tamm to leak the program in 2005.

"There was a lot of anger," one senior lawyer told me in early 2007, just as the unilateral Stellar Wind program was winding down. I soon discovered what he meant by this cryptic comment. In vivid testimony before the Senate Judiciary Committee in May 2007, James Comey, the deputy attorney general, described the now famous "hospital crisis" that was continuing to reverberate through the intelligence community.[25] Comey's decision to stand up to the Bush White House in this dramatic internal battle over NSA surveillance contributed to President Obama's decision to name him FBI director in June 2013 and helped ensure his near unanimous confirmation in the aftermath of the Snowden leaks.[26]

"That night was probably the most difficult night of my professional life," Comey recalled in his testimony.[27] The crisis occurred in 2004, before the NSA's program was leaked and well before Comey's firing by President Trump in May 2017. Jack Goldsmith, the new head of the Justice Department's Office of Legal Counsel, had conducted a review of some of the more outlandish claims of presidential power that had been advanced after 9/11, with special attention to arguments made by Yoo. The conservative Goldsmith concluded most of Stellar Wind was defensible under the dubious theory that Congress had somehow approved surveillance of international terrorists outside of FISA requirements by authorizing the use of military force after 9/11. However, Goldsmith decided that aspects of the program, including aspects of the NSA's bulk collection of certain metadata, had been a bridge too far and were probably illegal. As a result, Goldsmith's boss, Jim Comey, informed the White House that the Justice Department could no longer sign off on Stellar Wind. Comey's news came at a bad time. Since 2001 the NSA had provided the telecommunications companies with letters on a regular, periodic basis, assuring them they were cooperating with a program that the president had authorized and that the attorney general had concluded was legal. The president's most recent authorization was set to expire within a few days.

The White House was desperate to get the attorney general's continued approval for Stellar Wind, even if that meant asking him to overrule Goldsmith's opinion on the internet metadata issue. However, Attorney General John Ashcroft was ill and recovering from surgery. Ashcroft had temporarily signed over his powers as attorney general to his deputy. Jim Comey made clear he would not budge. He found out that White House officials were planning to visit Ashcroft in his hospital room to get him to sign off on Stellar Wind. Comey ordered his security detail to rush him to the hospital. Comey arrived first. After the White House officials arrived, Ashcroft refused to overrule him.

While Bush initially reauthorized Stellar Wind without change—and without the attorney general's approval—the situation had clearly become untenable. Comey, along with other top officials, threatened to resign if the Justice Department's legal advice continued to be ignored. Either the NSA surveillance had to end or the lawyers had to find another way for it to continue. Jack Goldsmith supported an alternative to the presidential power theory that required the approval of the FISA court. This was a defeat for Cheney's lawyer, David Addington. While the FISA court's civil libertarian critics ordinarily get more attention, its strongest detractors are ideologues like Addington who object to any judicial role in reviewing intelligence surveillance. "We're one bomb away from getting rid of that obnoxious court," Addington had told Goldsmith shortly before the "hospital crisis."[28] While Stellar Wind continued for three more years, lawyers at the Justice Department and the ODNI were now laboring to phase out the program.

It was a painstaking process, requiring creative lawyering that stretched the letter of the law to its limit and beyond. The first step involved using the Patriot Act's expanded authority for metadata collection under FISA to provide a legal way for the NSA to engage in the surveillance of the particular metadata that Goldsmith had decided could no longer take place under Stellar Wind. In 2004 the surveillance court approved this collection under Goldsmith's Patriot Act theory. In May 2006 the court approved bulk collection of telephone records under a similar theory involving a different provision of FISA. It was the power to obtain "certain business records" that had been expanded by section 215 of the Patriot Act—the section we had successfully branded as the "library records" provision when I was an ACLU lawyer.[29] While section 215 was never used to collect library records, the surveillance court was now issuing court orders on a regular basis allowing the NSA to obtain in bulk the call detail records of several major telecommunications providers, including Verizon, the company named in the order leaked by Snowden in June 2013.

The FISA court authorized the bulk collection of internet metadata and telephone records under Patriot Act provisions that allow collection of records *relevant* to international terrorism—the standard that Kate Martin and I had discussed back when the law was reauthorized for the first time. As we have seen, "relevance" is a very low standard, far lower than probable cause. Still, it took some effort to convince the court that the language of the Patriot Act allowed bulk collection because the vast majority of records the NSA was collecting were plainly not relevant. The court was convinced only because the NSA promised to follow detailed privacy rules. Analysts had to start with a telephone number or other unique identifier. NSA officials had to document reasonable, articulable suspicion connecting this "seed number" to one of several international terrorist organizations. An analyst could then access all the telephone numbers that were in contact with the seed number, as well as the numbers that were in contact with those first-order contacts, up to three degrees of separation ("three hops") from the initial seed number. By requiring this reasonable suspicion stricture as the starting point for the NSA's use of the bulk database, the government convinced the FISA court that it could find that all of the telephone records met the relevance standard.

By the time I was briefed on Stellar Wind in late 2006, bulk collection of metadata had already been approved by the FISA court under this creative theory. Although I had not realized it, I had entered the intelligence community just in time to help the Bush administration finish the job of putting the remaining Stellar Wind activities under what Addington had derided as "that obnoxious court." Obtaining the court's permission for the NSA to collect content (rather than metadata) inside the United States proved far more difficult. The Patriot Act did not provide much help. Although the Patriot Act had lowered the legal standard for collection of metadata and had made it easier to share intelligence information with criminal prosecutors, it had preserved FISA's bedrock requirement of judicial review based on probable cause for collection of content. The government's creative theory was that the law could be read to allow for a single order authorizing surveillance of thousands of suspected foreign terrorists, with probable cause determinations left to NSA analysts.

At the time, I thought the government's reading of FISA was strained at best. Even colleagues who agreed with the argument said they understood it was a stretch, perhaps even more of a stretch than bulk collection of metadata. Surveillance orders normally covered particular phones or internet accounts, not the international gateways that carry massive quantities of digital communications along the internet backbone. Still, the FISA court initially went along with it. In January 2007 Judge Malcolm Howard approved a blanket order for surveillance of foreign targets. The court said that while foreign targets would still have to meet the law's basic requirement—namely, that there was probable cause they were acting on behalf of al-Qaeda or affiliated international terrorist groups—specific determinations of probable cause could be made by NSA officials.[30] The creative lawyering had saved the NSA's program. Still, as a legal matter, Stellar Wind was now over. For the first time since October 2001, all of the NSA's domestic collection of data was back under the authority of the surveillance court.

Howard's order was limited to foreign selectors—targets of what had been the NSA's Stellar Wind program who were reasonably believed to be outside the United States. As there were relatively few domestic targets, this limitation caused little concern at the NSA. When the order came up for renewal in March, it was assigned to another judge, Roger Vinson. Vinson decided the international gateway theory was simply too much of a stretch, even for targets outside the United States. The creative lawyering had reached its limits. The court had gone along with the government's "ground-breaking and innovative" bulk collection theory for metadata, but if the NSA wanted to continue its collection of content from international gateways under FISA, it was not enough for the court to rely only on a "highly abstract and generalized probable cause finding" to support the NSA's collection program and for the NSA itself to decide the issue of individual probable cause for targets. Instead, it would have to prove to the court that it had probable cause for each target, as the statute obviously required. If the administration thought this requirement made little sense for foreigners outside the United States, it should go to Congress. According to Judge Vinson, it was not the court's job to rewrite the law.[31]

THE FEELING INSIDE THE INTELLIGENCE COMMUNITY when we learned of the Vinson order verged on panic. Even those who thought Stellar Wind had been legally justified, and who therefore believed that the NSA could simply go back to collecting phone calls and e-mails without court approval, understood that restarting Bush's warrant-less wiretapping program would be politically disastrous. There were thousands of foreign targets, all suspected operatives of al-Qaeda or affiliated organizations, some of whom frequently changed their methods of communication in an effort to avoid surveillance. Even figuring out which targets and accounts to prioritize for a case-by-case review would be a massive undertaking. As lawyers scrambled to put together the information needed to satisfy the court's demand for probable cause on a target-by-target basis, there was a precipitous drop in the number of targets the NSA was monitoring.[32] For the first time since 9/11, the NSA was going dark.

The need for secrecy had always been the argument against going to Congress, but the new director of national intelligence, retired admiral Michael McConnell, decided the NSA needed the public on its side. Closing the "intelligence gap" could only be done if Congress agreed to amend the law. McConnell told us his plan was to make Congress understand the serious consequences that Vinson's decision had created. In other words, he said bluntly, we were going to "scare" them. After a summer of dire warnings from McConnell and other Bush administration officials, Congress obliged. In August 2007 the Protect America Act became law. It allowed the FISA court to au-thorize surveillance of "persons reasonably believed to be outside the United States" without individual review of targets. The stan-dard would not be probable cause but whether the NSA believed that monitoring the foreign targets would generate foreign intelligence information. The court would not review targets at all. Instead, the court would review the NSA's surveillance in an entirely new kind of procedure under a new section 702 of FISA.

Some Congressional staffers described section 702 as a "basket" or program warrant. In fact, the procedure was nothing like a war-rant. A warrant requires probable cause and a neutral magistrate, and must be specific. Arguably, traditional FISA orders meet this standard; at a minimum, they come close.[33] The court's role under section 702 would be a new one: reviewing an entire program of NSA signals intelligence collection. The NSA was not trying to satisfy the Fourth Amendment's warrant clause. Instead, the agency was arguing that the Fourth Amendment was satisfied because its targets were foreign and its privacy rules would protect incidentally collected U.S. person information. This was a familiar argument; it was the same one the NSA had always made for its foreign and satellite collection programs. The difference was that the NSA's mass surveillance would now be reviewed by a court. The FISA court would now be examining the NSA's procedures for determining that targets were located abroad and its procedures for protecting the privacy of U.S. persons. If the court agreed that these procedures were reasonably effective in limiting the NSA to foreign targets and adequately protected the constitutional rights of U.S. persons who might be in contact with those targets, it could authorize surveillance in a single order under section 702 of FISA that would be good for one year.

Although McConnell had won the day in Congress, he found himself frustrated with the public debate. The NSA had been forced to talk publicly about its most sensitive programs, revealing that many foreign communications were vulnerable to surveillance from inside the United States. Nonetheless, the public did not really understand the issue: it still had the mistaken impression that the NSA had been engaged in a dastardly plot to spy on Americans. A few weeks after the Protect America Act became law, McConnell's frustrations boiled over. On a trip to the U.S.-Mexican border, he had trouble keeping his focus on the homeland security issues he was there to discuss. During an interview with a local newspaper, the *El Paso Times*, McConnell said that excessive openness about surveillance "means that some Americans are going to die."[34] In other words, McConnell was arguing that the information the NSA had declassified and released as part of its effort to convince Congress to pass the Protect America Act might endanger its ability to collect the information needed to stop the next terrorist attack. McConnell said this without evidence, and he was rightly criticized for it. More important, McConnell used the interview to provide new details on the NSA's surveillance activities inside the United States. There was more than a little irony in this; these were the very details that he had insisted remain classified during the debate over the law.

While Stellar Wind had included both foreign and domestic targets, the number of foreign targets had always been much larger.

The government's insistence that the number of targets remain secret made this reality awkward to discuss, but it explains the disconnect between the public perception of Stellar Wind as primarily a domestic spying program and the understanding of intelligence officials that the program was mainly one targeting foreign terrorists, although it created complex legal issues because it required access to data inside the United States. Of course, McConnell and other intelligence officials themselves were to blame for this situation. Whenever officials complained about a debate over a classified program being misinformed, which was often, I reminded them that they should not complain if they were the ones who were refusing to make public the information that was needed to inform the debate. We had told Congress the number of foreign and domestic selectors in classified briefings, but the numbers remained classified. Nevertheless, McConnell told the reporter for the *El Paso Times* that by the time the program had come to an end, the number of domestic targets was "one hundred or less. And then, on the foreign side, it's in the thousands."[35]

McConnell's exchange with the *El Paso Times* shows that the debate over whether NSA programs that obtain data on foreign targets from inside the United States are domestic or foreign confuses more than it clarifies. In truth, NSA officials were struggling with a new type of surveillance altogether—surveillance that was neither domestic nor foreign, but transnational. McConnell had offered the public a glimpse of the NSA's new world of transnational surveillance. The data were inside the United States but belonged to people located all over the world. Those in Congress on the receiving end of highly classified briefings, such as Representative Jane Harman, were "shocked" to find the director of national intelligence had "decided to share these details with a small-town newspaper."[36] I was also surprised at the director's jolt of transparency. Weren't such details still classified, I asked a senior intelligence lawyer? Well, he said, since they are on the record in an interview from the head of the intelligence community, they are not anymore. We will be talking for years about the famous *El Paso Times* interview, he observed wryly—and accurately.

THE DEBATE IN CONGRESS OVER the Protect America Act did more than shed some needed light on the NSA's transnational surveillance. It also spurred new privacy safeguards—safeguards I would have a direct role in implementing. The Protect America Act required periodic reports on the NSA's compliance with its court-ordered procedures. Alex and I pushed the NSA and the Justice Department to go beyond the minimum required by law. We urged more frequent and detailed reports that would do more than simply report any violations; they would provide context and analysis. We wanted the NSA to use these reports to learn from its mistakes, and we briefed Congress on our efforts. This was a new responsibility for Alex and me. Our job had been to review broad policies, not to conduct compliance assessments of particular programs. After August 2007, our visits to Fort Meade involved poring over the logs that NSA analysts kept to justify why they believed targeting particular selectors would generate foreign intelligence, as well as the steps they took to decide that these targets were outside the United States. Our first assessment took place just two weeks after court-ordered collection began; it was followed by monthly visits.[37] We were not alone; we were joined by lawyers from the Justice Department, and Alex was staffing up to handle the increased workload.

In reality, the most important policy question has never been whether the NSA should engage in transnational surveillance but under what rules. Should transnational surveillance be treated more like domestic national security surveillance or more like the NSA's foreign and satellite programs? Most civil libertarians would urge domestic rules, especially if there is any possibility the NSA's target is in contact with an American. They would require something akin to the warrants required by the Fourth Amendment: individual court review, based on probable cause that the foreign target is an agent of a foreign power. The intelligence community disagrees. It urges foreign rules, arguing that data and communications belonging to foreigners outside the United States should not be clothed in the protections of the Fourth Amendment just because they happen to be on a switch or a server inside the United States. According to the NSA's rules for signals intelligence collection, the Fourth Amendment protects "all U.S. persons anywhere in the world and all persons within the United States,"[38] but its protections do not extend to include foreigners outside the United States. The data it collects may be from domestic sources, but the focus of transnational surveillance is on foreign targets. By requiring domestic rules for transnational surveillance, intelligence officials say, the United States risks giving up its home field advantage as the hub of the global internet.

The way Alex and I had approached the Protect America Act offered another approach: specific rules for control of transnational surveillance. It was a middle way, more exacting than the general oversight the NSA applied to all its programs but more flexible than the individual court review required by traditional FISA orders. These new checks and balances were a victory for the rule of law, but they also greatly expanded the NSA's collection of data inside the United States. The warrantless Stellar Wind program had been limited in scope. The secrecy surrounding it made it less useful than the court-approved surveillance that replaced it. As Stellar Wind was based on the president's wartime powers, it could only be used to monitor specific international terrorist organizations. The new court orders under section 702 of FISA allowed surveillance for a wide variety of foreign intelligence purposes.

Although the Protect America Act passed by comfortable margins in both houses of Congress, most Democrats voted against the law. They believed it did not do enough to protect civil liberties. One of them was an idealistic young senator from Illinois and candidate for president, Barack Obama. The law was a temporary measure. Congress would have a chance to review the issue in the summer of 2008—just as the nation was consumed with a historic election campaign.

4

STONE KNIVES AND BEARSKINS

FROM HIS POST IN GENEVA IN THE SUMMER OF 2008, EDWARD SNOWDEN, THEN A CIA computer specialist disillusioned by the war in Iraq, the National Security Agency's warrantless wiretapping program, and other George W. Bush policies, decided against becoming a whistle-blower—at least for the moment. It appeared likely that Barack Obama would become the next U.S. president. "I think even Obama's critics were impressed and optimistic about the values that he represented," Snowden later said in an interview with James Bamford, the author of several books about the NSA. "He said that we're not going to sacrifice our rights. We're not going to change who we are just to catch some small percentage more terrorists."[1]

Along with most Americans, I shared Snowden's optimism. However, I noticed nuances in Obama's language that were apparently lost on Snowden and many others. In his remarks on the campaign trail, Obama did not echo his supporters' harsh criticisms of the Patriot Act, nor did he object to the impact of the NSA's surveillance programs on privacy. Instead, Obama criticized Bush for sidestepping Congress and the courts in the "war on terror." As *New York*

Times reporter Charlie Savage would later note, Obama was offering a rule of law critique rather than a civil liberties critique of the Bush administration's legal strategy.[2] Obama saw the war paradigm as a threat to the separation of powers between the executive, legislative, and judicial branches. He did not voice a particularly strong opinion about whether Bush's surveillance policies violated individual rights.

It was a subtle but important distinction. The original, unamended Constitution describes the powers of the legislative, executive, and judicial branches. It guarantees liberty only indirectly, through structural checks and balances. The Bill of Rights enumerates specific rights, including the right against unreasonable searches, protected by the Fourth Amendment. Ordinarily, a search requires a warrant for it to be considered a reasonable one. By the final year of the Bush administration, the NSA's transnational surveillance was subject to judicial review, but that did not mean it was subject to anything like a traditional judicial warrant. As we have seen, what some were calling "basket warrants" under section 702 of FISA that started with the Protect America Act were anything but warrants: they authorized surveillance of thousands of foreign targets without probable cause or individual review by a magistrate. A civil liberties critique might find fault with Congress and the courts for going along with such warrantless surveillance, even if it was directed at foreign targets, because of the impact on the privacy of Americans. The rule of law critique was satisfied by the fact that the judiciary—that is, the Foreign Intelligence Surveillance Court—was now deciding whether the NSA's transnational surveillance was permitted by laws enacted by Congress and whether these laws were consistent with the Constitution.

In August 2008 then senator Obama made a choice that made the rule of law critique less relevant. Although Obama had voted against the Protect America Act, he decided to vote for its replacement, the FISA Amendments Act. In the intelligence community's effort to attract broader support in Congress among members like Obama who had opposed the earlier law, the new law contained a number of provisions to enhance oversight. One required the inspectors general of the multiple departments and agencies involved in Stellar Wind to conduct a review of the now terminated program. The government later released the final report of all the inspectors general, in redacted form.[3] Another provision fixed a loophole in the original FISA law. FISA's definition of electronic surveillance had always allowed the NSA to target Americans using its overseas collection authorities without going to the FISA court, as long as they were outside the United States. Under Executive Order 12,333, the NSA had been required only to obtain the permission of the U.S. attorney general for such surveillance. Now the NSA would have to take these cases to the surveillance court, a change that top NSA officials told me they welcomed (although, as we will see in chapter 7, this was at least in part to make it easier to defend section 702 against challenges by communications providers).

The FISA Amendments Act also undid a troubling change affecting FISA's definition of electronic surveillance made by the Protect America Act. The change left open the possibility that communications providers might voluntarily cooperate with surveillance "directed at a person reasonably believed to be located outside of the United States" without review by the FISA court.[4] The provision left open the possibility that the NSA could obtain such data inside the United States under the same rules that applied to its foreign and satellite surveillance instead of using section 702—that it could use foreign rules for transnational surveillance, if communication providers agreed. As communications providers insisted on court orders anyway, the language had little practical impact. Still, Nancy Pelosi, Speaker of the House, explained its omission from the FISA Amendments Act as a victory for privacy, one that was "very important to each and every person in America."[5] In effect, by repeating this provision Congress was endorsing the middle way for transnational surveillance that Alex and I had championed as the correct approach.

While the new safeguards had been enough to change the minds of Barack Obama and Nancy Pelosi, the American Civil Liberties Union and other civil liberties organizations were furious. The FISA Amendments Act did more than extend section 702. The law also put an end to lawsuits challenging Bush's warrantless wiretapping by giving immunity to telecommunications providers who had participated in Stellar Wind. Obama had made a commitment during his primary campaign to filibuster any law that let providers off the hook. By voting for the FISA Amendments Act, Obama violated this commitment. His flip-flop prompted a torrent of criticism on My.BarackObama.com, an innovative platform allowing his supporters to exchange views. Obama responded with a thoughtful post. "In a dangerous world," he said, the government needed to collect intelligence. While Obama agreed that the FISA Amendments Act was not perfect, he argued it was "far better" than the Protect America Act. He pointed to the provision that Pelosi had championed making clear that "no law supersedes the authority of the FISA court"—a reaffirmation of Congress's original decision in 1978 to make FISA the "exclusive means" for the intelligence surveillance it chose to regulate, and a repudiation of the Bush administration's various arguments that this provision had not really meant what it said.[6]

Obama was fighting the last war. Cheney had already lost his battle to prevent Congress and the courts from involvement in intelligence surveillance. Cheney's effort to use the attacks of 9/11 to erode the authority of the FISA court had failed; Stellar Wind had come to an end more than a year earlier. However, the surveillance itself was continuing. Congress and the courts had not told the NSA to end its transnational surveillance programs or subject them to traditional warrants but to expand them even further. The danger Stellar Wind had presented was that it allowed the president to engage in surveillance activities entirely on his own, without consulting the other branches. Now all three branches were on board with the NSA's new approach. This posed a quite different sort of danger to civil liberties, especially when the legal tools those branches had to safeguard privacy were relics of another age.

SHORTLY AFTER OBAMA TOOK OFFICE, I ran into a colleague, Ben Powell, the outgoing general counsel of the Office of the Director of National Intelligence (ODNI)—the chief lawyer for the intelligence community. As one of the intelligence community's few political appointees, Ben would soon be gone. He seemed relieved. Among his last duties was briefing the new president in the Oval Office on NSA surveillance. The briefings had gone well, he told me. It appeared there would be no major changes to the programs we had all worked so hard to put under the supervision of the FISA court.

Ben Powell was a good choice to explain the NSA programs to Obama and his legal team. As I knew well, his earnest manner has a tendency to win over skeptics. He often speaks softly, as if to include you in the select club of those who appreciate the tough choices needed to safeguard security and maintain the country's constitutional balance. Ben explained how Bush's unilateral approach to NSA surveillance had changed during the president's second term. The NSA's domestic collection of data (both metadata and content) had now been authorized by all three branches of government—legislative, executive, and judicial. For Obama, who had taught constitutional law at the University of Chicago, approval by all three branches was a compelling argument.

Ben Powell also had some bad news. The NSA had recently informed the Foreign Intelligence Surveillance Court that it had bungled its handling of the telephone metadata program. "I want my lawyers to look into this," Obama responded, indicating his new White House counsel, Greg Craig, and his new attorney general, Eric Holder.[7] Still, these appeared to be compliance issues. As long as the NSA and the Justice Department could make changes that satisfied the court's concerns, there would be no need to elevate them to the White House. Over the next few years, Obama turned his attention to a broader privacy agenda, including strengthening consumer privacy and the growing problem of cybersecurity.

Ben wasn't the only one moving on. I was headed to the White House. My colleague Melissa Hathaway had just completed a review of cybersecurity policy. Melissa worked a few doors down from my office, and she had consulted Alex and me on the civil liberties and privacy issues involved in her review. She recommended that the White House national security staff have a dedicated privacy position within its new cybersecurity office.

This time, there was no hesitation—I jumped at the chance. The threats to privacy and security on the internet were growing rapidly, and Obama seemed to get it. The civil liberties questions were complex. They included the delicate question of what role the NSA should play in monitoring cybersecurity threats that affected critical infrastructure. In May 2009 Obama announced the results of Hathaway's review. It was the first speech by an American president devoted entirely to the subject of cybersecurity.

Obama's remarks included a brief nod to my new job. The national security staff, Obama explained, would now include an official with "a portfolio specifically dedicated to safeguarding the privacy and civil liberties of the American people."[8] While the staff of the National Security Council had long had a small office to address human rights issues, it had never had a dedicated privacy official. The new job reflected how important privacy issues had become for national security policy. Obama's counterterrorism adviser, John Brennan, told me he thought I could be helpful not only on cybersecurity issues but on other cutting-edge issues as well.

My colleagues were delighted. They told me I was moving to where the action was. Inside the national security establishment, almost everyone thought that cybersecurity was the next big thing. There was no interest in rehashing the arguments over NSA surveillance that had consumed the last administration. With all three branches on board, the NSA was now under control.

ALTHOUGH I DID NOT KNOW it during my time at the White House, back at Fort Meade the NSA's compliance problems were more serious than we realized. They extended well beyond the problems with the telephone metadata program that Obama had learned about in those early days. Addressing them required an end-to-end review of the NSA's systems.[9]

Upstream collection was particularly challenging. The challenges were the result of how the NSA's surveillance devices worked. The devices were designed to look for selectors associated with the NSA's target (such as an e-mail address) within the transiting data. If a selector was found, the NSA would acquire the entire "internet transaction"—that is, the data surrounding the selector. This design resulted in two significant consequences.

First, the NSA obtained not only communications that were "to" or "from" the targets of its surveillance, but also communications between entirely unrelated people that happened to contain a selector associated with an NSA target. The NSA called this "about" collection because this was collection that was about the target rather than to or from the target. Congress had not discussed "about" collection when it passed the FISA Amendments Act in 2013; indeed, "about" collection remained highly classified until 2013. The FISA court was aware of "about" collection and approved it. It was another legal stretch, requiring the court to interpret the word "targeting" in section 702 of FISA in a very peculiar way: as meaning something other than obtaining the communications belonging to a target.

The second consequence was one that the FISA court had neither understood nor approved. In some cases, the "internet transactions" that the NSA acquired included more than one communication. This meant that the NSA was collecting communications that were neither to, from, or even "about" the target. In fact, they had nothing to do with the target at all. Still worse, some of these unrelated communications were entirely domestic. In 2011 the NSA was forced to file an embarrassing declaration with the FISA court, admitting its devices on the internet backbone were capturing some communications that did not belong to the foreign targets it was authorized to monitor. The court decided that upstream collection was "deficient on statutory and constitutional grounds," and had been for years. The "NSA has, as a practical matter, circumvented the spirit" of the law requiring that its domestic collection of content be limited to communications involving foreign targets located outside the United States, the court found.[10] On two separate occasions, involving different forms of collection, the NSA had illegally acquired entirely domestic content it was not authorized to collect as a result of the way its surveillance systems were designed. When the NSA asked for permission to use the data anyway, the court had to pointedly warn intelligence officials of the criminal penalties involved if they knowingly made use of the fruits of illegal surveillance.[11]

The FISA court concluded, based on a study it ordered the NSA to conduct, that internet backbone surveillance had captured tens of thousands of communications of Americans, including entirely domestic communications with no connection to a foreign target. The collection was unavoidable because of the way the NSA's surveillance devices worked: they often acquired multiple communications, including communications having nothing to do with the NSA's target. As the content of domestic communications unquestionably enjoys full Fourth Amendment protection, the finding was deeply troubling. The NSA agreed to new restraints on the use and retention of the data.[12]

The NSA's collection of telephone records also created greater risks to privacy than was initially understood. The initial telephone number or other unique identifier—called a "seed number"—that analysts needed to use the bulk database had to be associated with a suspected international terrorist. This was the principal privacy safeguard that applied to the NSA's bulk collection. Seed numbers had to be approved by a high-level official, based on a standard of "reasonable, articulable suspicion," or RAS for short. In 2009, however, the NSA had discovered that analysts had been using several systems, including an "alert list," that were not limited to approved numbers. Analysts could not query the database without obtaining approval, but the alert list allowed NSA analysts to know that a number was in the database and seek approval. NSA technical personnel had interpreted the court order to permit such use of the alert list, and the lawyers had failed to understand this. When the lawyers told the FISA court of the issue, the court said this was not allowed, chastising the agency for "what appears to be a flagrant violation" of its orders.[13] It took months to fix the problems.

The NSA's failures raised real questions among the judges of the FISA court as to whether the agency could comply with complex rules in transnational surveillance and bulk collection programs, and whether judges were equipped to oversee them. In the case of internet metadata, the NSA itself eventually decided that it was not worth it, but only after years of trying to make a program of bulk collection work. (Internet metadata provide routing information about internet communications, such as the e-mail addresses contained in the header of an e-mail.) When the presiding judge of the FISA court, Colleen Kollar-Kotelly, asked a government attorney at an early hearing on the NSA's bulk internet metadata program if it was reasonable to "conclude that there wasn't content" being collected, the attorney confidently replied such a mistake was not a "physical possibility." (Precisely which portions of an internet communication the FISA court considers to be metadata and which it considers to be content remains classified.)

Years later, the NSA was forced to admit that its bulk collection program had ensnared some internet data the court had not authorized it to collect, meaning it had collected content illegally—after telling the court such collection was simply impossible. The agency blamed "poor management" and a failure to communicate with technical personnel.[14] The court's stern warnings about the criminal penalties for illegal and unconstitutional surveillance got the agency's attention. The NSA conducted a review and decided the program was not worth the trouble. In 2011 the NSA ended its court-supervised program of domestic bulk collection of internet metadata, preferring instead to collect such metadata abroad, where it would not have to comply with the FISA court's rules.

It turned out that subjecting the NSA's transnational surveillance and bulk metadata collection programs to court review was even more difficult in practice than it had been in theory. While the NSA had managed to placate the court, the public had no inkling that the transnational surveillance authorized by section 702 of FISA had resulted in such serious privacy risks to Americans. From my perch at the White House, I had also failed to understand the scope of the problem. If anyone briefed President Obama on how the NSA's compliance problems in its court-ordered programs were continuing to affect the privacy of Americans before June 2013, I was certainly not aware of it.

AS I WAS LEARNING, WHILE positions at the White House may carry prestigious titles, the day-to-day work is usually that of playing traffic cop for a sprawling national security bureaucracy. At my level, this did not for the most part involve making policy decisions directly but rather ensuring that the agencies had clearly outlined their views and had attempted to find consensus before difficult questions were elevated to ever higher levels for decision.[15] One of my first duties was to put together a committee of privacy and civil liberties officials from across the executive branch. Most of our meetings were not in the West Wing but in another part of the White House complex, the Eisenhower Executive Office Building; Mark Twain once called it the "ugliest building in America." For our first meeting, I hoped to inspire a sense of seriousness and purpose, so I decided to hold it in the White House Situation Room.

One by one, my colleagues filed in. The committee included my old boss, Alex Joel of the ODNI, along with privacy and civil liberties officers from the Departments of Justice and Homeland Security. Other departments sent lawyers. Many of the "three-letter" spy agencies were represented by officials Alex had requested be designated to handle privacy issues—one of many improvements Alex and I had made to strengthen what we had taken to calling the intelligence community's "civil liberties infrastructure": its lawyers, compliance officials, and inspectors general. The NSA did not yet have a full-time privacy and civil liberties official. (It would create the position after 2013, following the Snowden disclosures.) For now it was represented by John DeLong, a lawyer with a degree in mathematics. DeLong had just been named head of a new compliance office, created as a result of the problems the NSA was having following the rules the FISA court had imposed on its transnational surveillance programs.

My job was made more difficult by Obama's delay in setting up the Privacy and Civil Liberties Oversight Board—an independent board recommended by the 9/11 Commission. The first such privacy board was short-lived, lasting from 2006 to 2008 as a body attached to the Executive Office of the President. Its sole Democratic member, Lanny Davis, resigned in protest when Bush White House officials demanded revisions to a board report.[16] Congress restructured the board as an independent agency, but Bush's nominees for a new board were never confirmed. The Obama White House spent years wrangling over what its board should look like. President Obama did not manage to nominate all of its members until December 2011. It was not until his second term that the board opened its doors again. In May 2013 its full-time chair was confirmed, allowing it to hire staff and begin work—just as Edward Snowden was sitting down with journalists in a Hong Kong hotel room to record his story.[17]

In the meantime, my committee of privacy bureaucrats took up the slack. Our main task was to review Obama's cybersecurity agenda, but we also exchanged information about our common challenges in protecting privacy and civil liberties in agencies better known for spying and surveillance. In one such meeting, John DeLong gave us a window onto how the NSA was handling the issue.

With the increasingly complex rules the NSA was facing as a result of court oversight, DeLong explained, the NSA leadership was viewing compliance as essential to the NSA's intelligence-gathering mission. Compliance failures were not only a danger to privacy, they could threaten national security. If the agency could not manage to comply with the rules it was given—whether by Congress, the courts, or the executive branch—vital surveillance powers might be curtailed. In a later interview, DeLong estimated that "about 300 people" within NSA were focused on "core compliance type things," such as audits, spot checks, and training.[18]

Compliance problems could be as straightforward as typographical errors or they could be indicative of larger issues. One recurring problem was "roamers," or foreign targets who moved inside the United States, where monitoring required a warrant based on probable cause. As the NSA's systems might continue collecting their communications, this was a problem. In the popular imagination, an intelligence analyst can determine a target's location within seconds and with complete accuracy. In fact, the NSA's system is far from foolproof. The NSA tracked roaming incidents even when it complied with its rules by turning off its surveillance within the time those rules allowed. I remember that Alex Joel and I had warned the agency it should be clearer about when the roaming incidents involved actual violations of its rules and when those incidents where being tracked only to keep tabs on the scale of the problem. If it didn't, the agency might be punished for the meticulous way DeLong and other compliance officials were doing their job. Every six months a detailed accounting of compliance incidents is provided to Congress and the FISA court. In 2013 an unconfirmed document provided to the *Washington Post* that appeared to be an internal compliance report resulted in a front-page headline—"NSA Broke Privacy Rules Thousands of Times per Year, Audit Finds"—a headline I found very frustrating, given the work that Alex and I had put into improving how the NSA kept track of its mistakes in order to assess its compliance with court-ordered safeguards.[19]

Court review of the NSA's transnational surveillance and bulk collection programs had focused new attention on the agency's imperfections and the serious consequences of seemingly small mistakes. Roamers are not a problem unique to collection authorized by the FISA court. The NSA mistakenly picks up phone calls inside the

United States from its overseas and satellite collection as well. In fact, the NSA's typical "compliance incident rate" for court-authorized surveillance—the compliance incidents during the reporting period as a percentage of the number of selectors tasked—was impressive, at under one-half of 1 percent.[20] It spoke well of the NSA's rules-based culture and DeLong's leadership, but in light of the volume of the NSA's collection, even if the agency's compliance rate for its foreign collection was as good as its rate for court-supervised programs of domestic collection of less than one-half of 1 percent, the absolute number of mistakes would be very large. Fewer resources and even less high-level attention were focused on the foreign collection programs. At meetings of our White House privacy committee, DeLong asked the kind of perceptive questions one might expect of a mathematician. There seemed to be a lot of resources devoted to compliance with privacy rules, but were we really getting more privacy? How could we measure that? As a result of the FISA court's attention, domestic collection of data had been put under a microscope. Yet the NSA's foreign collection under Executive Order 12,333 still consumed most of its resources and generated most of the data.

Our focus on the domestic collection programs that had started after 9/11 distracted us from other programs whose impact on privacy would make them as or even more controversial after June 2013, when press articles appeared that said they were based on the Snowden leaks—articles that said the NSA was engaged in programs targeting foreign leaders and aid organizations, mass surveillance of the communications of foreign nations, and pervasive efforts to undermine internet security.

DELONG WAS RIGHT TO QUESTION the focus on a handful of domestic programs. I was missing the privacy implications of global surveillance. Our job at the White House cybersecurity office was to ensure an open, interoperable, and secure communications infrastructure. Still, I failed to see the privacy impact of much of what the NSA did. Although it was the NSA's increasingly aggressive operations that were affecting the security of the internet, I largely dismissed the danger its overseas programs posed because they did not affect U.S. persons as much as domestic collection did—or so I thought. After I left government, an Obama administration official who worked on internet freedom for the State Department argued that overseas NSA surveillance might have a greater impact on American privacy than the collection of domestic data, which was at least overseen by a court.[21]

In part, my blindness was a product of the law's myopia. The NSA and other intelligence agencies are charged with finding a vast array of information about foreign governments, organizations, international terrorists, and other "foreign persons." These programs collected information not only about terrorism and other security threats but also for broad "foreign affairs" purposes. The FISA court does not review the NSA's overseas activities unless they intentionally target a U.S. person. I did not know, and I did not want to know, whether the NSA or other agencies were targeting foreign leaders, even friendly ones, as long as the agencies were following the rules and were doing so to collect foreign intelligence. Executive Order 12,333 governs foreign programs. It authorizes "all means" to collect "intelligence information," consistent only with the law "and this Order." While "full consideration" must be given to "the rights of United States persons," foreigners did not receive such consideration.[22]

NSA analysts enjoy a great deal of freedom. While Edward Snowden certainly did not have "the authority," as he later claimed, to target the e-mail account of the president of the United States—or of any U.S. person, absent a court order—software tools such as the XKeyscore program later leaked by Snowden do give analysts broad desktop access to an array of signals intelligence databases. The NSA inspector general later revealed that a handful of analysts in Fort Meade had used signals intelligence resources to target current and former romantic partners, most of whom were foreign nationals. This use of NSA resources for what people at Fort Meade jokingly called "LOVEINT" was, at a minimum, a violation of intelligence oversight rules. NSA employees are permitted to use its surveillance capabilities only for authorized foreign intelligence requirements, not for personal reasons.[23] Still, if the analysts had targeted Americans in this way, they could have been prosecuted. Instead, they received internal discipline.

Nevertheless, in the absence of intentional abuse, surveillance of foreigners is fair game, so long as the analyst articulates a valid intelligence purpose. During my time in government there was no law, executive order, or policy designed to protect the privacy of foreigners, although the inspector general's actions to combat LOVEINT shows that the compliance system still provided some de facto protection against the worst abuses. Nevertheless, as an official charged with protecting privacy and civil liberties, I was told that my concerns should be about the impact of intelligence programs on U.S. persons. At the time this made perfect sense to me. Neither my colleagues nor I thought very much about the broader consequences for privacy of the NSA's mass surveillance of foreigners in the digital age.

In retrospect, my biggest blind spot during my stint in the Obama White House was the impact of the NSA's methods of breaking into global communications on the security of the internet. Of course, the NSA was founded as a spy agency precisely to read protected foreign communications. Yet if the NSA's capabilities are directed toward a valid end—obtaining foreign intelligence—and if rules to protect the information of U.S. persons are followed, then "all means" are authorized. The NSA also has another mission. While the NSA's "Signals Intelligence Directorate" is devoted to surveillance, its "Information Assurance Directorate" protects the security of U.S. military and national security systems. We hoped to leverage the NSA's Information Assurance Directorate to protect other government agencies and privately owned critical infrastructure from foreign cyberattacks. A single-minded focus by the NSA on "enabling" signals intelligence by undermining internet security would frustrate this goal. I understood the problem in general terms, but I failed to appreciate just how serious these risks were becoming.

For example, while the National Institute of Standards and Technology (NIST), an agency of the Department of Commerce, has the lead on technical standards development when it comes to cryptography, by law the NSA also participates. Engineers often design secure hardware and software based on such NIST standards. Randomness is a key element in setting up and using a secure cryptosystem. At a leading conference of cryptographers in 2007, Dan Shumow and Niels Ferguson of Microsoft pointed out a weakness in one of four random number generators NIST had recommended in 2006. There was speculation about an NSA "backdoor." When the issue resurfaced based on press reports in 2013, the crypto community felt its worst fears had been confirmed. "Trust has been violated," remarked Matt Green, a cryptographer at Johns Hopkins University. Deeply embarrassed, NIST withdrew the standard.

While countering Chinese and Russian hackers was at the top of our cybersecurity agenda, we should have spent more time thinking about what our own intelligence agencies were doing to the security of everyone's communications, including our own. After these operations became known, the heads of both Google and Facebook said the NSA's approach risked "breaking the Internet."[24] This is untrue, but only because the internet was broken already; it never had been secure. In large part the insecurity is because Silicon Valley giants ignored the problem. The NSA simply took advantage of the internet's insecurity in order to do its job, just as it was told to do. Still, some of the agency's more aggressive operations could not help but diminish everyone's privacy.

VALERIE CAPRONI WAS THE GENERAL COUNSEL of the FBI for most of the time I was in government. She is now a federal judge. Valerie has a dry sense of humor. Unlike those NSA people up at Fort Meade, she said in more than one meeting during Obama's first term of office, our agents at the bureau still have to use "stone knives and bearskins" for surveillance. It took me a while, but I finally figured out what she meant. She was referring not to the FBI's use of old technology but to its insistence on a venerable legal procedure—individual court review, based on probable cause—for its surveillance in national security investigations. The concept of probable cause is far older than FISA. It is a constitutional requirement, dating to the ratification of the Bill of Rights in 1791.

Caproni was poking fun at the jargon that intelligence community lawyers were using to describe the court orders for transnational surveillance that replaced Stellar Wind. We called the orders "new FISA." They have little in common with traditional FISA orders. A single order for bulk collection of telephone records allowed the NSA to amass a nationwide database of call detail records, including re-

cords of domestic calls. Another order under section 702 of FISA allowed the NSA to monitor the e-mail accounts and telephone calls of
tens of thousands of targets believed to be outside the United States.
As Caproni reminded us, the FBI was still going to the FISA court for
traditional national security surveillance orders based on probable
cause. We called these orders "old FISA" or even "Stone Age FISA"—
which explains Caproni's quip about "stone knives and bearskins."

The Fourth Amendment is the part of the Bill of Rights that protects
against "unreasonable searches and seizures," usually by requiring a
warrant. For a search to be reasonable, probable cause is a bedrock
requirement, even in cases where a warrant is not required. As we
have seen, while the NSA's programs of transnational surveillance
and bulk metadata collection were now subject to judicial review,
they did not require probable cause. Although all three branches had
struggled with complex legal issues involving the precise wording of
FISA in order to sign off on these programs, the constitutional issues
had received far less attention. This was because the Supreme Court's
decisions made decades earlier had made approval of the NSA's mass
surveillance approach surprisingly straightforward, both for content
and for metadata.

The surveillance court had no trouble issuing broad orders, allowing the NSA to collect the content of communications of foreign
customers under section 702 of FISA. In 1989 the Supreme Court had
decided that foreigners outside the United States lack Fourth Amendment rights. In *United States v. Verdugo-Urquidez*, Chief Justice
William Rehnquist reasoned that foreigners outside the United States
are not part of "the people" protected by the Fourth Amendment.[25]
While inadvertent and incidental collection of American communications could and did raise significant constitutional questions, the
simple fact that the NSA was forcing American companies to help
the government spy on their foreign customers raised no issues under
the Bill of Rights. When one e-mail provider, Yahoo, challenged the
constitutionality of the Protect America Act in secret proceedings
before the FISA court, it focused exclusively on the law's impact on
its American customers. As we will see in chapter 7, Yahoo did not
even bother to argue that its foreign customers had constitutional
rights.

Collecting massive quantities of domestic metadata in bulk also posed surprisingly few constitutional issues. The FISA court required some convincing that it could approve bulk collection of telephone records and internet metadata under Patriot Act provisions requiring these records be "relevant" to a counterterrorism investigation. While satisfying the Patriot Act had required some creative lawyering, satisfying the Fourth Amendment was a breeze. For decades the federal courts have refused to give meaningful protection to records that have been provided to a third party. In *Smith v. Maryland*, decided in 1979, the Supreme Court decided that call routing information lacks protection under the Fourth Amendment because a caller must provide it to the telephone company in order to complete the call. Under this "third-party doctrine," there was no constitutional problem with collecting phone records or other metadata without probable cause or individual court review. *Smith* involved a single suspect, while the NSA's program collected records in bulk. According to the FISA court, this did not matter. Since metadata have zero constitutional significance, the court simply saw "no Fourth Amendment interest" in amassing a database that included the calling records of millions of Americans. Any number multiplied by zero is still zero, the court reasoned.[26]

Many civil libertarians object to the government's continuing reliance on *Smith* at a time when our phones have become such a ubiquitous part of our lives. They believe the courts have failed to consider just how much communications metadata can reveal of a person's intimate activities and associations. Of course, as an intelligence agency, the NSA is interested in metadata precisely because it can provide valuable insights. Michael Hayden, a former director of the NSA and of the CIA, has made this point dramatically. "We kill people based on metadata," he said in 2014, referring to drone strikes—although he was quick to add that this was not how the government uses domestic metadata.[27]

The FISA court had little trouble finding the NSA's activities under its bulk metadata and transnational surveillance programs to be consistent with the Fourth Amendment prohibition on "unreasonable searches" because collection of metadata did not count as "searches," and foreigners were not part of "the people" the amendment protects.

As we will see, however, this was not because the surveillance court is a rubber stamp. The Fourth Amendment, at least as it had been interpreted by the Supreme Court, does not limit searches of metadata, or of people outside the United States. The problem is not so much that *Smith* is wrong about metadata or that *Verdugo-Urquidez* is wrong about searches of foreign citizens outside the United States. There will always be exceptions to the Fourth Amendment's warrant requirement; a judicial warrant cannot be required for everything. The problem is that in an era of global mass surveillance, the inevitable consequence of these exceptions is that the Fourth Amendment protects only a tiny fraction of the world's data.

All three branches had agreed that the NSA's transnational surveillance and bulk metadata programs were consistent with the Fourth Amendment, yet they, like me, had failed to appreciate just what this meant for privacy in the digital age. Valerie Caproni turned out to be right in more ways than one. As a result of the federal judiciary's analog-era interpretation of the Constitution, relying on the Bill of Rights to limit the NSA's transnational surveillance in the digital age was like using stone knives and bearskins to fight missiles and drones.

Part II

OUT OF THE SHADOWS

5

BREAKING THE SECRECY HABIT

AS EDWARD SNOWDEN WAS SITTING DOWN WITH JOURNALISTS IN A HOTEL IN HONG Kong in May 2013, I was wrapping up the details involved in my own decision to leave the government. Since January I had been on leave at Brown University, where my wife teaches computer science. Brown had offered me a permanent position, and I had accepted. I would be helping Brown put together a new degree program on cybersecurity. I was planning to focus my teaching, research, and writing on issues such as online identity management and international norms for conflict in cyberspace. As the surveillance programs that had consumed much of my attention for the past six years were highly classified, I never expected to say or write anything about them.

During my seven years in the intelligence community, I had become accustomed to its culture of secrecy. Generating secrets had become second nature. Our office still had old-fashioned "secret" and "top secret" stamps in the supply closet, but I never had the satisfaction of using one. Instead, the word processing, e-mail, and other software we used on our classified computers was configured with a "classify" drop-down menu listing reasons for classifying information. With a click of the mouse, the software automatically generated the appropriate markings. Before the intelligence community's post-Snowden transparency drive, it was a pretty good working assumption that if I wanted to draft a document containing the kind of meaningful details about surveillance discussed in this book—such as the specific safeguards that apply to court-ordered bulk collection of metadata or the number of targets affected by an order of the Foreign Intelligence Surveillance Court—I would need to select at least "secret" from my "classify" drop-down menu.

I do not know how many documents I classified, but I am sure it was too many. For decades, the Information Security Oversight Office of the National Archives has kept detailed statistics on classification decisions, providing the public a way to quantify just how many new secrets are generated each year. High-ranking officials make "original" classification decisions, deciding what information the government should be keeping secret and justifying those decisions by describing the damage to national security that would result from release. The number of original classification decisions has actually been trending down in recent years. However, the vast majority of decisions to classify are made at a lower level, and they have skyrocketed.[1]

In 1997 Senator Daniel Patrick Moynihan chaired a commission that was deeply critical of the national security establishment's penchant for secrecy. With the end of the Cold War, the commission urged "a new way of thinking about secrecy." "The best way to ensure that secrecy is respected," the report argued, "is for secrecy to be returned to its limited but necessary role. Secrets can be protected more effectively if secrecy is reduced overall."[2] In the same year in which the Moynihan Commission released its report, government employees made 6.4 million lower-level classification decisions. By 2013 that figure had grown to 80 million, a twelvefold increase.[3] In theory, lower-level classification decisions are less significant because they do not involve an independent decision to classify. Such "derivative" classification simply reflects the judgment of a lower-level official that a document, report, or e-mail contains information that already has been classified. In reality, most derivative decisions are based on agency "classification guides" that instruct legions of officials to mark classified documents based on broad categories of possibly secret information that provide no real guidance.

Along with almost everyone I knew with a security clearance, I had derivative classification authority. My "classify" drop-down menu was linked to the classification guide for the Office of the Director of National Intelligence (ODNI). As a result of a Freedom of Information Act (FOIA) request, a version of the sixty-three-page guide was released in 2016.[4] Despite its length, the descriptions in the guide are abstract and general, providing little guidance on what is secret and what is not. For example, while the guide makes clear that the bare fact that the agency "relies on the results of IC collection sources and methods" is not classified, almost everything else about collection potentially is. For years, as I stared at a draft e-mail on my "high-side" computer—the computer connected to the government's top-secret computer network—I would think about how to apply the classification guide. Did the e-mail reveal a "general U.S. or foreign collection capability, or interest"? If so, I should choose the drop-down option of "secret," indicating that disclosure would cause "serious damage to the national security." If it revealed a *specific* "collection capability, interest, or vulnerability," I should select "top secret," indicating the potential for "exceptionally grave harm to the national security" if the e-mail were ever disclosed.[5]

My struggles with the government's vague classification standards were not unique; indeed, virtually everyone I know who has ever dealt with classified information has experienced the same frustration. During the 2016 election campaign, Barack Obama said in an interview with Chris Wallace of Fox News that he thought the use of a private e-mail server by his former secretary of state, Hillary Clinton, had "not jeopardized America's national security," even though more than 2,000 of the e-mails she turned over to the government were later found to contain classified information. "There's stuff that is really 'top secret' top secret," Obama explained, but there is also "stuff you could get in open source," meaning information from foreign news organizations and open websites, and this material may also be classified.[6]

Indeed, the State Department's classification guide—which has also been released under FOIA—urges diplomats to classify "negative commentary" on foreign government officials at the secret level or higher, even when derived from "unclassified sources," because of the potential damage to foreign relations. The guide urges special sensitivity when discussing royalty, a deference that does not apply equally across the globe. Europeans "have a much more relaxed attitude toward their royals than do the citizens of certain Asian countries," the guide notes. While Europeans might be "unfazed" by American diplomatic chatter about royal scandals in the local tabloids, Asians "could be offended" by such talk, warranting higher levels of classification.[7]

President Obama's acknowledgment of the innocuous nature of much of the classified material he saw every day meets one definition of a Washington "gaffe"—when a politician "accidentally reveals something truthful."[8] In testimony before the House Judiciary Committee in 2010, longtime transparency advocate Thomas Blanton reported estimates he had collected of the volume of classified material encountered by top officials going back to the Reagan administration that they said plainly should never have been secret. The estimates ranged from 50 percent to 90 percent.[9] Obama's complaints about overclassification were nothing new. Still, because the power to create government secrets derives from the president's foreign affairs responsibilities and his role as commander in chief under Article II of the Constitution, it was striking to see the very man holding the office whose authority is invoked to classify information at a rate of 80 million times a year—twice each second—bow to the obvious. Obama's attempt to put the Clinton e-mail controversy in context did not convince the public. Hillary Clinton's failure to handle classified information appropriately when she was secretary of state probably cost her the presidency.

When I was in government, I tried to follow the rules as best I could, but the incentives were heavily tilted toward overclassification. If I was a bit too quick to click "classify," I knew the staff that handled FOIA requests could easily downgrade my markings. As Clinton learned in 2016, a mistake in the other direction could result in far more serious consequences. If I failed to appropriately mark and handle properly classified material, I might jeopardize my security clearance—and my career.

THANKS TO SNOWDEN, THE GOVERNMENT'S classification markings are now familiar to anyone who has spent time reading the documents he leaked and that journalists have chosen to make public. The first was published on June 6, 2013. It was an order to Verizon Business Services, requiring it to produce "on an ongoing daily basis . . . all call detail records or 'telephony metadata'" belonging to the company, both for international and for purely domestic calls.[10] Perhaps the most explosive of the secrets I had ever learned in government had become public knowledge in an instant. The order was marked "TOP SECRET//SI//NOFORN," almost certainly generated with a "classify" drop-down menu command like the one I had used. SI means "signals intelligence"—a type of sensitive compartmented information. In other words, this information is so sensitive that "Top Secret" is not good enough. We must limit access even further. NOFORN means the document should not be released to any foreign government, not even the other "Five Eyes" nations, the NSA's closest intelligence partners: the United Kingdom, Canada, Australia, and New Zealand. The document appeared to be genuine. Any doubts about the order's authenticity were dispelled when Director of National Intelligence James Clapper issued a statement confirming that the order "is used to support a sensitive collection operation" and providing further details about the program's safeguards in order to "address the misleading impression" left by the leak of the order without any context.[11]

The court order to Verizon was confirmed by Clapper only a few days after I signed the paperwork making final my separation from the ODNI. I immediately found myself talking with the press about a troubling program that I had known about for years but had never discussed publicly. In a studio in New York in the middle of June, CNN host Christiane Amanpour grilled me about NSA surveillance, demanding to know why Clapper had not disclosed the telephone records program much earlier, so that it could have been the subject of an open debate in Congress. "You were in the administration and you were part of this 'safeguards' group," Amanpour noted. "Why didn't you suggest that?"

Good question, I thought. "Well, you know, we're part of a large team and I probably should have been more forceful in advocating that," I said, squirming a bit. "But it's difficult for the intelligence community to break out of its culture. Its culture really prizes secrecy—and for good reasons."[12]

My colleagues were facing much tougher questions about the "sensitive collection operation" that Clapper had finally confirmed. One of them was Robert Litt, the general counsel of the ODNI. After my White House detail ended, I had worked for Bob Litt in the ODNI general counsel's office. A former federal prosecutor, Bob enjoyed sparring with me, the American Civil Liberties Union lawyer who had somehow ended up working in his office. As a boss, Bob was both caring and no-nonsense. He is deeply devoted to the rule of law. Among the headaches Bob faced in the summer of 2013 were calls for the resignation of the director of national intelligence for lying under oath to Congress. The accusation came as a shock.

Retired Air Force general Jim Clapper radiates honor and integrity. His long and distinguished military career includes service in Vietnam, where he flew more than seventy combat support missions and earned a Bronze Star. While his three predecessors had struggled in the new job, none lasting more than two years, Clapper had a solid reputation as a manager known for his blunt talk. In my meetings with Clapper I found him direct, pragmatic, and more than a little intimidating.

The accusation that Clapper had lied to Congress was based on his appearance at a rare public hearing of the Senate Select Committee on Intelligence in March 2013, just a few months before the Snowden revelations began. A member of the committee, Senator Ron Wyden of Oregon, had asked Clapper a carefully worded question: "Does the NSA collect any type of data at all on millions or hundreds of millions of Americans?"

"No sir," Clapper said. "Not wittingly."[13]

The answer, of course, was false, as anyone with knowledge of the NSA's bulk collection programs knew. Snowden said later that Clapper's "lie under oath" was the "breaking point" for him. "Seeing that really meant for me there was no going back," he said.[14] This claim has become a sore point for Snowden's critics, who note that he was amassing the archive of documents he would later leak long before Clapper's testimony and had been in touch with journalists for months. They argue Snowden would have gone through with his plans to leak documents anyway. Of course, only Snowden can know what was in his mind in March 2013.

As a courtesy, Wyden's staff had provided the question to Clapper a day before the hearing. Bob Litt said later that he had not had a chance to prepare Clapper ahead of time and that they had not discussed how to handle Wyden's question. There is no doubt in my mind that Bob is telling the truth about this. I know him too well to believe he would ever advise a client to give a false answer under oath under any circumstances. Clapper maintains that the NSA's program of bulk collection of telephone records had simply escaped his mind; he was thinking about the NSA's collection of content. This is a plausible explanation; the complexities of NSA surveillance can sometimes flummox even the most knowledgeable experts and insiders. Still, after the hearing, Wyden's staff invited Clapper to send a letter clarifying the public record. Clapper declined, knowing it would be hard to do so without revealing the existence of the NSA's bulk collection program. After he confirmed the program in June, following the Snowden leaks, Clapper sent the letter that Wyden's staff had requested months earlier. Clapper later explained, "I responded in what I thought was the most truthful, or least untruthful manner, by saying no."[15] Clapper's explanation had more than a whiff of Pontius Pilate. It earned him nothing but scorn. Senator Rand Paul of Kentucky, a Republican candidate for president in 2016, later quipped that Clapper and Snowden should share a jail cell, where they could have long talks about liberty and security.[16]

Although Clapper's answer certainly misled the public, it did not mislead and could not have misled his questioner. Wyden already knew all about the NSA's bulk collection, as did every other member of the Senate Select Committee on Intelligence, along with other members of Congress who had taken advantage of the classified briefings the administration had offered in advance of the 2009 and 2011 debates on whether to extend the expiring provisions of the Patriot Act, including section 215, the basis for the NSA's bulk collection of telephone records. Wyden opposed bulk collection, but he had found it hard to persuade his colleagues of his position and was hoping to force a public debate.

Wyden's most recent source of irritation was a public appearance

by NSA director Keith Alexander at DEF CON in the summer of
2012. DEF CON is a popular hackers' convention held each year in
Las Vegas. The three-star general cut an unlikely figure at the event,
dressed in a t-shirt and faded jeans. He was hoping to build goodwill
with the crowd, and possibly win a few recruits. When Alexander
was asked whether the NSA had "a file on everyone," Alexander said,
"No, we don't. Absolutely no. . . . The story that we have millions or
hundreds of millions of dossiers on people is absolutely false."[17] Alexander's reply was defensible. The NSA certainly did not and does not
create files or dossiers on millions of Americans. Still, the NSA director's denial plainly rankled Wyden, who saw it as misleading, and
he decided to use Clapper's public appearance before the Senate in
March 2013 to grill him about it. He was careful to explain that his
question was not about "dossiers" but about "any type of data at all,"
knowing this would make it harder for Clapper to avoid revealing
the NSA's bulk collection program. It was a classic legal move. In *To
Kill a Mockingbird*, Harper Lee ascribes to Atticus Finch some sage
advice for every lawyer. "Never, never, never, on cross-examination
ask a witness a question you don't already know the answer to."
Wyden was not seeking information. Frustrated with his inability to
force the public debate on the NSA he had been urging for years, he
was publicly cross-examining the head of the intelligence community
about a highly classified program.

Faced with such an aggressive questioner, secrecy whipsawed Clapper with competing duties. Of course, like all sworn witnesses, Clapper had an obligation to tell the truth, the whole truth, and nothing
but the truth. Yet transparency about the intelligence community's
secret work involves by definition half-truths, giving answers that are
the "least untruthful" possible without revealing the government's
secrets. Under the National Security Act, one of the core duties of the
head of the intelligence community is to protect sources and methods of intelligence.[18] Clapper's statutory responsibility to protect the
government's secrets uniquely disabled him from giving the "whole
truth" about NSA surveillance, or any other classified programs, in
public. At the beginning of public hearings, Clapper had a habit of
reminding everyone of his reluctance to answer questions that might
involve classified programs. At this hearing, Clapper had again ex-

pressed his "serious reservations about conducting open hearings on the worldwide threat, especially the question-and-answer sessions."[19] If intelligence officials stay in the shadows, there is no risk that their duty to tell the truth may conflict with their duty to keep secrets. During the Church Committee investigation, Senator John Tower of Texas, the ranking Republican, strenuously opposed the first ever public appearance of an NSA director in October 1975, arguing it would harm national security.[20] It is only because of the reforms of that era that U.S. intelligence officials like Clapper appear in open hearings at all, where they may be questioned publicly under oath.

If Clapper had sought the advice of his counsel before answering, what might Bob Litt have whispered in his ear? Clapper was certainly entitled to refuse to give the "yes or no" answer that Wyden was demanding. In other contexts, federal courts have long upheld the government's right to "neither confirm nor deny" the existence of classified programs—the unsatisfying "Glomar response," named after the subject of a FOIA lawsuit involving a secret ship, the *Glomar Explorer*, built by the CIA to salvage a Soviet submarine.[21] The Glomar response is now a cliché. When the CIA decided to get a Twitter account, its Public Affairs office had some fun: "We can neither confirm nor deny that this is our first tweet."[22] In part because the response has become so familiar, it is a very poor way to keep a secret. If Clapper had provided the classic Glomar response in response to Wyden's question in March 2013, it would certainly have raised eyebrows, implied the true answer was yes, and increased the risk of disclosure. Of course, this was Wyden's goal. Clapper could have escaped his dilemma if he had declassified the NSA's program of bulk collection of telephone records, as should have been done years earlier. This was partly my fault, as Amanpour rightly pointed out when she pressed me on this point on CNN in June. In hindsight, I could have saved Clapper a great deal of trouble if I had been more forceful in urging the NSA to come clean about bulk collection.

It was soon Bob Litt's turn to face sharp questions. In July 2013 Robert Goodlatte, the chair of the House Judiciary Committee, asked Bob Litt if he really believed "a program of this magnitude . . . could be indefinitely kept secret from the American people?"

"Well, we tried," Bob shot back.[23]

No doubt—and that was the problem. Some secrets are not worth trying to keep. Before we try to keep a secret, we should think about whether it is realistic to believe we can do so. We should also ask whether doing so is worth the cost: to transparency and democratic values, and to the reputation and integrity of the public servants we ask to keep our secrets.

TO MAKE ITS CASE TO the public in the summer of 2013, the Obama administration began by using the same playbook its predecessors had used successfully during the Bush years. Officials claimed the NSA's programs had successfully thwarted dozens of terrorist attacks. They pointed to the "United States person" rules and the oversight of the surveillance court. They denounced Snowden for betraying government secrets. They assumed that the public would trust they had got the balance right and would see Snowden as the villain. The strategy fell flat. Despite Snowden's theft of top-secret documents, his flight to China, and his decision to seek asylum in Russia, more Americans initially viewed him as a whistleblower than as a traitor.[24] They did not trust the NSA's assurances that their data were protected by privacy rules.

The backlash surprised intelligence officials, who had become accustomed since 9/11 to receiving the benefit of the doubt when it came to programs they said were needed to fight terrorism. One reason is because the NSA programs leaked in 2013 were focused on much broader foreign intelligence goals than the Bush-era leaks of warrantless wiretapping in the "war on terror." Still, the backlash also surprised me. Along with other lawyers and oversight officials, I had been working for years to make sure the NSA was under control, and yet all this work to subject NSA surveillance to checks and balances did not seem to matter much to the public. A twist on Obama's 2008 campaign slogan "Yes, We Can" and the famous "Hope" poster by artist Shepard Fairey, featuring a thoughtful candidate shaded in red, white, and blue, captures the post-Snowden mood. The parody outfits Obama with an eavesdropper's headphones. The slogan reads "Yes, We Scan." In an interview, Fairey said he was "pleased to see people subvert my Obama images" because he felt "sickened and betrayed" by Obama's support of the NSA's spying programs.[25]

Obama asked Clapper to reveal more about the NSA to put the revelations in context. With little fanfare, Clapper embraced his role as truth-teller with the zeal of a convert—if only a last-minute convert who fears being burned at the stake. Beginning in July, Clapper released an avalanche of material about the NSA's domestic collection programs that had been the subject of FOIA lawsuits and requests from journalists and civil liberties advocates. They were mostly opinions, legal briefs, and other materials from the FISA court. As these documents detail the privacy safeguards that the NSA's domestic collection programs must follow, they offered a counterpoint to the headlines generated by the Snowden documents, which focused mostly on the scale and intrusiveness of the programs. In August Clapper launched a new website, *IC on the Record,* to make these authorized dumps of declassified documents more user-friendly. The site is hosted on Tumblr, a popular social media site. Users can create their own sites, or "Tumblrs." Many discuss celebrities and other pop culture topics. The intelligence community's Tumblr was soon hosting thousands of pages of documents the government had been fighting for years to keep secret. These were not dusty Cold War files from decades earlier, primarily of interest to historians. They contained rich detail about ongoing NSA programs. In some ways, the documents declassified through *IC on the Record* were more embarrassing than some of the Snowden documents. The narrative of the Snowden documents was that of a powerful mass surveillance state in which there would be "no place to hide." *IC on the Record* showed the NSA's embarrassing missteps in adapting its transnational surveillance to judicial review—failures that made stark the agency's management woes and other flaws.

Over the next several months, I tried to convey to reporters the magnitude of the secrets the government was making public in the interest of transparency. I called the new attitude "Big Transparency" in a *Wall Street Journal* op-ed and at a forum I sponsored at Brown University.[26] Later, I wrote another article celebrating the transparency trend and other Obama reforms—an article for which I found few takers, although it was eventually published.[27] Understandably, reporters were skeptical. The government was revealing these documents only because it had no choice, many told me. I did not see it that way. When I was in the intelligence community, the typical response to embarrassing stories based on leaks was to say nothing so as to avoid giving reporters more material, and it sometimes worked. (As we saw in chapter 3, this strategy proved extremely effective in the case of the *USA Today* scoop about bulk collection in 2006.) While the Obama administration had no control over journalists working with the Snowden documents and which NSA activities those journalists chose to reveal, it certainly had a choice about how to respond. The administration could have dug in, refusing to comment on the Snowden stories except perhaps in background briefings to reporters. It could have exhausted every last appeal in its FOIA cases instead of releasing materials on *IC on the Record*. Of course, this strategy would have come at a cost, as the intelligence community would have been giving up its chance to make a more public case for itself. Yet if transparency about the NSA's programs was at least at first primarily a tactical move, it too was not without cost.

ONE REASON I WAS SURPRISED by the volume of information about classified NSA programs that was officially released in 2013 is that the law provides an array of defenses against legal challenges to surveillance that depend on secrecy. From the government's perspective, transparency about surveillance can seem like unilateral disarmament.

In the summer of 2013, a judge in San Francisco, Jeffery White, was considering what to do about a challenge to the NSA surveillance that had begun with Stellar Wind and was now authorized by section 702 of FISA. The case had been pending for several years, brought by the Electronic Frontier Foundation (EFF), a civil liberties organization. Government lawyers had asked Judge White to dismiss the case entirely, asserting the strongest form of the "state secrets privilege." Essentially, the government's lawyers were saying that because so much of the case against the NSA involved classified information, it was impossible for the court to hear it without compromising national security. If the judge agreed, the government would win by default. Transparency advocate Steven Aftergood has described this form of the state secrets privilege as the government's "nuclear option" because it "terminates the lawsuit."[28]

The Obama administration's decision to opt for greater transparency defused the NSA's most potent argument. In July 2013 Judge White ruled against the government on the state secrets issue. White's opinion specifically noted "multiple public disclosures of information" about NSA surveillance. According to White, "'[T]he government's many attempts to assuage citizens' fears that they have not been surveilled now doom the government's assertion that the very subject matter of this litigation . . . is barred by the state secrets privilege.'"[29] Clapper's lawyers surely advised him that while he might not want to remain silent, anything he said could and certainly would be used against the NSA in court—and it was, almost immediately. The quandary is not unlike that of an innocent person under criminal investigation who is bursting to tell his side of the story. Any competent lawyer will caution her client that answering even the most innocuous questions under oath may later be ruled a waiver of his constitutional rights under the Fifth Amendment not to be a witness against himself. The safest course of action is to say nothing—to "take the Fifth"—no matter how guilty this makes him look. In much the same way, while excessive secrecy makes the NSA look guilty, transparency creates what any government lawyer is sure to advise are serious legal risks. Continued secrecy is a much safer option.[30]

Judge White did not dismiss the government's secrecy concerns entirely. He only said that they could not be used to dismiss the entire case—at least not immediately. Still, the government's lawyers can be counted on to caution officials that even anodyne statements about classified programs may come back to haunt them. The EFF's mission is to defend civil liberties on the internet, reflecting the hopes of the tech community that the "electronic frontier" can remain a domain that is free from government control. I have worked closely with the EFF for years; it is perhaps the most effective voice for internet freedom in the world. As a rule, its activists are not fans of the NSA. One of its founders, John Berry Barlow, once referred to the NSA as the "American Occupation Army of Cyberspace."[31] Although the EFF may win a few cases by arguing that increased transparency waives the government's defenses, these will be pyrrhic victories if the intelligence community reacts by going back to its bad habits of excessive secrecy.

Transparency may best be served by disarming both sides of their most potent weapons. Judges should be skeptical of arguments that the government has waived the right to keep information classified simply because it has chosen to make some information public. Still, if judges are more likely to reject the state secrets privilege—or at least its nuclear version—excessive secrecy might lose some of its appeal. Secrecy may sometimes be the only way to safeguard national security. Secrecy should not be a legal strategy. The potency of the secrecy argument has made it extremely attractive to government lawyers.

For this, a too credulous judiciary must share the blame. Sitting on a bookshelf in my office is an unusual book, published in 1974. It is full of blank spots to mark where it has been censored. *The CIA and the Cult of Intelligence,* by John D. Marks and Victor Marchetti, is one of the first critical books about the agency by insiders. The book is also the first book the U.S. government ever went to court to censor before publication, based on the authors' secrecy agreements. The judge upheld the agreements—the same type of agreement that required me to submit the book you are now reading to prepublication review by the ODNI to ensure it does not contain classified information. The publisher, Alfred A. Knopf, decided to print the book in censored form. There are blank spots to show the passages that the government succeeded in suppressing. Hundreds more are printed in boldface type, indicating that the CIA had originally argued that these portions were also secret, but had relented during the course of the case. I still remember leafing through the passages incredulously when I first came across it in a used bookstore. Did the U.S. government actually censor books? The proof that it did was in my own hands.

In the ACLU office where I once worked, I found another copy. It was full of the handwritten notes of the ACLU lawyers who had fought for the right of Marks and Marchetti to publish their manuscript in full. Mort Halperin, the former Nixon White House official I met after 9/11, was an expert witness for the ACLU in the case. He testified before Judge Albert Bryan in a federal district court in Alexandria, Virginia. The key issue was how much deference the judge should give to the executive branch. Did the CIA have to prove that the passages were classified, or should the judge defer to the agency's judgment? "Our view," writes ACLU legal director Melvin Wulf in the book's introduction, "presented through the expert testimony of Morton Halperin, was that concrete proof of classification was required." Judge Bryan agreed and found that only 27 of the 168 passages that the CIA was seeking to censor were actually classified. He said the remaining passages could be published. The government appealed, and the CIA won. The book was published with all 168 passages deleted.[32]

Today *United States v. Marchetti* is known mainly as the first case in which a court upheld the intelligence community's "mosaic" theory of secrecy, or the idea that sometimes apparently innocuous information must be classified because a foreign intelligence service could fit it together with other information, like a mosaic, to form a picture the government is urgently trying to hide. "What may seem trivial to the uninformed, may appear of great moment to one who has a broad view of the scene and may put the questioned item of information in its proper context," the appeals court reasoned. As judges are not intelligence specialists, they "are ill-equipped" to make such judgments. As a result, the court decided not to question the CIA's claims about the damage the uncensored book might cause.[33] Ever since, the mosaic theory has featured prominently in the government's arguments demanding that classified documents stay secret. For a brief moment following the end of the Cold War, it appeared that the theory might be scaled back. President Clinton's executive order on classification in 1995 featured what the Justice Department called a "somewhat more restrictive form" of the theory. The courts did not seem to notice. In any event, the mosaic theory came back with a vengeance after 9/11, when it was frequently used by lawyers to justify the Bush administration's secrecy claims in the "war on terror."[34]

If even innocuous information may be kept secret because it might be used by an adversary, it becomes almost impossible to challenge a culture of secrecy. While it is undoubtedly true that foreign intelligence services can piece together valuable insights from routine information—or, as our own agencies do, from open sources—as a legal argument the mosaic theory demands excessive deference to the intelligence community. More than forty years ago the Nixon administration went to court in an attempt to stop the *New York Times* from publishing news stories based on a secret history of the Vietnam War, stolen and leaked by a whistleblower, Daniel Ellsberg. The Supreme Court ruled against the government, infuriating Nixon and setting in motion the events that led to Watergate. In his opinion for the Court, Justice Potter Stewart warned against pursuing "secrecy for its own sake." "For when everything is classified, then nothing is classified," Stewart wrote.[35] It would be wise to heed Stewart's pragmatic advice. Given the overwhelming problem of overclassification, if the government cannot give a simple and straightforward answer to a judge's question, "Why is this document classified?" the most likely explanation is because it should not be.

IN THE FALL OF 2013, I invited transparency advocates, reporters, and government officials to Brown University to explore the NSA's new "Big Transparency." Steven Aftergood was a guest at my forum. As director of the Federation of American Scientists' Project on Government Secrecy, he had been challenging the intelligence community's culture of secrecy for more than two decades. His blog, *Secrecy News*, began as a newsletter. It has an avid readership among both activists and intelligence agency employees. I expected Steven, like the skeptical reporters I had tried to convince of the intelligence community's new openness, would say that *IC on the Record* and other transparency reforms were mere window dressing—too little, too late. Instead, he had nothing but praise. "We're living through a slow-motion earthquake in government secrecy policy," Aftergood marveled later in an interview. "Already we've seen a more extensive disclosure of classified information about current intelligence programs than we've seen for at least forty years, and maybe ever." By March 2014 *IC on the Record* had released more than twice as many previously classified documents as journalists working with the Snowden documents had published.[36]

Of course, if the intelligence community's new openness about surveillance was surprising, that was at least in part because it had been so secretive for so long. The new transparency may seem unremarkable—just a case of long-delayed common sense. For the intelligence community, however, it was a painful shift. At the forum at Brown University, my old boss Alex Joel tried to put into words just how unsettling the new openness was for many inside the government. "The intelligence community is not designed and built for transparency," he observed with wry understatement. "Our culture is built around finding our adversaries' secrets and keeping our own secrets secret."

Slavish adherence to the secrecy culture contributed to myths about surveillance that frustrated insiders to no end. When Congress enacted FISA in 1978, it required the Justice Department to release yearly reports. More detailed, classified reports are provided to Congress. Before 2013 the government argued that virtually any details about its use of FISA surveillance were classified unless they were required by law to be included in the public reports. The public reports required disclosure only of the total number of applications for surveillance and the total number granted, modified, or denied. For years, these numbers were invariably the same, or almost the same, leading to the persistent belief that the FISA court was nothing more than a rubber stamp.[37] As we will see in chapter 7, the court documents released after 2013 show that the FISA court system has many shortcomings, but not because its judges fail to take their jobs seriously.

Through *IC on the Record*, the intelligence community has begun to release more meaningful annual reports about FISA surveillance. Crucially, the new transparency reports include the estimated number of targets affected by such surveillance. A comparison of the public reports that are still made by the attorney general under FISA to the post-Snowden transparency reports released by Clapper's office shows just how vital that number has become in today's era of transnational surveillance. For the year 2014, the Justice Department reported only that there were 1,416 applications for surveillance orders, of which 22 were modified and none was denied. For the same year, the intelligence community's transparency report gives the number of targets in addition to the number of court orders. Its transparency report discloses that probable cause orders for targeted surveillance and physical search—what we called "old FISA"—affected 1,562 targets. A single order under section 702 of FISA—"new FISA"—is reported separately. It affected 92,707 targets.[38]

THE INTELLIGENCE COMMUNITY HAS OFTEN been, in the words of former Justice Department official Jack Goldsmith, "self-defeatingly secretive and insular, and terrible at explaining what it was doing and why."[39] Nowhere has this been more true than in its attempts to make the case that Snowden's disclosures of classified information caused real damage. In light of the volume of secret information compromised by Snowden, it should have been easy for the intelligence community to make the case that his actions caused grave harm to the United States. A survey by the *National Journal* in 2014 of more than 100 defense and foreign policy experts from across the political spectrum showed that an overwhelming majority, 80 percent, said any benefit to privacy from the debate that the Snowden disclosures forced was not worth the national security costs.[40] Yet while the intelligence community may have persuaded the national security establishment that Snowden caused serious damage with his disclosures, it has failed to make a convincing case to the wider public. The culprit, ironically, is excessive secrecy.

Even the basic facts remain hotly disputed. Snowden downloaded about 1.5 million classified documents from two of the government's most sensitive computer networks, NSANet and a separate top-secret Defense Department network, JWICS. However, he provided only a fraction of these documents to journalists—according to the Canadian Journalists for Free Expression, about 50,000. (This number is in dispute, but the CJFE's information appears to be reasonably reliable; the organization has worked with journalists and activists supporting Snowden. It says it does not have the documents, but it hosts an archive of those Snowden documents that have been made publicly available.) Yet when this book went to press, fewer than 1,200 of these documents had been made public, sometimes with redactions.[41] Why so few, and why do they contain redactions? Snowden trusted Glenn Greenwald and other top journalists at major media outlets such as *The Guardian,* the *Washington Post,* and *Der Spiegel* to keep details out of their stories that might cost lives, and to be selective about the documents they uploaded to accompany them. Greenwald argues this shows that Snowden was "the classically responsible whistleblower."[42] No one I know who has been entrusted with access to highly classified documents believes giving journalists a huge trove of documents is responsible behavior, but it is true that Snowden's approach lessened the potential damage his actions might otherwise have caused. Snowden did not give his documents to WikiLeaks or dump them on the internet. Indeed, Snowden later criticized Julian Assange's organization for its more indiscriminate approach. After WikiLeaks began releasing hacked documents obtained from the Democratic National Committee in 2016, Snowden gently rebuked them. "Democratizing information has never been more vital, and @ Wikileaks has helped," Snowden said in a tweet. "But their hostility to even modest curation is a mistake."[43] In the same way I had once exercised derivative classification authority delegated to me by the U.S. government, Snowden delegated to journalists what might be called derivative leaking authority through his "modest curation" approach.

Of course, the public is harmed if journalists misjudge the damage their derivative leaks may cause. Journalists do not have experience with declassifying documents, so they are likely to make mistakes—and they have. In one particularly egregious error, the *New York Times* attempted to redact the name of an NSA employee and other details about an operation in Iraq from a Snowden document, but the information was still embedded in the file. It was impossible to unring the bell: when the error was noticed, an antisecrecy website had already captured the original file. In an otherwise sympathetic interview with Snowden, the political satirist John Oliver called the incident a "fuck-up," saying Snowden had to "own" the damage his disclosures caused along with whatever benefits they may have provided. When Oliver pressed Snowden to say whether he had read all the documents he took before giving them to journalists, Snowden said only that he had "evaluated" them. As Snowden dodged Oliver's questions, he sounded like a politician trying to evade responsibility.[44]

Naturally, the NSA considers the entire trove of documents compromised, not just those that have been made public. There is at least some risk they are in the hands of the NSA's adversaries. Snowden insists that he encrypted the documents he took with him to Hong Kong and gave nothing to the Chinese government. Snowden says he took no files with him when he left China, and that he no longer has access to any of them. Snowden says he taught a course as an NSA contractor on protecting against Chinese hacking and is confident his precautions were sufficient. Security expert Bruce Schneier argues that even if we accept all of this as true, the Russian and Chinese intelligence services might still have some or all of these files. While they may not have gotten them from Snowden, he argues it is reasonable to assume the journalists and activists who worked with him are soft targets for two of the most sophisticated cyber adversaries of the United States.[45]

In January 2014 the Defense Intelligence Agency provided a classified "damage assessment" of the Snowden leaks to Congress. Representative Mike Rogers, the chair of the House Permanent Select Committee on Intelligence, announced that the assessment "confirms my greatest fears." Rogers said the report showed that "Snowden's actions are likely to have lethal consequences for our troops in the field." The committee's ranking Democrat, Dutch Ruppersberger, agreed. "Snowden handed terrorists a copy of our country's playbook and now we are paying the price, which this report confirms," he said.[46] The DIA's assessment of the damage from the Snowden disclosures is classified. In May 2014 the government released a declassified version under FOIA. Every one of its thirty-nine pages was almost entirely redacted. Only the report's conclusion remained: "The scope of the compromised knowledge related to US intelligence capabilities is staggering." No information in support of that conclusion survived the agency's declassification review. The DIA took the position that it had to classify even the headlines of newspaper articles concerning the Snowden leaks. "Confirmation that these specific newspaper articles contain classified information through the release of these references under the FOIA would cause harm to national security by offering validation that the stolen information is classified," one official argued.[47]

In 2016 the House intelligence committee issued its own report on Snowden. The bulk of the report consists of a highly critical account of Snowden's employment history. "Despite his lack of experience, the 23-year-old Snowden told the Deputy Director of Support"—who the report wants us to understand is "one of the ten most senior executives of CIA"—that "he felt 'pretty disenfranchised' because his immediate superiors did not take his unsolicited recommendations to heart." (Perhaps the intelligence community needs some advice about how to manage its millennial workforce.) Later the report informs us that "Snowden had few friends among his co-workers at NSA Hawaii." Apparently, they said, Snowden was "'smart' and 'nerdy,' but also someone who was 'arrogant,' 'introverted,' and 'squirrelly.'" We are also told that Snowden came into work late because "he stayed up late playing video games." The brief section that actually discusses the impact of Snowden's disclosures claims the leaks caused "tremendous damage to national security," but this discussion is entirely redacted.[48]

Continued secrecy about the damage caused by the Snowden disclosures distorts the debate, allowing Snowden's critics to make statements that cannot be challenged and Snowden's defenders to claim there was no damage at all. Intelligence agencies maintain that classified information remains classified even if it is leaked. There are times when this rule makes sense: as we have seen, even a front-page story in a major newspaper like *USA Today* has not always led to the full and lasting disclosure of secret programs. Still, some leaks may not plausibly be denied. Denying reality saddles the public with the costs of secrecy but none of the benefits. Like all of us, sometimes the government simply fails to keep a secret. Whether the damage is "staggering," "tremendous," or considerably less than originally feared, the public should know. Censoring the damage assessment serves no good purpose. The damage is done.

GREATER TRANSPARENCY NEED NOT BE a threat to keeping genuine secrets. Keeping bulk collection a secret provided the NSA and telephone companies a temporary respite from having to answer tough questions. In the long run it did nothing to help Clapper protect the intelligence community's sources and methods. Indeed, if we believe Snowden when he says that it spurred his final decision to leak his trove of top-secret documents, it may have contributed to the worst breach of the NSA's secrets in history. More than a century ago the Dutch cryptographer Auguste Kerckhoffs warned against the practice of "security by obscurity," or keeping a system secret in the hope your adversary will not discover its weaknesses. His second principle for the design of military ciphers was that the design "should not require secrecy, and it should not be a problem if it falls into enemy hands." Today basic texts on cryptography teach that the security of a system should depend on minimal secrecy. Ideally, the only thing that should have to remain secret is the cryptographic key.[49] The NSA is well aware of Kerckhoffs's principle when it comes to designing cryptosystems. Far too often, it has failed to apply its insights more broadly. Over the past four years, the public learned more about surveillance—good, bad, and ugly—than it had in the previous four decades, and the intelligence community has come out better for it. If the new transparency has taught us anything, it is that the intelligence community can make much more information available than it ever thought it could, if it has an incentive to do so.

The Snowden crisis appears to have prompted a genuine and lasting change in the culture of the intelligence community. For the first time ever, the government's rate of creating new secrets has dropped substantially. In July 2016 the Information Security Oversight Office reported "good news"—a 32 percent drop in the number of derivative classification decisions, from almost 77.5 million in fiscal year 2014 to 52.8 million in fiscal year 2015.[50] My old boss Alex Joel has even changed the name of the office where I used to work. The Civil Liberties and Privacy Office is now the Office of Civil Liberties, Privacy and Transparency. Still, the public is right to be skeptical. Old habits are hard to break. While writing about NSA surveillance on my Brown University laptop, I still sometimes find myself looking for that missing "classify" command.

6

PASSING THE BUCK

Steve Roberts, an NPR host, was doing an in-depth show on the National Security Agency and was looking for a guest to provide the government's perspective on the NSA's controversial domestic collection programs, including its bulk collection of American telephone records. As I began to prepare for the interview, I remembered that when our office had briefed Congress on the NSA's collection under the Foreign Intelligence Surveillance Act (FISA), we had often cited examples of how these programs had helped prevent terrorism. I called my former colleagues at the Office of the Director of National Intelligence (ODNI) to get the latest information. During the course of my interview with Roberts, I told NPR listeners that one reason there had been so few terrorist attacks since 9/11 was that the NSA was on the watch. The NSA had "accurately documented to the Congress fifty-four terrorist plots that have been thwarted by FISA authorities," I said. The bulk collection program of American telephone records that had proved so controversial was responsible for twelve of these successes. "That's pretty powerful," I added confidently.[1]

My confidence was misplaced. The examples I had cited were real, but the NSA's massive telephone records database had provided no unique value. Five months later, the Privacy and Civil Liberties Oversight Board, an independent government agency established to review counterterrorism programs, completed a comprehensive examination of the NSA's collection of telephone records under section 215 of the Patriot Act. After examining each case in detail, the board concluded that there was not "a single instance involving a threat to the United States in which the program made a concrete difference in the outcome of a counterterrorism investigation."[2] While the NSA had tipped information to the FBI in each of the twelve cases, the FBI already had access to those records. Defenders of bulk collection made other arguments. The program was an insurance policy against potential future attacks. It helped the government allocate scarce resources against the real threats. Still, the strongest case for bulk collection had crumbled, along with much of the NSA's remaining credibility.

Obviously, the government's success stories should have been put to the test many years earlier. For this failure, the buck stops with me. Along with other privacy officials, I had been in a position to scrutinize the NSA's claims. On visits to Fort Meade, I had checked the logs of NSA analysts, making sure their queries were legitimate and properly documented and that they were following the rules imposed by the FISA court. However, I did not challenge claims that the data the bulk collection program was generating had been useful in terrorism cases. My job was to make sure privacy rules were followed, or so I believed. Surely there was someone else who was investigating whether the programs were effective.

One of the framers of the Constitution, James Madison, argued that the design of a democratic government could not depend on trusting any one person or institution to do the right thing. "Ambition must be made to counteract ambition," Madison explained. (Madison knew something about ambition: his coauthor in the series of essays known as the Federalist Papers, the famously ambitious Alexander Hamilton, later tried to take credit for some of his work, including this essay on checks and balances, number 51.)[3] Madison's argument for the separation of powers assumes that those who are looking for advancement, whether judges, politicians, or government officials, will seek to outdo one another out of self-interest, maximizing their power at the expense of the other branches. There is a weakness in Madison's argument. It is not always in the best interests of the ambitious to take responsibility for hard choices. Passing the buck has been a persistent problem when it comes to issues of surveillance, civil liberties, and national security. When any decision might result in criticism, either for a controversial surveillance program or for the failure to prevent the next terrorist attack, the ambitious may think the smarter move is to sidestep those choices. Why not let someone else take the heat if something goes wrong?

A PARTICULARLY EGREGIOUS EXAMPLE OF passing the buck involves a member of Congress who simply refused to do his job, and then professed outrage when he discovered what had been done with the law he had championed. James Sensenbrenner of Wisconsin, a conservative Republican and the former chair of the House Judiciary Committee, describes himself as the author of the Patriot Act. He is at least the author of the law's name; most of the words were written by lawyers in the Justice Department. He shepherded Bush's counterterrorism proposal through the House in the weeks after 9/11. While he raised a few objections to the Justice Department's original draft, he also ran roughshod over any opposition. Sensenbrenner continued to strongly support the Patriot Act through its multiple reauthorizations, in 2005, 2009, and 2011.

Sensenbrenner enjoyed dismissing the Patriot Act's critics, including me and other civil libertarians who appeared before his committee, as victims of our own Orwellian fantasies. During debate on the House floor over the last reauthorization in 2011, Sensenbrenner lamented that the debate over the Patriot Act "has been plagued by myths and misinformation for ten years." He specifically praised section 215 of the Patriot Act, the business records provision. He said it had "numerous protections," had been carefully scrutinized by the courts, and was constitutional. Sensenbrenner also claimed that section 215 had helped prevent "countless potential attacks."[4] In June 2013 Sensenbrenner learned for the first time that the Bush and

Obama administrations had used his law—specifically, section 215—
to authorize bulk collection of American telephone records. The critics had been right and he had been wrong. "Big Brother is watching,"
he said. According to Sensenbrenner, however, this was not his fault.
He said it was not true that "every member of Congress has been
briefed on this program," as Obama had claimed mistakenly in his
first public statement on the NSA controversy. On the contrary, he
said, "most, including myself, were not."[5]

Sensenbrenner blamed Obama for his ignorance, but he should
have blamed himself. While George W. Bush had sharply limited
access to his Stellar Wind program, Obama's national security team
was determined to avoid this mistake. Intelligence officials offered
multiple briefings about bulk collection well in advance of both
the 2009 and 2011 votes on the Patriot Act. While we could not
force members to attend, we took pains to ensure all members were
invited, not just those on the intelligence committees who had reviewed the program in some detail. In 2009 the leadership of the
intelligence committees in both the House and the Senate circulated
letters urging all members to review material about a classified program before voting on Patriot Act renewal. Most did not. In 2011
the Obama administration again provided briefings to Congress (although in the House, it turned out that the House Permanent Select
Committee on Intelligence failed to circulate the letter this time).[6]
In a speech on the Senate floor in May 2011, Senator Ron Wyden of
Oregon, the member of the Senate Intelligence Committee who later
cross-examined Clapper about NSA collection of data on "millions
of Americans," implored his colleagues to take advantage of classified briefings. Clearly irritated, Wyden informed his colleagues that
he could not fully explain in public why he was planning to vote
against Patriot Act renewal. "And I want to deliver a warning this
afternoon—when the American people find out how their government has secretly interpreted the Patriot Act, they are going to be
stunned and they are going to be angry." He reviewed the history of
intelligence abuses that had led to the reforms of the 1970s, including
FISA. One was the NSA's Shamrock program, involving bulk collection of international telegrams.[7] Wyden's cryptic words did not move
many members. In 2011 both houses of Congress voted by wide mar-

gins to renew the expiring provisions of the Patriot Act for another four years, until 2015.

The briefings in 2009 and 2011 were the right thing for intelligence officials to do, but they also served a pragmatic purpose: self-preservation. Inside the intelligence community there was a persistent fear that politicians who had gone along with surveillance programs when briefed in private would, if those programs were leaked and proved controversial, feign outrage, like Captain Louis Renault from the film *Casablanca*. ("I'm shocked, shocked to find that gambling is going on in here!") Each time we went up to Capitol Hill, we were careful to document it. This turned out to be prudent. Sensenbrenner's complaints did not gain much traction in 2013, despite his claims of being shocked—shocked!—to find that his Patriot Act was being used to authorize a broad surveillance program. The evidence that Congress had indeed been briefed on the NSA's bulk collection of telephone records was overwhelming and undeniable, although it was also true that most members, like Sensenbrenner, had failed to take advantage of these briefings. By choosing not to attend, Sensenbrenner became a victim of willful blindness as to how his own law had been interpreted. As a member and former chair of the House Judiciary Committee, Sensenbrenner had ample opportunity to engage in oversight of the program. When pressed on why he was unaware of the NSA's bulk collection program, he explained that he typically skipped classified briefings. He said closed briefings are a "game they use to suck members in" by giving them information and then forbidding them from speaking about it publicly.[8] Yet Sensenbrenner's failure to acquaint himself with how the Patriot Act was being used did not stop him from vouching for its effectiveness in stopping terrorism.

Sensenbrenner's defenders argue that his stand can be regarded as principled, not opportunistic. They point to the predicament of Senator Wyden, who was unable to make the real reasons for his objections to the Patriot Act public.[9] By refusing to play that game, they say, Sensenbrenner avoided being captured by the intelligence community. This gives Sensenbrenner far too much credit. While secrecy complicated Wyden's efforts to rally public support to his side, he took his oversight obligations seriously. Wyden, a liberal Democrat, could have used the support of a senior Republican lawmaker like Sensenbrenner. Instead, Sensenbrenner ended up vigorously supporting a law he later professed to abhor, even to the point of ridiculing its opponents. Once the truth became public, he refused to take responsibility for the part he had played in enabling mass surveillance.

There is a legal doctrine that Congress is presumed to be aware of judicial interpretations of the law. Accordingly, when Congress reenacts a law without changing the words that a court has interpreted, courts ordinarily say that Congress has "ratified" that interpretation. After 2013 the government argued that this doctrine of "ratification" should be applied to the FISA court's secret interpretation of section 215 of the Patriot Act allowing bulk collection. In its successful challenge to the NSA's bulk collection of telephone records before a federal appeals court in New York in 2015, the American Civil Liberties Union argued that because most members had not taken advantage of the classified briefings, Congress should not be regarded as having "ratified" the FISA court's bulk collection theory when it reauthorized section 215 of the Patriot Act in 2009 and 2011.[10] While I believe the ACLU was right, this is not because the intelligence community had not at least tried to brief Congress (it had) or because Congress should get away with passing the buck (it shouldn't). The problem with the ratification argument is that it punishes the public instead of Congress for Congress's failure to do its job. It does not follow that because Congress was remiss in its constitutional responsibilities, government lawyers get a free pass to impose the FISA court's decisions on the rest of the federal judiciary. A better solution to the problem of Congress's passing the buck is for the public to hold Congress accountable. Voters should know whether their members are doing their jobs. Members' decisions to attend or to skip relevant classified briefings should be recorded, just as votes are. When Congress approves new surveillance powers, it must be willing to investigate how those powers are being used. If members are unwilling to do so, perhaps they should not vote for such powers—or voters should think twice about electing them.

THE INTELLIGENCE COMMITTEES OF THE House and Senate are charged with oversight of surveillance programs, ensuring they respect constitutional rights. They are also supposed to ask the tough questions about whether intelligence agencies are doing their jobs effectively. Far too often, they have given the government a pass. Neither committee offered much resistance to Stellar Wind, or to the NSA programs under FISA that replaced it. Ron Wyden was joined by only one other senator, Mark Udall, in objecting to the NSA's bulk collection of telephone records. The remaining members of both parties strongly supported it. After that program was revealed, it was the intelligence committees that sought most vigorously to preserve it. In the summer of 2013, members of the intelligence committees and others in Congress who had supported the NSA were on the defensive. Two members of the House from Michigan who were not on those committees—Justin Amash, a tea party Republican, and John Conyers, a liberal Democrat—teamed up to sponsor an amendment to end the NSA's bulk collection of telephone records. In the face of dire warnings from the NSA director, it was defeated, but the vote was a squeaker: 205-217, with more than 100 Democrats joining almost as many Republicans to vote against the administration.[11]

In the first article in *The Guardian* detailing the NSA's bulk collection of telephone records in June 2013, Glenn Greenwald described only the scale of the program that Snowden had leaked to him, without discussing any of the rules that restrain it. Whether or not Congress eventually decided to end bulk collection or to keep it, I wanted the debate to be an informed one. In an op-ed in the *Wall Street Journal* in August, I tried to put into plain language the detailed legal rules that the surveillance court had imposed on bulk collection to protect privacy. "I've seen the safeguards," I wrote. The public would be "reassured" if they were more generally known.[12] A month later, Senator Dianne Feinstein, chair of the Senate Select Committee on Intelligence, invited me to testify about NSA surveillance and to suggest possible reforms to FISA. Glenn Greenwald promptly denounced me as a "virulent NSA defender," arguing the hearing was nothing more than a sham to head off real surveillance reform.[13]

My testimony did not offer the unqualified defense of the NSA that both Greenwald and Feinstein herself seemed to be expecting. Instead, I argued that the public's support for Edward Snowden in the summer of 2013 showed a crisis in public confidence that was the most serious the intelligence community had seen in decades. The NSA programs that Snowden had leaked highlighted a major transformation that had taken place out of public view. While I discussed the NSA's telephone records program, I also described other NSA programs that had until then received less public attention, including Prism and the NSA's collection of data from the internet backbone. These programs were the subject of newly released FISA court opinions, and they created serious risks for privacy. FISA had been a shield to protect civil liberties. After 9/11, it became a sword to compel cooperation with transnational surveillance. It was clear this was not the message Feinstein was expecting from the former ACLU lawyer who had been defending the NSA. "Whoa, there," she said, interrupting me at one point. I highlighted specific problems with the way the NSA had administered its upstream collection program. The problems in upstream collection had resulted in what the FISA court had called years of illegal collection of domestic communications. Feinstein interrupted me again. The committee had reviewed this question, Feinstein assured me. The problems had been addressed.[14]

The Senate Select Committee on Intelligence and its counterpart in the House are a product of the intelligence reforms of the post-Watergate period. The idea is to ensure that intelligence agencies are subject to the same checks and balances as other parts of government by creating special institutions to review classified programs. The reforms have had the unintended consequences of extending the club of national security insiders beyond the executive branch. Regardless of which party controls the House or Senate, the intelligence committees have too often been staunch defenders of the status quo—so much so that in the immediate post-Snowden period, the executive branch did a far better job of investigating itself than Congress did of providing oversight.

In 2013 Obama was under pressure to produce credible reform, and to produce it quickly. Some of Obama's strongest supporters, such as top executives of Silicon Valley firms, were in crisis mode. Foreign competitors argued that U.S. companies could not be trusted to store data because they were in bed with the NSA. Initial estimates of lost business from the "Snowden effect" ranged from $35 billion to $180 billion.[15] The Obama administration's constant talk about protecting "U.S. persons" was not helping. In fact, it was counterproductive, the technology executives told Obama, as it implied that no one else's privacy mattered. Obama decided he could not wait for Congress. He needed to show he was doing something, and he needed to do it fast. While the independent Privacy and Civil Liberties Oversight Board had finally opened its doors in May, the board's members made clear to the White House that they intended to take a deliberative, step-by-step approach to reviewing NSA programs, beginning with the NSA's bulk collection of telephone records. The broader concerns that the technology community was communicating to Obama would have to wait.

Impatient to show progress, Obama created the President's Review Group on Intelligence and Communications Technologies and set a quick timetable for the panel to produce recommendations. In December 2013 the five-member review group released a comprehensive report, touching on privacy, foreign relations, and cybersecurity. The report devoted an entire chapter to protecting the privacy of non-U.S. persons.[16] Many inside the national security establishment were surprised at the way the group had challenged the status quo in ways Congress had never done.[17] While the committees created in the late 1970s to act as a check on the president's intelligence powers were busy arguing that the intelligence community did not need to change, a hand-picked group of the president's confidants was offering a fresh look at surveillance.

In response to the report, Obama issued new rules on signals intelligence. Presidential Policy Directive 28 extended the mechanisms for protecting "U.S. person" information to protect information belonging to anyone, anywhere in the world.[18] Retention and minimization limits that once applied only to U.S. persons now applied to all personal information. The directive imposed limits on the use of signals intelligence collected in bulk and explicitly banned abusive practices. Signals intelligence cannot be used to disadvantage anyone, anywhere in the world, on the basis of race, gender, sexual orientation, or religion. The directive also codified the government's long-standing unwritten policy against using intelligence agencies to steal foreign trade secrets for the benefit of American companies. Obama's review group prompted significant reforms that challenged decades of conventional wisdom in the national security establishment, but there were weaknesses in the way it went about its job. The review group had urged some changes in the NSA's bulk collection of telephone records, but it made the same mistake that I had made of accepting the government's claims of effectiveness at face value. With its broad focus and short deadline, the review group had simply not had time to examine any one program in detail before it disbanded at the end of 2013. By the group's own admission, it spent only a single day at Fort Meade.[19]

The Privacy and Civil Liberties Oversight Board took a more methodical approach, one that complemented the review group's broader policy assessment. In January 2014 the Privacy and Civil Liberties Oversight Board completed its review of the NSA's telephone records program, finding it had not been valuable and recommending that the program be terminated. Yet the board's next report vindicated the government. In July 2014 it completed a detailed review of the NSA's surveillance of foreign targets from inside the United States under section 702 of FISA. This law authorized the NSA's Prism program and its upstream collection program, which obtains content from the internet backbone. The board found these transnational surveillance programs had been quite valuable. Surveillance conducted under section 702 had "led to the discovery of previously unknown terrorist plots . . . enabling the disruption of those plots." These included the fifty-four cases I had cited in my radio interview along with additional examples, leading to well over 100 arrests.[20] By taking a careful look at specific surveillance programs instead of accepting the government's claims at face value, the privacy board provided a unique public service where Congress had fallen down in providing oversight of the NSA.

As an independent executive branch agency, the Privacy and Civil Liberties Oversight Board enjoyed credibility with insiders and outsiders alike. Unfortunately, it was fully operational for only three years during the entire Obama administration. President Obama took five years to get the board up and running. In the summer of 2016 its full-time chair resigned, leaving the board hobbled for the remainder of Obama's presidency. During the short-lived tenure of the Privacy and Civil Liberties Oversight Board, this small and little-known independent institution inside the executive branch was extraordinarily successful in providing accountability for surveillance.

BY CONTRAST, CONGRESS CONFRONTED THE issue of NSA surveillance only because it was forced to do so. Two years after the NSA's bulk collection of telephone records was disclosed by Snowden, lawmakers finally took action, after failing time and time again to find a compromise on the issue. While Congress knew that the law providing authority for the NSA program, section 215 of the Patriot Act, was set to expire on June 1, 2015, it nevertheless failed to meet its self-imposed deadline. On June 1 section 215 of the Patriot Act actually expired. A day later, Congress passed a law it had been debating for years that replaced the NSA's bulk collection program with an alternative that allows NSA analysts to query call detail records stored at the telephone companies. The law gave the NSA six months to transition to the new system.

Leading the effort to find a compromise were Representative Sensenbrenner and Senator Patrick Leahy of Vermont, a Democrat—the same members who had sponsored the USA PATRIOT Act, the Uniting and Strengthening America by Providing Appropriate Tools Required to Intercept and Obstruct Terrorism Act. With their USA FREEDOM Act, they atoned not only for the mass surveillance the Patriot Act had allowed but also for its name, inventing a new and equally awkward acronym. The Freedom Act's full title is the "Uniting and Strengthening America by Fulfilling Rights and Ensuring Effective Discipline Over Monitoring Act," which is, fittingly, a slight softening of the original title, which had promised to fulfill rights by "Ending Eavesdropping, Dragnet-collection and Online Monitoring." As a result of the Freedom Act, the NSA may no longer use the Patriot Act to amass a nationwide database but instead must use a "specific selection term" to retrieve telephone or other metadata from providers. Much of the debate over the Freedom Act concerned how this limit should be defined. The government sought to avoid a narrow definition that might quickly become obsolete. Civil libertarians were suspicious that a secret and overly broad interpretation of "specific selection term" by the FISA court might resurrect something like the bulk collection that Congress was seeking to outlaw.

Efforts to find a compromise had stalled several times in the two years after the Snowden leaks revealed the use of the Patriot Act for the NSA's bulk collection of telephone records. For months before section 215 was set to expire, the Senate had failed to find the sixty votes needed to allow a vote on the Freedom Act. The bill was opposed by an odd combination of overzealous civil libertarians and misguided national security hawks. Their champions were Rand Paul and Mitch McConnell. Both senators were Republicans from Kentucky. Both opposed the Freedom Act, but for very different reasons. Paul's and McConnell's last-minute gamesmanship almost resulted in scuttling the reform bill.

Mitch McConnell was determined to be more zealous in defending NSA surveillance than the NSA was, and it almost cost the NSA dearly. He yearned for the days when Republicans ran circles around Democrats on terrorism. McConnell saw support for surveillance reform as a threat to his party's traditional political advantage on national security. McConnell's opposition to the Freedom Act dovetailed well with the Republican Party's strategy for the 2016 presidential election. At that time, the candidate most people in Washington believed would be the nominee, former Florida governor Jeb Bush, had already put together an impressive roster of foreign policy advisers. Two of them—Michael Hayden, who had been director of both the NSA and the CIA, and Michael Mukasey, a former attorney general—had blasted the Freedom Act in a *Wall Street Journal* column. The law was reform that "only ISIS could love," they said. They derided its painstakingly crafted provisions, endorsed by the Obama administration and its intelligence community, as "exquisitely crafted to hobble the gathering of electronic intelligence."[21] McConnell took to the Senate floor, waving a copy of the *Journal* as evidence the changes to NSA surveillance that Obama was pushing were dangerous.

In fact, not only had the NSA said it could live with the Freedom Act, it needed the Freedom Act to pass if it was to preserve its access to the call detail records of American telephone companies. By 2015 it had become clear that bulk collection was on very shaky legal ground. Although the FISA court was continuing to issue orders for bulk collection, the ACLU was challenging the program in other federal courts. In May 2015 the United States Court of Appeals for the Second Circuit sided with the ACLU, ruling that bulk collection was illegal. The appeals court did not find that the program was unconstitutional, but it sharply disagreed with the FISA court's reasoning that all call detail records could be regarded as "relevant" and therefore subject to the Patriot Act's business records provision. In doing so, the court focused its attention on the language I had discussed with my colleague, Kate Martin, in 2005, requiring a "statement of facts" justifying relevance—vindicating her view that this language had banned bulk collection.[22] Despite this ruling, McConnell continued to urge Congress to reauthorize the Patriot Act without change. Even if it did so, the NSA's bulk collection program was in deep trouble, and intelligence officials knew it. McConnell's position blithely ignored this reality.

Kentucky's other senator also had the 2016 election in mind. The Freedom Act compromise had disappointed many civil liberties and privacy advocates. Rand Paul's quest for the presidency depended on bringing new people into his party's primary process, especially younger, libertarian-minded voters. By demonstrating his fierce opposition to NSA surveillance with a dramatic filibuster, Paul was sure to attract their attention and burnish his image as a different kind of Republican. He showed little concern that his antics threatened a delicate compromise that had made possible the most important surveillance reform legislation in decades. Meanwhile, McConnell was hoping the threat would force supporters of the Freedom Act to agree to a short-term extension of the Patriot Act, depriving Obama of a victory and giving Republicans credit for saving an important NSA program. As the deadline rapidly approached, it became clear the Senate would not be able to break Paul's filibuster in time. The NSA began to wind down bulk collection, without any replacement program. On June 1 the Patriot Act actually expired. For the first time since 9/11, NSA analysts would not have a ready way to query new telephone metadata from domestic sources. It was the surveillance equivalent of a government shutdown. McConnell finally relented, allowing a vote to proceed. On June 2 the bill passed by a wide margin, 67-32.[23] Obama signed it the same day, and the NSA's bulk collection temporarily resumed to allow the agency time to work out the new rules it would apply to querying telephone records without collecting them in bulk.

After the six months allowed by the law, the NSA fully transitioned to the new system. On midnight of November 29, 2015, bulk collection came to an end for good. On the presidential campaign trail in December, Senator Marco Rubio of Florida issued dire warnings that the end of bulk collection would compromise the NSA's intelligence capabilities. He argued that one of his opponents, Senator Ted Cruz of Texas, who had voted for the Freedom Act, had helped take away a "valuable tool" in the fight against terrorism. In fact, the Freedom Act was a major success for the NSA. In a little noticed post on a national security blog, the NSA's top lawyer revealed that the Freedom Act actually gave the agency access to "a greater volume of call records" than it had under the old program, which had been limited for reasons including logistics and trust to a few large providers. In 2016 the NSA reported that it had collected more than 151 million call detail records using the Freedom Act.[24]

While Congress had not exactly covered itself in glory during its debate on the Freedom Act, the result represented a shift in the politics of surveillance. Beginning in 2001, Congress had passed surveillance measures mainly out of fear—both genuine fear that without new powers, the country would be at risk of attack, and political fear that opposing surveillance laws would leave a member exposed to charges of being soft on terrorism. The Freedom Act upended this tired political playbook, offering a hopeful model for a more constructive politics of surveillance reform. Those Republican candidates for president in 2016 who were serving in the Senate were forced to defend their positions for or against the NSA's collection of telephone records because they had voted on the issue. Congress had to decide because the legal authority for the program was an expiring provision of FISA. Politically, there was no place to hide.

The Freedom Act offered a rare moment of accountability during which members of Congress had to go on record on the issue of NSA surveillance. The debate in 2017 over section 702 of FISA is another such moment, forcing members to vote on whether they agree with the NSA's Prism program and its domestic collection of data from the internet backbone, the programs that the law authorizes. Still, for much of what the NSA does, Congress can continue to pass the buck, as it has done for decades. Most NSA programs are not subject to FISA and therefore are not subject to review by the FISA court or another body outside Congress. As we have seen, when Congress was considering FISA in the late 1970s, it largely dodged the question of what to do about the NSA's overseas programs. According to the report of the Senate Judiciary Committee, its decision to exempt signals intelligence from judicial review "should not be viewed as congressional authorization of such activities." While "it is desirable to develop legislative controls in this area, the Committee has concluded that these practices are sufficiently different from traditional surveillance techniques, both conceptually and technologically, that except when they target particular United States citizens or resident aliens in the United States, they should be considered separately by the Congress."[25] Congress never considered separate legislation.

One might expect Congress to pay more attention to programs that do not require review by the FISA court in order to make sure that they are overseen by someone outside the executive branch. Perversely, the NSA's foreign and satellite collection programs receive even less attention than those authorized by FISA. In the fall of 2013 a story appeared that reporters said was based on leaked documents from Edward Snowden, detailing what the reports described as an NSA collection program that obtained metadata from overseas sources under Executive Order 12,333. A senior staffer on the Senate Select Committee on Intelligence explained, "In general, the committee is far less aware of operations conducted under 12,333." The staffer elaborated, "I believe the NSA would answer questions if we asked them, and if we knew to ask them, but it would not routinely report these things, and, in general, they would not fall within the focus of the committee."[26] The other bulk collection program that grew out of Stellar Wind, the NSA's domestic collection of internet metadata (discussed in chapter 4), illustrates the problem. When this program became public in 2013, it attracted far less attention than the telephone records program for the simple reason that the NSA had decided to terminate it two years earlier. One astute independent journalist, Marcy Wheeler, speculated that the NSA had probably done so only because it could get all the internet metadata it needed from its collection sites overseas. An NSA inspector general report released in response to a FOIA request proved Wheeler had been on to something. The report makes clear that the NSA decided it could end domestic collection of metadata in bulk in part because it had loosened internal rules on the handling of metadata collected overseas that belong to U.S. persons. With the NSA's newfound ability to exploit metadata collected abroad that involve Americans, it was not worth the effort to collect metadata under the watchful eyes of the FISA court.[27]

There has been no debate in Congress on the NSA's mass collection of metadata or its other foreign and satellite collection programs. There is no reason to think these programs have any less impact on American privacy than its programs authorized by FISA, such as its domestic metadata collection under the Freedom Act, Prism, and "upstream collection" of data and communications from the internet backbone. Transnational surveillance does not operate in one direction only. The ease with which data travel across jurisdictions makes a territorial approach to protecting civil liberties arbitrary and problematic.[28] Just as the internet age has given the NSA access to foreign data inside the United States under section 702 of FISA, it gives the agency access to more American data outside the United States under Executive Order 12,333. Modern internet protocols can even be manipulated to route traffic through a favored jurisdiction, according to a computer science professor who studies internet routing, Sharon Goldberg of Boston University. She speculates that the NSA might consider shifting internet traffic abroad to take advantage of the looser rules that apply to the NSA's foreign collection.[29] Congress's lack of focus on the NSA's foreign and satellite surveillance is itself a choice that allows members to wash their hands of the issue even as Congress appropriates funds for NSA activities it says it has not authorized. This decision not to decide is a cynical evasion of responsibility.

CONGRESS IS NOT THE ONLY branch of government that has passed the buck on issues of surveillance. Outside the FISA court, federal judges have often been obliged to sidestep important legal and constitutional

questions about the NSA's mass surveillance operations. This is because the Supreme Court has made it difficult, if not impossible, for
federal courts to hear many challenges to secret surveillance. (The
Second Circuit's decision in the ACLU's challenge to bulk collection
is a rare exception.)[30] This evasion of the judiciary's core constitutional responsibilities stems from the triumph of Justice Antonin Scalia's narrow philosophy on when courts should entertain challenges
to government action, a philosophy that was influential among his
fellow conservatives. Unlike the high courts of many other countries,
the Supreme Court may not issue advisory opinions on whether a law
is constitutional. Article III of the U.S. Constitution, which concerns
judicial power, limits the federal courts to deciding "Cases" or "Controversies." Federal courts may only hear the complaints of people
who say they have been injured by something the government has
done and are asking the courts to vindicate their rights. The idea is
called "standing." A broad view of the injuries that can provide standing to sue makes it easier to challenge government action, giving the
courts power to say whether those actions are legal or constitutional.
Scalia believed that a narrower view of standing was critical to limiting the power of the federal judiciary.[31] In a case decided only a few
months before the world learned of Prism and surveillance of the internet backbone, a five-member conservative majority rejected a challenge to section 702 of FISA. In *Clapper v. Amnesty International*,
the Supreme Court said nothing about the law's constitutionality.[32]
Instead, it ruled that because the challengers could not show that their
communications had been intercepted under that law, the case could
not be heard at all.

When the ACLU decided to challenge the constitutionality of section 702 of FISA in 2009, its lawyers knew that it would be an uphill
battle to establish standing. Still, they managed to make a strong case.
The people the ACLU represented were not wearers of tinfoil hats. Instead, they were international human rights lawyers, reporters, and
researchers whose communications put them in touch with the sort
of people—including associates of terrorist organizations—who were
likely enough to be NSA targets. Nevertheless, in an opinion written by Justice Samuel Alito in February 2013 (joined, of course, by
Scalia), the Supreme Court said that reasonable fears of surveillance
are not enough—the surveillance had to be "certainly impending."

There is good reason to revisit the issue, and not only because Scalia is no longer with us. For one thing, Alito embraced a government argument that has since been discredited. Obama's solicitor general, Donald Verrilli, argued the case for the government in *Clapper*. Verrilli told the Supreme Court that because the government would disclose surveillance under section 702 of FISA, if there were a later criminal prosecution resulting from the NSA's intelligence collection, the federal courts would have a chance to consider the constitutionality of the law when the defendant challenged evidence that had been derived from it. After the case was decided, the Justice Department embarrassed Verrilli when it revealed that it had not been disclosing its use of information derived from section 702 surveillance to criminal defendants. Prosecutors provided notice in some cases in which evidence derived from section 702 surveillance was being used, and the Justice Department reformed some practices. Still, it appears that after-the-fact judicial review of intelligence surveillance is not as straightforward as the Supreme Court believed it to be.[33]

More significant, the reasoning of the Court's conservative majority simply makes less sense in a post-Snowden world. Justice Alito argued in his opinion in *Clapper* that fears of surveillance depended on a "highly attenuated chain of possibilities." The intelligence community's own transparency drive has made that chain of possibilities much less speculative. Surprisingly, allowing foreigners to challenge NSA surveillance might be the best way to allow Americans to hold their own intelligence agencies to account. A foreign citizen would actually have an easier time establishing standing. Because foreigners' communications can be targeted directly under section 702, their fears of surveillance are less speculative that those of Americans who fear incidental collection. The absence of Justice Scalia has also affected how the Supreme Court addresses the issue of standing. In 2016 a commercial privacy case raised alarm bells among privacy advocates. They believed the five conservatives were going to make it difficult for people whose personal information had been mismanaged, but who had suffered no other harm, to have their day in court. In an extremely narrow opinion, possibly written to avoid a 4-4 deadlock, Justice Alito offered a somewhat more generous view of standing than many were expecting, saying that the mere "risk of real harm" from a privacy violation may be enough to satisfy the rule, even if the harm was intangible.[34] In a post-Snowden world, it may be easier for civil liberties advocates to find challenges that can show risks that are concrete enough to meet the hurdle of standing. The Supreme Court should reconsider its approach to surveillance challenges, an approach that amounts to passing the buck on its basic obligation to say what the Constitution means.

IDEALLY, CHECKS AND BALANCES OFFER a kind of layered defense of civil liberties, but this defense depends on each branch doing its job. The goal of surveillance reform is to ensure that the ambitious in each branch of government compete to keep intelligence agencies under control. Agencies must live with the constitutional limits that judges impose—but only if they are able to review surveillance. Congress may draw the line of what is allowed well short of the constitutional limit, but to do so effectively, Congress must understand what is being done with the powers it has given the intelligence agencies. The third limitation, often overlooked, is in the executive branch itself. The president may always choose not to push surveillance to the limits of what is permitted by law, based on prudent advice from national security officials, informed by oversight officials within the agencies and by independent review boards—but only if they ask the right questions about both privacy and effectiveness.

Far too often, the three branches of government have competed with each other not in keeping surveillance within bounds but in avoiding accountability. President Obama rightly defended his NSA programs of transnational surveillance by pointing to the separation of powers in his first remarks on the NSA controversy in June 2013. The public did not have to trust him, he argued: "That's not how it works." Three branches of government had signed off on the NSA's activities. "And if people can't trust not only the executive branch but also don't trust Congress and don't trust federal judges to make sure that we're abiding by the Constitution, due process and the rule of law, then we're going to have some problems here."[35] Obama was prophetic: people did not fully trust the three branches of government on matters of surveillance, and the Obama administration was going to have some problems as a result. It turns out there was good reason for this lack of trust.

In a subtle way, Obama was using the checks-and-balances argument to pass the buck for his own decisions to continue and expand NSA surveillance. It was not persuasive. While Obama was right that three branches offer more protection than one, his argument was, like the unamended Constitution, an incomplete one. "If men were angels, no government would be necessary," Madison noted in his famous essay on checks and balances, urging the ratification of the draft that the constitutional convention in Philadelphia had hammered out in the summer of 1787. Still, Madison and his fellow federalists failed to convince the public that the separation of powers was a complete answer to the imperfections of human nature. The framers only won the argument for ratification of the Constitution when they finally agreed to add a bill of rights. Obama could not forever evade responsibility for the impact of his surveillance choices on constitutional rights by pointing to Congress and the judiciary. He had himself twice sworn an oath to uphold the entire Constitution.

For each branch to fulfill its constitutional obligations, each branch must do its job. The president should welcome tough scrutiny by a strong Privacy and Civil Liberties Oversight Board. Congress should build on the Freedom Act's success in its approach to section 702 of FISA and future surveillance debates. Members must do their jobs by overseeing surveillance powers. The Supreme Court should reform legal doctrines, such as "standing," which are an obstacle to judicial review.

Still, if Madison's system is to work, it is not enough for the three branches of government to check each other. In fact, Obama had it backward. It is only when people have little faith in the executive branch but also do not trust Congress or federal judges that Madison's system of checks and balances can work. While public cynicism is corrosive to democracy, skepticism is essential. Healthy skepticism requires transparency about surveillance. Checks and balances that operate entirely in the shadows can provide little more than the illusion of accountability. Without active pressure by an informed public to keep the government's powers in check, it is far too tempting to pass the buck. If the ambitious see little benefit in taking their oversight obligations seriously, they are sure to be too quick to give the government the benefit of the doubt—just as I was.

7

BEHIND THE JUDGE'S CURTAINS

IN A SMALL LECTURE HALL AT BROWN UNIVERSITY, JUDGE BRUCE SELYA WAS HOLD-
ing forth on his experience as the chief judge of the secret appeals
court created by the Foreign Intelligence Surveillance Act (FISA).
Critics such as Glenn Greenwald had been denouncing the FISA
court system as providing nothing more than a "fig leaf" for government surveillance.[1] On that gloomy February evening in 2014, the
judge was eager to set the record straight.

Bruce Selya is a judge of unimpeachable integrity. His erudite
opinions are legendary well beyond the tight-knit legal community
in his beloved state of Rhode Island, where he has spent his entire
career. I had met Judge Selya almost two decades earlier, as a law
clerk for one of his colleagues on the U.S. Court of Appeals for the
First Circuit. While we had seen little of each other in the interven-
ing years, it turns out we had both played a role in keeping the NSA's
transnational surveillance programs in check.

In his remarks, Selya insisted on referring to the "FISA courts"
to emphasize that the law had actually created two courts, a lower
court to hear government applications for surveillance and an ap-

peals court to review the lower court's decisions. The Chief Justice of the United States designates members of both courts from among sitting federal judges. The statute requires that three of the eleven district court judges who sit on the lower court, the Foreign Intelligence Surveillance Court, reside within twenty miles of Washington, D.C. The three judges of the appeals court, the Foreign Intelligence Surveillance Court of Review, can be drawn from among any of the hundreds of federal district or appeals court judges, although typically appeals court judges are chosen. All of the FISA judges are "Article III judges," meaning they are appointed by the president and confirmed by the Senate, with life tenure to ensure independence. The judges who agree to serve on the FISA courts serve part time for a period of seven years, as a temporary additional responsibility even as they continue to hear ordinary cases.

From 2005 to 2012 Selya served on the Foreign Intelligence Surveillance Court of Review. In 2008 Chief Justice John Roberts elevated Selya to the role of chief judge. Shortly after this, Selya told us, he remembered receiving a call from Washington. There was a classified document for him to review. As there were not yet any secure communication facilities at the federal courthouse in Providence, Rhode Island, the document had to be sent by courier. A man in a trench coat arrived with a briefcase handcuffed to his wrist, much to the judge's amusement. After dismantling the judge's telephone, the courier insisted on trying to close the judge's "entirely decorative" drapes. Eventually he gave up and lowered the unused blinds, sending up clouds of dust. The judge was deprived of his fine view of College Hill, where Brown University and the Rhode Island School of Design are located.

The judge could not resist a wisecrack. "Oh, you must be afraid that whatever you're going to show me might be observed by those subversives up at Brown," he said.

"Not just Brown, RISD too!" the courier replied.[2]

The document, it turned out, was entirely routine. The FISA court of review does not get "much business," Selya recalled. This was an understatement. In the history of the FISA courts, from their creation in 1978 until Selya's remarks in 2014, we know of only two appeals. The reason is straightforward. The lower FISA court usually hears only from the government. If only one side appears and it (almost) always wins, an appeals court has little to do.

As it turned out, however, Selya was lucky. During his tenure as chief of the FISA appeals court, he got to hear a case. Anyone managing to peek into the federal courthouse in downtown Providence during the summer of 2008 would have witnessed a milestone in surveillance. Judge Selya's court was considering the constitutionality of section 702 of FISA, enacted the previous summer when Congress passed the Protect America Act. (This is the law discussed in chapter 3 that was the subject of Director of National Intelligence McConnell's unusual interview with an *El Paso Times* reporter.) The government was seeking to use section 702 to expand the NSA's transnational surveillance operations beyond the telecommunications companies that maintain the internet backbone, to include the Silicon Valley giants that provide services such as webmail. Its success resulted in the type of collection known as "downstream collection," or Prism, a program later leaked by Edward Snowden.[3]

The government was intent on winning its appeal before Judge Selya because Prism opened up an entirely new way for the NSA to collect communications. The NSA's Stellar Wind program involved only surveillance of communications in transit. Stellar Wind depended on the voluntary cooperation of the telecommunications companies that maintain the internet backbone. As discussed in chapter 3, the Stellar Wind program ended in January 2007. The FISA court initially approved the NSA's request to continue such surveillance for foreign targets without individual probable cause determination, based on a creative legal argument. In March Judge Roger Vinson of the FISA court rejected this argument. In August Congress responded by passing section 702 of FISA, requiring companies inside the United States to cooperate with surveillance of foreign targets "reasonably believed to be outside the United States." The NSA used section 702 to restart its "upstream collection" program, which acquires the communications of foreign targets transiting the domestic internet backbone, with the assistance of telecommunications providers—now compelled, instead of voluntary.

Section 702 also opened up a new type of "downstream" surveillance for the NSA: surveillance of stored content, such as the e-mails on the servers of internet companies that provide free webmail accounts. Despite President Bush's authorization after 9/11 of warrantless surveillance in the "war on terror," the NSA never used Stellar Wind to obtain such content. Silicon Valley firms were never likely to comply with a voluntary program like Stellar Wind. Unlike telecommunications companies, internet companies do not have decades-long relationships with the NSA, and their executives typically are far more libertarian in outlook. As a result, the NSA continued to use individual "old FISA" orders based on probable cause from 2001 to 2007 to obtain stored e-mails and other communications from internet companies, even when those e-mails belonged to foreign targets. The passage of the Protect America Act of 2007 gave the government another option. While the debate in Congress had concerned telecommunications companies, section 702 allows the government to compel assistance from any "electronic communications service provider." After the law passed, the government began to serve internet companies with orders under section 702 demanding access to accounts of users that NSA analysts wanted to monitor and who were believed to be outside the United States. This type of collection became known as Prism collection. Prism soon eclipsed the NSA's older "upstream collection" program. By 2011 Prism collection encompassed more than 90 percent of the NSA's collection under section 702, according to one FISA court opinion (although this number may be exaggerated).[4]

In 2007 Yahoo was served with its first order under section 702 of FISA. Yahoo argued that because the orders did not require individual review based on probable cause, they violated the Fourth Amendment. Yahoo lost in the FISA court. The company appealed to the FISA court of review. Yahoo's request for a stay pending appeal was rejected. In May 2008, under threat of ruinous fines—$250,000 a day, doubling every week—Yahoo began complying with the NSA's demands for user data.[5] On June 19, 2008, in a specially secured courtroom—the entire floor of the federal courthouse in Providence had been emptied—the FISA court of review was in session for only the second time in its history, Chief Judge Selya presiding. To make the case for the NSA, the government brought in its heaviest hitter, Gregory Garre. Garre was the acting U.S. solicitor general, the lawyer who normally argues cases before the Supreme Court. While the amendments to FISA that Garre was defending had technically expired, the order against Yahoo was still valid. At the time, Congress was considering whether to renew the NSA's authority, and it did so in August for another four years by passing the FISA Amendments Act. (In 2012 Congress reauthorized section 702 for another five years, until the end of 2017.)

Yahoo's attorney, Marc Zwillinger, argued that the law did not satisfy the Fourth Amendment, saying that judicial review of an entire program of NSA collection, despite court-imposed privacy safeguards, was not enough to protect the interests of Americans whose communications might be collected by the NSA.[6] As evidence, Zwillinger brandished the tasking order Yahoo had just received, listing e-mail accounts that it was required to put under surveillance. "Why I show you this is because I think it's a perfectly fair question to ask the Solicitor General of the United States how a name gets on this list," Zwillinger said, pressing his point home. It was not good enough to leave targeting decisions to NSA analysts, he argued. In the absence of individual review by a judge there was a strong risk of error. What is more, the tasking list suggested this was just what was happening. A significant number of accounts "do not exist," Zwillinger observed. "They aren't accounts at Yahoo. Whether the government is misinformed, or using stale information, we don't know." Of course, there could be no harm from surveillance of a nonexistent account. Still, an inaccurate target list might be "indicative of a problem" in the NSA's system. Any problem could have serious ramifications. Zwillinger noted that in a seminal Supreme Court case on domestic intelligence surveillance in 1973, one of the justices had "said he was aghast at the notion that 900 conversations had been intercepted" without a warrant. Zwillinger continued, "We are just one provider. We have [redacted] accounts placed under surveillance in [redacted]. That's the magnitude of the surveillance we're talking about." The government has now released the transcript of this argument. It has insisted on deleting this number, despite its decision to declassify similar information after 2013. Whatever number Zwillinger gave the court in 2008, in 2016 the total number of foreign targets affected by section 702 surveillance was above 106,000, and the number of times that data were queried for information about U.S. persons was well over 30,000.[7]

Of course, the NSA's foreign and satellite programs also swept up communications of U.S. persons, but Zwillinger argued that transnational surveillance presented unique risks. If there was a problem in the NSA's Prism target list, the agency was far more likely to obtain the constitutionally protected digital correspondence of Americans, Zwillinger argued. "This is not a phone exchange in Abu Dhabi where if they're off by one digit, they're likely to get a different telephone user in Abu Dhabi," he noted. Yahoo's servers were in Sunnyvale, California. Most of the data stored on those servers belonged to Americans and were plainly protected by the Fourth Amendment.[8] The judges were unmoved. After all, even in ordinary wiretap cases the government might make a mistake and get the wrong number. The law presumes the government acts in good faith. "Why do you think the FISA Court is going to discover these errors?" one judge wanted to know. Federal judges did not have the time or the manpower to scrutinize the vast databases in Fort Meade. That is why the NSA must follow the minimization and other procedures the lower FISA court had reviewed and found acceptable. Did Yahoo really expect the court to send someone to "check on whether the government is telling the truth?"[9]

In August 2008 the FISA court of review ruled on Yahoo's appeal. True to his reputation for eloquence, Judge Selya wrote an opinion that provided a ringing endorsement of the judicial role, making clear that "the government cannot unilaterally sacrifice constitutional rights on the altar of national security." Selya's opinion reminded the government that the "judiciary's duty is to hold that balance delicate and true." Selya's language echoed that of Chief Justice John Marshall in *Marbury v. Madison*, the landmark 1803 case in which the Supreme Court first established the principle of judicial review: "It is emphatically the province and duty of the Judicial Department to say what the law is." Yet, as in that venerable case, the outcome was a win for the government. Yahoo, like Marbury, lost its challenge. As the "government has instituted several layers of serviceable safeguards," Selya concluded, "its efforts to protect national security should not be frustrated by the courts."[10]

Selya had to fight hard to have his opinion released to the public. "We immediately met a stone wall because the national security folks were very resistant to declassifying anything," Selya recalled later. It was a struggle to ensure any part of his opinion remained meaningful. The text "would come back with everything struck out except two 'thes' and maybe an 'of.'"[11] One reason was the intelligence community's insistence that the name of the provider who had challenged the law remain secret. In January 2009 a blacked-out version was made public. While it was clear that the FISA court of review had upheld the law and the basic reasons why it had done so, key details about the case remained unclear. There was "a specific privacy concern" that the company had raised at the last minute. What was it? A footnote explaining what the NSA had agreed to do about it was redacted. Did the surveillance involve telephone calls or internet communications? It was impossible to tell. Even the name of the case was mysterious. It was *In re Directives [redacted text].*[12] The redactions obscured the fact that the FISA court of review had done much more than uphold the law Congress had passed to authorize NSA surveillance that had started with Stellar Wind. The court had provided a green light for a new kind of surveillance—Prism—that would soon dwarf the NSA's earlier upstream collection program.

ONE OF THE FIRST NEWS stories published in June 2013 was based on the Snowden disclosures about Prism. It was based on an unconfirmed document that reporters said revealed that the program involved collection directly from the servers of several providers. That allegation turned out to be false. To the amusement of many, the articles also revealed what was said to be the program's clumsy logo. It bore a resemblance to the album cover art for Pink Floyd's *Dark Side of the Moon.* On a website dedicated to improving business presentations, one user offered a more elegant version. "Dear NSA, you can do whatever with my data. But not with my eyes."[13]

The government quickly issued a statement saying it "does not unilaterally obtain information from the servers of U.S. electronic communication service providers." Prism was simply an "internal government computer system" for implementing section 702 of FISA. The law had numerous safeguards, including judicial review.[14] Still, the image of NSA analysts surfing through user data stored on the servers of American technology companies was a powerful one. Naturally, Yahoo wanted its users around the world to understand that it had fought Prism from the beginning and was only participating because it had lost. For more than a year, Yahoo urged the government to allow it to identify itself as the company that had challenged section 702. It was not until September 2014 that the government agreed, releasing a new version of Selya's opinion in the case that we now know by its full name: *In re Directives to Yahoo! Inc.*[15]

There was at least a kernel of truth in the stories about Prism. As Zwillinger had explained to the FISA court of review, the companies are simply given a list of the accounts the NSA wants to put under surveillance. Obtaining the data was seamless enough that the confusion about whether the NSA had direct access to the servers of the companies is understandable. The companies have no way to check on the NSA's compliance with the "serviceable safeguards" that Judge Selya's court had decided were enough to make Prism constitutional. As a practical matter, neither does the FISA court. Both the court and the companies are dependent on audits by lawyers from the Justice Department and the Office of the Director of National Intelligence (ODNI), like the ones I had conducted in my visits to Fort Meade with Alex Joel. As discussed in chapter 4, these reviews eventually revealed significant shortcomings in the NSA's implementation of its transnational surveillance programs. During the Obama years, the NSA was forced to admit it had engaged in illegal and even unconstitutional surveillance under section 702 of FISA. Although upstream collection had created the most serious issues, the NSA's problems forced it to engage in an overhaul of its entire compliance process. In hindsight, the faulty tasking list that Yahoo's attorney had dramatically displayed in a sealed courtroom in Providence was an early warning sign.

In defending the FISA court system in his remarks at Brown University in 2014, Judge Selya did not give much credence to the idea that it might need reform. Judges are "used to sizing up these things," Selya argued. He especially disliked a proposal that President Obama was considering and that I strongly favored, an outside lawyer who would argue for privacy. "I think it's an awful idea," he told me. An outside advocate would just "slow up the process" for "no real gain."[16] Selya's views were shared by his colleagues—indeed, they reflected the official position of the federal judiciary. In a letter on behalf of the Administrative Office of the United States Courts, Judge John Bates, former head of the lower FISA court and the man who had expressed such concern when faced with the NSA's compliance problems, nevertheless strongly objected to the advocate idea. An adversarial process would be "counterproductive," "cumbersome," and "resource-intensive," he wrote. Because of the need to include the advocate in communications with the government, the court could no longer receive "complete and accurate information" in an informal setting. Other proposals for changes to the court, such as increased transparency, fared no better.[17]

By contrast, President Obama was open to reforming the FISA courts. If a judge "hears only one side of the story," he mused, it was natural for people to think the court would lean "too far in favor of security" and would "not pay enough attention to liberty." He made clear he was open to an "independent voice" to make sure that government lawyers are "challenged by an adversary."[18] The President's Review Group on Intelligence and Communications Technologies, created by Obama in the summer of 2013, also urged another voice in the FISA process. The surveillance court's decisions touched on "serious and difficult questions of statutory and constitutional interpretation about which reasonable lawyers and judges could certainly differ," they said. The solution was to employ the law's great "engine of truth," the adversary system.[19] When Congress passed the Freedom Act eighteen months later, it included a much modified version of the review group's proposal for outside lawyers, written to address the objections of the FISA court judges. While it does not provide anything like a fully adversarial process, the law does require the appointment of an amicus curiae, a friend of the court, if the court believes an application presents "a novel or significant interpretation of the law."

Amici are drawn from a pool of people designated by the court with "expertise in privacy and civil liberties, intelligence collection, communications technology," or other relevant areas. They must be eligible for the top security clearances required to do their jobs. Amici present "legal arguments that advance the protection of privacy and civil liberties," "information related to intelligence collection or communications technology," or other areas as directed by the court.[20]

While the amici are formally independent of the government, care must be taken to ensure that subtle pressures do not influence their work. A lawyer who is hoping for a long and fruitful career in the field of national security might be reluctant to win arguments against government surveillance powers a bit too often. A court that hears regularly from weak or timid amici would be worse than the old system, where at least the judges knew that they were only hearing one side. The court has now appointed some of the finest lawyers in the field of national security law in the country to serve as amici curiae, including Marc Zwillinger, Laura Donohue, and David Kris. They have diverse backgrounds and philosophies. As we have seen, Zwillinger is a lawyer with experience in challenging the NSA. Donohue is a law professor and the author of a critical book on FISA and NSA surveillance. David Kris is a former head of the Justice Department's National Security Division and the coauthor of a well-regarded treatise on FISA and national security investigations.[21]

If the FISA courts are to act as a meaningful check on the NSA's transnational surveillance programs, outside lawyers are not enough. The court's new role requires new expertise to help judges ask the right questions about complex technical issues. Buried in the Freedom Act's amicus curiae provision is language that could be used to greatly aid the court in understanding the complex nature of NSA surveillance, if the lawyers who dominate the FISA process are sensible enough to recognize it. Under the law, amici need not be lawyers. Amici may also be appointed to provide technical expertise. Many of the most serious problems faced by the NSA in adapting its programs to court oversight have resulted not from one-sided rulings by the FISA court but from a basic misunderstanding about how the surveillance itself works. These misunderstandings were often the result of failed lawyer-technologist communication. Judges at the FISA court, advised by a professional staff of lawyers, hear arguments from lawyers at the Justice Department, who typically consult with the NSA's lawyers. Serious compliance problems persisted for years both because lawyers did not accurately describe to the court what the NSA was doing and because lawyers did not convey to NSA technical staff the limits of what the court had imposed.

In ordinary civil cases, federal judges appoint technical experts as "special masters" to facilitate discovery of relevant data, monitor compliance with court orders, adjudicate legal disputes, and conduct inspections of computer systems.[22] For similar tasks, FISA court judges rely on the NSA's own compliance staff and periodic audits by the Justice Department and the ODNI—the sort of reviews that Alex and I began conducting in 2007. If the court employed its own technical experts, it would have more granular insight into the nuts and bolts of how the NSA's systems are working—or not working. Lawyers tend to be verbal and overconfident. In my experience, technical personnel are often less likely to speak up in meetings. In recent years, privacy and civil liberties organizations that have typically been staffed by lawyers have defied the legal profession's insularity and hired technologists. They include Chris Soghoian, who served as the ACLU's "principal technologist" until 2016, Daniel Kahn Gillmor, another computer scientist at the ACLU, and Joe Hall of the Center for Democracy and Technology. The surveillance court would be wise to follow their lead.

The court's complex responsibilities also require new resources to address the workload. One way to ease the burden on FISA judges would be to make use of magistrates. The Supreme Court has said that magistrates are "indispensable," accounting for a "staggering volume of judicial work."[23] They do not require presidential appointment and Senate confirmation. Instead, they are appointed by the judges of their district and serve terms of eight years. Many judicial functions could be performed by magistrates without provoking any constitutional concerns. Magistrate judges issue search warrants every day. Increasingly, they grapple with the complex privacy and civil liberties questions involved in searching computers and digital devices.[24] It was a federal magistrate judge, James Ornstein, who heard arguments in the fierce battle in 2016 over the FBI's demand for Apple's assistance in circumventing the security features of an iPhone. Although FISA does not permit magistrates to issue traditional surveillance orders, it does allow them to issue orders for business records and for metadata. Despite this, the FISA court does not employ magistrates at all.

The use of magistrates would have been particularly helpful in easing the judges' workload as they managed the NSA's bulk collection of telephone records. As a result of compliance problems with bulk collection in 2009, judges temporarily took over the task of designating the seed telephone numbers from which the NSA analysts began their search of the database. In doing so, judges had to decide whether the hundreds of numbers provided by the NSA met the court's standard of reasonable, articulable suspicion. From 2013 to 2015, the Obama administration again asked the court to perform this function, in response to public criticism of bulk collection after the program was disclosed by Snowden. A magistrate corps could have provided this kind of review, allowing the judges to focus on more complex issues.

Magistrates could also make it possible to subject more decisions to judicial review, instead of leaving such decisions to the NSA and other intelligence agencies. Congress has given the FBI power to obtain some business records in national security cases without review by any court by issuing written demands, known as "national security letters" or NSLs. The president's review group recommended judicial review of NSLs. The idea went nowhere because the volume of NSLs is simply too great for judicial review to be practical. In 2016 the government issued over 12,000 NSLs, more than eight times the number of traditional FISA orders. Subjecting the NSA's targeting decisions in its Prism and upstream collection programs to individual judicial review would plainly be impossible without substantial new resources. In 2016 a single order issued under section 702 of FISA affected more than 106,000 targets selected by NSA analysts. For the FISA court's eleven judges to review targets individually, each judge would have to consider more than 9,600 cases a year. If the FISA court's role were limited to reviewing only U.S. person queries, the task would still be formidable. In 2016 there were 5,288 queries using U.S. person identifiers of the contents of communications collected under section 702. There were 30,355 such queries for non-content information, such as metadata. (These figures exclude queries by the FBI.) Even if the FISA court reviewed only U.S. person queries involving content—what we might call true "backdoor searches"—requiring such review would quadruple the total number of cases the FISA court considered in 2016.[25] If the court employed magistrates, Congress could make the NSA and other intelligence agencies submit at least some of these decisions to judicial oversight without flooding an already overworked court with an impossible workload.

PUT SIMPLY, THE FISA COURTS need more help to navigate the new world of transnational surveillance, whether or not the judges themselves realize it. Any institution may become entrenched. Yet the opposition to reform by the FISA court judges themselves reflects more than the ordinary human tendency to resist criticism. It is also a result of the rightward tilt of the FISA courts. The tilt is a structural one, as the Chief Justice of the United States names every member of both the lower FISA court and the court of review, and designates their chief judges. Of course, there is the practical constraint that the Chief Justice must persuade an independent federal judge to do extra work without additional compensation. Still, the Chief Justice has a great deal of discretion. Only three Chief Justices have ever exercised this power: Warren Burger, William Rehnquist, and John Roberts, all of them conservatives.

With each selection, the current Chief Justice has shaped the FISA court even more aggressively than his predecessors. Roberts was the first Chief Justice to be named after 9/11. He was chosen by George W. Bush, who made the "war on terror" a central focus of his presidency. Roberts has chosen judges like himself—conservative, appointed by Republican presidents, and with executive branch experience, likely to make them sympathetic to the government's positions on national security issues. By the time the public got its first look at the broad opinions authorizing NSA surveillance in the summer of 2013, Roberts had made sure that all of the court's eleven judges were drawn from his side of the political spectrum.[26]

We now know there was a particularly compelling reason for Bush to be concerned about the FISA courts in 2005. When Chief Justice Rehnquist died, the FISA court was in the middle of secretly adapting the NSA's Stellar Wind programs to court review. The court's decisions were critical in interpreting FISA in a way that allowed the NSA's transnational surveillance programs to continue. Of course, all of this was highly classified at the time. Still, the way Roberts made his mark on the FISA courts should not have been a surprise to anyone who was paying attention. At his confirmation hearing, Roberts was questioned by Senator Mike DeWine of Ohio, a Republican member of the Senate Select Committee on Intelligence. DeWine urged Roberts to take a "hands-on approach," arguing the FISA court judges would be making "sometimes life or death decisions for our country." Roberts promised that he would take great care to name only those judges "who are most sensitive" to issues of national security.[27] While this exchange might seem like nothing more than a routine discussion of one of the Chief Justice's administrative responsibilities, the historical context makes it clear what DeWine meant by a "hands-on approach." After 9/11 the FISA court had come under intense public scrutiny. The 9/11 Commission blamed the lower court's rulings—or at least the way those rulings had been interpreted inside the national security establishment—for erecting a "wall" between intelligence and law enforcement surveillance, impeding efforts to prevent the attacks. When Roberts said his appointments would be "most sensitive" to issues of national security, he was promising to select judges that would give the government a freer hand.

In the aftermath of the Snowden leaks, Senator Richard Blumenthal, a Democrat from Connecticut, argued for reform of the judicial selection process. Under his proposal, the Chief Justice would no longer have the sole power to name judges. Instead, he would share that power with the chief judges of the thirteen federal courts of appeals and with the other Supreme Court justices.[28] Blumenthal's proposal was not adopted. For the foreseeable future, the Chief Justice of the United States will have the sole power to name judges to the FISA courts. To restore public confidence, bringing balance to the court's membership is as important as bringing balance to the arguments it hears. While the federal judiciary became more diverse and less conservative during the Obama years, the current selection process all but guarantees that the FISA courts will remain a right-leaning redoubt. At his confirmation hearing, Roberts famously described judges as umpires who do no more than "call balls and strikes."[29] As every baseball fan knows, however, an umpire's calls can be decisive in close games.

THERE ARE MANY GOOD REASONS to regard the FISA court system with suspicion. While a fair reading of the opinions released since 2013 shows that the rubber-stamp accusation is unfair, the judges have embraced an expansive view of the government's surveillance powers. For the Snowden generation, the secret court appears to be just one more cog in the surveillance state. Some critics have even gone so far as to describe the FISA court as a "modern-day Star Chamber," arguing it should be abolished.[30] Yet the realistic alternative to the FISA court system is not review of intelligence surveillance by regular courts but surveillance by the executive without court review at all. In matters of national security, the president holds the trump card. If Congress abolishes the executive branch's special powers under FISA, the president may always invoke his constitutional powers, as presidents have in the past. This was understood well by Vice President Dick Cheney and his counsel, David Addington. It is why they fought a rearguard battle to keep the FISA courts from reviewing post-9/11 surveillance. It was a victory for civil liberties that they lost. It is only because of the FISA court that the government may not eavesdrop intentionally on an American—or anyone inside the United States—based on mere suspicion. Instead, the government must persuade a federal judge that there is probable cause to believe the target is an agent of a foreign power.

Before the FISA court system was created, warrantless surveillance of civil rights leaders, peace activists, and others was not only common, it was widely accepted as a perfectly ordinary exercise of executive power. As a warning of the dangers of warrantless surveillance, FBI director Jim Comey kept on his desk a memorandum from his predecessor, J. Edgar Hoover, requesting surveillance on Dr. Martin Luther King Jr. The memorandum is directed not to a judge but to Attorney General Robert F. Kennedy, who approved it.[31] Hoover's rationale for the wiretap was King's decision to employ two advisers who were former communists, on the theory they might be agents of the Soviet Union. It was a flimsy excuse for an FBI campaign to discredit King. It was barely enough for an attorney general fearful of making the administration of his brother, John F. Kennedy, look soft on communism. Hoover's request would never have stood up to judicial scrutiny.

Jim Comey began his government service as a federal prosecutor in 1987; he was the first FBI director who has lived with the FISA court his entire professional career.[32] As abuses like Hoover's wiretapping of King pass out of living memory, there is a risk government officials and critics alike may fail to recognize just how vital the FISA court has been to preserving civil liberties. The FISA court may not last forever. During the 2016 election campaign, Donald Trump said he would consider "warrantless searches of Muslims" in order to prevent terrorism.[33] Whether the FISA court system or something like it is actually required by the Constitution is still an open question. While the Supreme Court has said that a warrant is required for surveillance involving domestic security threats, it has still never decided whether a judge must sign off on surveillance of suspected foreign agents.[34] David Addington may yet be proved right in a crisis: we may still be "one bomb away" from a demand by the president to abolish court review of national security surveillance.

The FISA court system was an experiment. Despite fears that involving judges would create red tape that would impede time-sensitive intelligence operations, the experiment was clearly a success in collecting intelligence. Legitimate national security surveillance expanded after it was subject to court review. During the era of J. Edgar Hoover, the FBI conducted a total of 10,559 warrantless wiretapping and bugging operations in the thirty-four years from 1940 to 1974. In the thirty-four years of the FISA court's operation from 1979 to 2013, there were 35,333 surveillance applications. In other words, following the enactment of FISA, the government engaged in more than triple the number of surveillance operations in national security investigations, with far fewer abuses.[35]

Perhaps the FISA court has been a success for the government, but does it really protect civil liberties? As critics point out, during that same period of 1979 to 2013, only twelve FISA applications were rejected—an approval rate in excess of 99.9 percent. Since 2003 the Justice Department has reported applications that were modified by the court, in addition to denials. The number of reported modifications ranged from a high of ninety-four in 2004 to a low of two in 2008. This is still a yearly rate for approving applications without change that ranges from under 95 percent to well over 99 percent, consistent with the public image of the FISA court as a rubber stamp.

These statistics give a misleading impression. As discussed in chapter 5, it is the government's own excessive secrecy that is largely responsible for the mistaken view that the FISA court is a rubber stamp. While I was in government, everyone I knew with first-hand experience of the FISA process said it was more, not less, exacting than the process for criminal wiretaps, and far more onerous than obtaining an ordinary search warrant. The numbers do not tell the whole story. First, lawyers at the Justice Department play a gatekeeping role. They have traditionally viewed their role not as zealous advocates for government surveillance but as trusted mediators between the court and the intelligence community. If they have doubts about an agency request, an application will never be prepared. Second, the government shares its applications with the court before they are formally filed. If the court's small professional staff or the judges themselves express concerns, the application is often changed, and these informal changes are not counted as orders that have been modified by the court. If the government cannot meet the court's objections, the application is typically withdrawn, instead of being filed and then denied. In October 2013 Judge Reggie Walton, the presiding judge of the lower FISA court, wrote a public letter to Senator Charles Grassley in an effort to explain this process. For a three-month period in 2013, Judge Walton kept track of this more informal back-and-forth between the FISA court and the government. According to Walton, from July 1 through September 30, 2013, "we have observed that 24.4% of matters submitted ultimately involved substantive changes . . . as a result of Court inquiry or action."[36] In other words, only about three in four proposed applications are simply approved without any change in response to the FISA court's concerns. Judge Walton's letter in 2013 is the first significant effort to provide a more realistic view of how the FISA court works behind the scenes. One three-month period in 2013 is not enough to make a definitive judgment, of course. The FISA court should provide similar information on a regular basis.

The statistics are less important than the results. Edward Snowden exposed complex transnational programs of mass surveillance, bulk surveillance of domestic telephone records and metadata, surveillance of foreign leaders and foreign populations, and the undermining of internet security by the NSA. While all these programs pose grave risks to privacy in the digital age, Snowden revealed no intentional targeting of American journalists, political figures, or activists for reasons that would be an obvious pretext for political spying. For all its faults, the secret court system appears to have done exactly what it was intended to do: prevent a future Hoover from spying on a future King.

Nevertheless, further reform is vital if the FISA court is to continue to protect civil liberties. The job of the court has changed. The privacy concerns that the FISA court addresses in the digital age go far beyond the simple national security wiretaps it was designed to review. To paraphrase a decision by Chief Justice John Roberts involving the search of digital data on a mobile phone, if an ordinary FISA order is like a "ride on horseback," the NSA's transnational surveillance programs under section 702 of FISA are like a "flight to the moon."[37] Yet as we have seen, the judges of the FISA courts often bristle at the notion there is anything wrong with the secret court's status quo.

When Judge Selya was defending the FISA court's secret, one-sided process for my students at Brown, he argued that what the FISA did was really not much different from what a local judge in Providence does when the police are seeking a search warrant. Selya did not seem to give much thought to the idea that in an era of mass surveillance, judges need to probe deeper.

The FISA court's civil libertarian critics are wrong to call it a rubber stamp, much less a Star Chamber. (No one who has ever had experience dealing with the FISA court system needs much convincing on this point.) Yet the critics are right that the FISA courts are flawed. A system designed mainly to review individual national security wiretaps is simply out of its depth when it comes to review of complex transnational programs of surveillance. The judges need help to fulfill their responsibilities, and this means strengthening the FISA court system as a whole. FISA judges need skilled technologists to ask the right questions, and a corps of magistrates to bring more decisions inside the judiciary. The judicial selection process also needs reform to restore public confidence in the wake of Chief Justice Roberts's success in packing the court.

These reforms should happen even if the FISA judges themselves say they are not needed. Georges Clemenceau, the leader of France during World War I, is credited with saying that "war is too serious a matter to leave to military men." Likewise, judicial review is too important to leave to the judges. In an age of mass surveillance, for the FISA court to fulfill its duty to "hold that balance delicate and true," in the words of Judge Selya, it is going to have to embrace a more ambitious role.

Part III

THE STRUGGLE FOR REFORM

8

TECHNOLOGICAL MAGIC

AT A CONFERENCE HELD IN AN ELEGANT MANSION IN NORTHWEST WASHINGTON, I met one of the world's leading cryptographers. At the time, I was working at the White House. A computer science professor at Brown University, Anna Lysyanskaya wanted me to know that modern cryptography was not just about encrypting communications to protect them from eavesdroppers. There were a host of amazing capabilities that her field had now made possible. She was eager to see these capabilities put to work to protect privacy in the digital age. Like me, she was optimistic that President Obama could make progress in protecting privacy.

Anna glossed over the complex mathematics involved in cryptography. Instead, her talk was peppered with pop culture and literary references. Privacy-enhancing cryptography was like "the Force" from *Star Wars*, she said. You do not have to understand how it works. You just have to "use the Force." Anna's slides also featured the figure of Alice from *Alice in Wonderland*. In Lewis Carroll's tale, Alice tells the Queen of Hearts that there's "no use trying" to believe impossible things. "I daresay you haven't much practice," the Queen replies, saying she could believe "six impossible things before breakfast." Anna took the Queen's side of the argument. She described many impossible things that her field has made a reality. She explained that you can prove you know the answer to a question without revealing what the answer is, establish basic facts about your identity without saying who you are, search what would seem to be meaningless encrypted data without decrypting the data first, and retrieve a particular record from a massive database with an iron-clad guarantee you have learned nothing about anything else.

Anna was intent on showing me and anyone else from the government who would listen about how modern cryptography allows us to have our cake and eat it too. We could have the benefits of the digital age without sacrificing privacy. There were alternatives to intelligence programs that rely on massive collection of data. It seemed like magic, I thought—until I remembered a quotation from one of my favorite authors, Arthur C. Clarke: "Any sufficiently advanced technology is indistinguishable from magic." Anna and I went from discussing impossible things at conferences to talking about them before breakfast. In January 2013 we married.

A MONTH AFTER THE SNOWDEN revelations began in June 2013, a reporter at the *Washington Post* asked me for my impressions of General Keith Alexander, then the director of the National Security Agency. Alexander was well known inside the intelligence community for saying things like "Why can't we collect all the signals all the time?" At least in part, his way of speaking was intended to be tongue in cheek, designed to boost the morale of his troops. Alexander's rhetoric had been awkward for me and other privacy officials. In more than one classified briefing, I had found myself wishing the general might curb his enthusiasm, or at least confine it to the battlefield.

Ellen Nakashima found her headline in three words one source had used to sum up Alexander's approach: "Collect it all." I told Ellen that while that assessment was fair, Alexander also voiced sincere concern that the NSA stay within legal boundaries. He was not shy about pushing those boundaries as far as they could go. "He certainly believes you need to collect everything you can under the law,"

I told Ellen, "and that includes pushing for pretty aggressive interpretations of the law."[1] The NSA has always had very broad authority to collect intelligence overseas and from satellites. During Alexander's tenure, the Foreign Intelligence Surveillance Court had also approved broad programs of domestic collection (discussed in chapters 3 and 4), including the bulk collection of American telephone records and internet metadata.

Alexander's passion was a deadly earnest one. It saved lives on the battlefield. The NSA grabbed every possible signal in Iraq—text messages, phone calls, and e-mails. It used these signals in innovative ways to combat a raging insurgency. At the same time, the collect-it-all approach also resulted in global surveillance on a truly massive scale. In a report released in the summer of 2013, the NSA revealed that it "touched" 1.6 percent of daily internet traffic, apparently believing this would reassure the public. It did not. While the NSA report did not define what it meant by "touching," one reporter calculated that the amount of data came to 29 petabytes per day. A petabyte is 1,000,000,000,000,000—one quadrillion—bytes. By comparison, at the time Google was analyzing a smaller, although still quite vast, 20 petabytes per day.[2]

If "collect it all" became the NSA's unofficial motto only under Keith Alexander, the idea was not new. In the first public appearance by any NSA director before Congress in the mid-1970s, one senator described the NSA's satellite collection as akin to "a huge vacuum cleaner." He did not mean it as a criticism; he believed the NSA's "awesome technology" was vital to national defense.[3] Nor will Alexander be the last NSA director to collect bulk data. Shortly before Alexander retired in 2014, President Obama issued Presidential Policy Directive 28. It affirmed the NSA's policy of collecting signals intelligence in bulk. It also imposed the first-ever constraints on the practice. PPD-28 limits the use of data collected in bulk to six specific national security threats. They are espionage, terrorism, weapons of mass destruction, cybersecurity threats, threats to U.S. or allied military forces, and transnational crime.

Bulk collection has become synonymous with mass surveillance—in other words, surveillance of any kind without individual warrants that affects a large number of people. In the intelligence community, bulk collection has a narrower meaning. It refers only to programs where there are no targets at all, at least not at the collection stage. PPD-28 defines bulk collection as "the authorized collection of large quantities of signals intelligence data which, due to technical or operational considerations, is acquired without the use of discriminants (e.g., specific identifiers, selection terms, etc.)."[4] In other words, the NSA is acquiring all the data transiting a facility or stored in a large database without any prior effort to filter out communications that do not belong to its specific targets. Bulk collection has a host of downsides; privacy risk is only one of them. As the sheer volume of personal data continues to skyrocket, vacuuming up such information has become very expensive. Power surges have been a recurring problem for the NSA for decades. At a cost of well over $1 billion, the NSA has constructed a new facility in Bluffdale, Utah. Electrical problems delayed its opening by at least a year. It finally became operational in 2014. With a million square feet of space for servers and supercomputers, the facility's capacity easily exceeds Google's largest data center. Its electric bills alone are more than $1 million a month.[5]

Why does the NSA collect information in bulk at all, instead of collecting the data and communications only of specific foreign intelligence targets? The NSA's critics think they know why. The danger to privacy from bulk collection is not a bug, they argue; it is a feature. Glenn Greenwald argues that it is actually the goal of the NSA to eliminate privacy. According to Greenwald, the NSA is about political and social control, about inducing "passivity, obedience, and conformity."[6] If it is, the agency has done an exceptionally bad job. Glenn Greenwald and other journalists working with the Snowden documents won Pulitzer Prizes. Greenwald's collaborator, Laura Poitras, won an Oscar for her documentary, *Citizenfour*. Critics of Big Brother were treated less gently in George Orwell's novel. More fundamentally, if the government wants to intimidate people at home or abroad with the breadth of its surveillance programs, it makes no sense to keep them secret. If the NSA regards the impact of bulk collection on the privacy of ordinary people not as a bug but as a feature, it was both undocumented and highly classified—at least before Snowden came along.

DURING MY TIME IN GOVERNMENT, I spent many hours discussing the true reasons for bulk collection with technical staff. As targeted collection clearly poses fewer risks to privacy, I wanted to understand why the NSA did not just forgo bulk collection altogether. To my surprise, I learned that bulk collection has nothing to do with the more exotic claims of NSA critics—and even a few of its defenders—about monitoring everyone in order to somehow predict who might later become a terrorist. The problem of the "unknown unknowns" of Donald Rumsfeld's infamous locution has yet to be solved, and it is far from clear that it ever will be.[7] Instead, the NSA uses bulk collection mainly because it makes it easier and quicker to identify and trace new intelligence targets as they switch between different phones, e-mail accounts, and modes of communication.

In PPD-28, Obama ordered Director of National Intelligence Jim Clapper to study the technical feasibility of alternatives to bulk collection. Clapper assigned the task to a committee of experts under the National Research Council. In January 2015 the committee issued its report *Bulk Collection of Signals Intelligence: Technical Options*.[8] Perhaps the report's most valuable contribution was its description of why the NSA collects in bulk. When I first learned of these capabilities, we could discuss them only at a highly classified level. The National Research Council study described them in more detail than any unclassified document ever had before.

First, assembling a bulk database of communications metadata can be useful for contact chaining—tracking networks of contacts among intelligence targets, such as terrorists or other clandestine groups like weapons proliferators. While collecting the metadata of a particular individual is enough to show to whom that person talks directly, it will not uncover a link between two people that depends on one or more intermediaries—"cutouts," in the jargon of espionage. If Alice and Bob never talk to each other but they do talk to Charlie, data collection targeted on Alice alone may not uncover Bob's significance. Analysts may not realize that Alice is part of a network that includes Bob. Perhaps Bob is in contact, directly or through an intermediary, with someone who is known to be part of the broader network. If there is more than one intermediary, bulk collection becomes even more useful.

Of course, if we can obtain the metadata not only for Alice but also for every one of Alice's direct contacts over a given period of time, we might eventually discover that Alice is using Charlie to communicate with Bob even without bulk collection. However, targeted collection will likely result in uncovering a connection between Alice and Bob much more slowly than bulk collection. This has nothing to do with how quickly the NSA obtains the data, but if Alice and Bob are new targets, the NSA will not have as much data about their communications—and, more important, their first- and second-order contacts. If the NSA is able to query past data on Alice and Bob that reveal their communications for a substantial period of time before they were targets—a possibility if data are either retained by providers for that period or are collected in bulk—an analyst could uncover much more quickly that they are communicating through Charlie. If Alice and Bob stop talking to Charlie before either is identified as a target, the connection will never be discovered.

A second way in which bulk collection is useful is in helping analysts track targets who often change phones, e-mail accounts, or other identifiers. Since the pattern of calls or e-mail contacts for the new phone or account will be similar to the old one, NSA analysts can quickly pinpoint the new target if they are able to look for it within a bulk database. To be sure, even if the NSA can only obtain data through targeted collection, analysts might still be able to identify a target's new phone or other account. If a target switches phones or e-mail addresses, analysts may discover the new one through targeting someone who is in regular contact with the real target, in order to see whether a new identifier has appeared that may be a replacement for the old one. Of course, for this technique to work, the true target's contact must be one the analyst is lawfully permitted to single out for surveillance.

Assuming there is a contact available whom the NSA may validly target, the issue is mostly one of speed. Monitoring the contact of a target is likely to take more time than searching a comprehensive database of metadata collected in bulk because the analyst will need to wait for a pattern to emerge in which the new identifier is in touch with the contact the NSA is monitoring. The technique will not work at all if the target makes sure not to be in touch with people who were in direct contact with the old phone or account. A bulk database solves this problem. An analyst may trace a new phone or account that is in touch with other members of a terrorist or other network based only on communications patterns, even if there are one or more "hops" between targets.

Finally, bulk collection may be useful to the NSA as a form of triage, allowing analysts to quickly assemble a relatively complete picture of a previously unknown group in the event of a terrorist attack or other new developments. Perhaps a government that was thought to have abandoned a nuclear program is discovered to have cheated. Policymakers will want as much information as quickly as possible about the undisclosed program. If the NSA already has a database that includes the communications metadata of that nation's government, industry, and scientific establishment because it routinely collects such information in bulk, it will be much easier to meet that demand.

This points to a fundamental difference between bulk collection and targeted collection. It is the NSA's need for historical data, not the desire to put everyone under surveillance, that makes bulk collection particularly helpful. The analysis techniques that the NSA says bulk collection makes easier, such as contact chaining, finding alternative identifiers, and triage, all depend on historical data. While the NSA can engage in all three techniques—contact chaining, finding alternative identifiers, and triage—using only targeted collection, it is only with a collect-it-all approach that the NSA can be sure it will always have the past data of new targets. As the report put it, "For investigations that have little or no prior targeting history, bulk collection may be the only source of useful information."[9] Putting the same point in a more Orwellian fashion, the NSA must make everyone a target if it wants to be sure it will have the data of everyone who might later become a target. Whether bulk collection is worth the loss of privacy depends in part on how much—and whose—privacy we are willing to sacrifice.

Some threats may be so catastrophic that bulk collection is worth the cost, such as the risk that terrorists might acquire weapons of mass destruction. While such fears have been used to justify disastrous policies such as torture and waging preventive war in Iraq, there is a crucial difference between these policies and NSA surveillance. Torture provides inaccurate information, and the war in Iraq was based on faulty intelligence. Good intelligence provides accurate warning. More comprehensive intelligence allows us to take actions short of war to address threats well before they become imminent, and to alleviate fears of threats that prove unfounded. Intelligence will be a vital tool for monitoring the deal with Iran to end its nuclear weapons development program, concluded in 2015. The NSA can do more than help us win wars. It can help us avoid them.

IF COLLECTING SIGNALS INTELLIGENCE IN bulk is sometimes necessary, what should be done about the cost to privacy? One answer is to define the problem away. Intelligence agencies must follow privacy procedures whenever they "collect, retain or disseminate information." Under its classified rules, the NSA applies a rather peculiar definition to the word "collection," which means that much of what it does simply does not trigger those rules.

The way the NSA's lawyers play games with a simple word like "collection" is a sore point for civil libertarians. When Jim Clapper was searching for a rationale for his false answer to Wyden's question— "Does the NSA collect any type of data at all on millions or hundreds of millions of Americans?"—Clapper focused on the word "collect." Clapper said, "When someone says 'collection' to me, that has a specific meaning, which may have a different meaning to him." Even Clapper admitted his explanation was "too cute by half."[10]

While the NSA's full definition of collection is classified, the rule is not quite as permissive as some have suggested. The most recent declassified version of United States Signals Intelligence Directive 18—the NSA's internal privacy rules—describes collection as the "selection" of "identified nonpublic communications for subsequent processing." "Selection," in turn, is defined as "the intentional insertion of a [redacted], telephone number, e-mail address, [redacted] into a computer scan dictionary or manual scan guide."[11] While I have heard some argue that this rule means the NSA escapes its responsibility for "collection" of data unless it is viewed by a human being, the definition is broader than this. Information is collected as soon as it is selected for further processing, even if only by a computer. Still, as much of the data that the NSA ingests is never selected in this fashion, the data are never "collected." In a meeting, I once described this curious phenomenon as the mystery of the "immaculate collection."

In August 2016 the Obama administration issued new privacy rules for intelligence activities that apply throughout the Department of Defense, replacing an exceedingly old regulation that was issued in 1982. The old rules said that information is collected only when an employee "officially accepts" it. Under the new rules, information is collected as soon as it is "received"—a much more sensible rule that conforms more closely to the practice of intelligence agencies. Data that "only momentarily passes through a computer system" still do not count.[12] The NSA's classified rules remain unchanged, including its more specific definition of collection.

Of course, there may be situations in which it makes sense to give the NSA leeway in applying its rules to unknown data it has obtained—or "collected," in the way the word is normally used. The NSA obtains data all over the world, in a dizzying variety of formats, sometimes on the battlefield. An exemption to some of the NSA's rules for such situations may make sense, but the legal fiction that the data have not been collected invites mischief; it could obscure real privacy issues. The opposite is also true. We may want the NSA to apply privacy rules even when its systems do not collect data, even in the ordinary use of the term. What if a company scans all data passing through its systems but only provides some data to the NSA? While the scanned data have not been collected *by the NSA* in the ordinary sense of the word, it does not follow that the agency should be able to wash its hands of responsibility for the program's broader privacy implications. The bottom line is that both intelligence officials and privacy advocates may ascribe too much importance to the way the NSA defines collection. The definition is not a get-out-of-jail-free card. Even if data are not "collected" under the agency's internal definition, that does not mean the agency may violate federal laws or the Constitution. The doctrine of immaculate collection should not be used as an excuse for the NSA to evade responsibility for mass surveillance.

IF WORD GAMES ARE MY specialty, Anna is usually more interested in math. When it comes to privacy, my marriage is a special case of "West Coast Code" meets "East Coast Code." The idea, popularized by Larry Lessig, is that technology can define the rules that guide our lives as much as—and sometimes more than—law. East Coast Code is law—the U.S. Code and other regulations and rules made in Washington, D.C. West Coast Code is computer code—the software, protocols, and standards most famously written in Silicon Valley.[13]

The East Coast Code idea of privacy originates in a paper by Louis Brandeis and his law partner, Samuel Warren, published in the *Harvard Law Review* in 1890. In "The Right to Privacy," Warren and Brandeis argue that invasions of privacy require a legal remedy, just as the law provides a remedy for physical harms. When Brandeis later became a Supreme Court justice, he continued to champion privacy in other contexts, including in the context of what was then a new form of surveillance, wiretapping. In *Olmstead v. United States*, the Supreme Court's majority found the government needed no search warrant to engage in wiretapping of a telephone line on a public street, focusing on the fact that there was no physical intrusion into the suspect's home, only an intangible invasion of his privacy. In one of his famous dissents, Brandeis protested that wiretapping was no less a search for being intangible. He wrote that "every unjustifiable intrusion by the Government upon the privacy of the individual, whatever the means employed, must be deemed a violation of the Fourth Amendment." In 1967 the Supreme Court repudiated the narrow approach to surveillance it had taken in *Olmstead*, vindicating Brandeis's dissent.[14]

Eloquence aside, there is a wiggle word in Brandeis's definition of privacy. It is only *unjustifiable* intrusions that violate the Fourth Amendment. Lawyers like wiggle words. It gives them power because lawyers and judges are the ones that say what the words mean. Intelligence officials often look to their lawyers to figure out creative ways they can get the data they need—or think they need—without violating the rules. When the Justice Department was seeking to justify the NSA's bulk collection of telephone records under the Patriot Act, its lawyers praised the FISA court's opinions approving bulk collection of internet metadata as "ground breaking and innovative."[15] As we have seen, that program of domestic bulk collection turned out not to have been particularly valuable. When lawyers think in innovative ways, the results can be bad for privacy.

The West Coast Code idea of privacy offers no wiggle room. It is perhaps best captured in a paper written by three computer scientists at the Massachusetts Institute of Technology, Ron Rivest, Adi Shamir, and Len Adelman. The paper outlines the first practical system of public key cryptography, the "RSA algorithm," its name incorporating the initials of its inventors. Public key cryptography solves the problem of how to encrypt communications without the need to agree on a key ahead of time. Two keys are used, one for encryption, which can be made public, and one for decryption, which must remain private. Without the RSA algorithm, privacy on the internet would be an impossibility. To define privacy, the RSA paper introduced the characters of Alice and Bob, now familiar to generations of computer scientists. Bob can make his encryption key public, allowing Alice to use it to encrypt her message to him. Alice cannot reverse the process, however. Bob's public key cannot be used to decrypt her encrypted message; only Bob's secret key can do this. The bulk of the paper consists of a detailed mathematical analysis supporting its claim that it is "not possible" to reverse engineer the secret decryption key from the public encryption key. Of course, it is impenetrable to me, but not to Anna. Anna assures me that RSA remains sound as long as the key is large enough.[16] Many computer scientists thought the encryption debate was settled in the 1990s, when the Clinton administration decided to loosen regulations to promote digital commerce. After the Snowden revelations, the battle erupted again as technology companies began to offer more secure products and services. The FBI warned that law enforcement would soon be "going dark." In 2016 the FBI sought Apple's assistance in defeating the security features of an iPhone belonging to one of the perpetrators of a terrorist shooting in San Bernardino, California. Apple CEO Tim Cook said that it would not do so, because the government was asking it to "build a backdoor into our products" that would weaken user security. In remarks at a technology conference in Austin, President Obama accused technologists of being "absolutist." They were building "black boxes" that no one could break, he said, not even with a warrant.

While the quarrel between Obama and Cook was a fight between government and the technology community, it was more than that. The dispute also reflected the way the two men were used to thinking about privacy. For Obama, the Harvard-trained lawyer, privacy is a balancing of interests. For Cook, privacy is defined not by a malleable legal standard but by the rigorous logic of West Coast Code.[17]

IN THE AFTERMATH OF THE Snowden disclosures, there were multiple reviews of surveillance by the Obama administration. The report by a committee of the National Research Council on alternatives to bulk collection is the only one that was not written by lawyers. Anna and I both had high hopes for it. If West Coast Code could render bulk collection obsolete, there would be less reason to stretch East Coast Code to allow it. The study dashed our hopes. Although the report provided several examples of techniques that could "more effectively target collection" and enforce controls on data that had been collected, it discounted the more ambitious goal of replacing bulk collection altogether. The study found that "there is no software technique that will fully substitute for bulk collection; there is no technological magic."[18]

Anna was furious, and she was not alone. Other cryptographers have told me they were similarly shocked by the way the study seemed to ignore important cryptographic solutions to the NSA's problems. It is hard to imagine how the authors could have chosen words that would be less helpful to efforts to promote privacy-preserving cryptography. While the study's authors were not entirely wrong, they seem to have missed the point. The study concluded there was no technological magic that could substitute for bulk collection because the value of bulk collection was in the knowledge a bulk database can provide about past events, and there is no guarantee that data about past events will be available to the NSA unless they are collected by the agency in bulk. This point at least is valid. Technology cannot recreate data that no longer exist. Yet if the NSA knows that the data are being stored by someone else, technology may offer an alternative to bulk collection that allows the NSA to query data if and when it becomes useful—in a variety of seemingly magical privacy-preserving ways.

Imagine that one party, such as the NSA, would like to retrieve metadata from a large database held by another party, such as a communications provider, based on a highly classified list of selectors belonging to its intelligence targets. Assume the NSA does not trust the provider. Even if it does, perhaps it does not have time to vet the provider's employees and provide them with security clearances. Without magic, it would seem the only solution for the NSA is to demand the provider give it a copy of its entire database. One of Anna's colleagues, Seny Kamara, has explained that the NSA's problem can be solved quite easily, and that the technology to do so was developed almost two decades ago. Private information retrieval, first introduced in a paper in 1995, offers an alternative for the NSA—an alternative in which the NSA does not have to reveal its selectors or obtain the provider's data in bulk. Encryption is used to mask the NSA's query from the provider. If there is a match, the NSA will learn the result while the provider will never learn anything.[19]

There are downsides to using private information retrieval in this way. It guarantees privacy for the NSA, but not for the provider: the NSA might learn information about people other than its targets, although the technique is still a huge improvement over obtaining the *entire database*. Second, the provider must trust that the NSA's queries are valid, a problem I had never even considered. (I have found that cryptographers are sometimes so far ahead of me—and other lawyers—that they offer solutions to privacy problems before I even know to ask for them.) Yet both problems can be addressed, Kamara says—you just need more magic, using technologies that have been developed more recently. To protect the privacy of the provider, you need a form of private information retrieval with stronger properties—oblivious transfer—along with another extraordinary cryptographic technology—secure multiparty computation. To ensure that only authorized queries are posed, you provide an authorizing body such as the Foreign Intelligence Surveillance Court with a cryptographic key to sign them and incorporate that body into the whole scheme. Kamara later developed a more sophisticated privacy-preserving method of encrypted search that would apply not only to individual queries of metadata but also to the call graph, the connections between callers that the NSA analyzes.[20] Again, if I asked for an explanation of exactly how all this worked, I would be lost because the math is too advanced. To me, the explanation might just as well involve magic.

The intelligence community itself has funded significant research into privacy protection technologies, through the Intelligence Advanced Research Projects Activity.[21] The name indicated IARPA's intent to pursue innovative scientific projects that could crack the toughest intelligence problems—those that are both "high risk" and "high reward." Its acronym was chosen deliberately to mirror that of the Defense Advanced Research Projects Agency, or DARPA. DARPA is most famous for creating ARPANET, the predecessor of the internet—now such a pervasive aspect of modern life that many writers (including me) do not typically capitalize it. IARPA has similar ambitions. IARPA's privacy protection program was designed specifically to address the problems posed by the NSA's mass surveillance programs; I worked with IARPA on its early efforts to fund this research shortly after I joined the government. The hard problem was that incorporating privacy protection techniques into the NSA's workflow would slow down processing time dramatically because of the extra computational work required by employing advanced cryptographic techniques to offer ironclad privacy guarantees for large data sets. Over the next decade, federally funded research has made possible advances in the state of the art that helped make these encrypted search technologies feasible at the scale required by the NSA, with significant results in 2013 and 2014.[22]

Researchers continue to find ways to provide technical privacy guarantees. Such techniques could prove useful in implementation of the Freedom Act, which ended the NSA's bulk collection of telephone records from American companies in 2015. Under the Freedom Act, the records remain with the companies. The NSA may rapidly query metadata about people in communication with its targets out to two "hops." To do so, the NSA must be able to query different providers for metadata securely, using a suspected terrorist's identifier as a starting point. What if one of the providers proves untrustworthy, leaking information about the NSA's intelligence investigations? A privacy-preserving cryptographic scheme like Seny Kamara's would permit the NSA to find the records that it needed by posing an encrypted question in a federated manner across several telephone companies. The NSA would learn nothing about data that it did not need. The telephone companies would learn nothing about the NSA's queries. Of course, if national security officials are ignorant of techniques like these, they might think the only answer to the NSA's problem is to give up and repeal the Freedom Act, or, worse still, ask the FISA court to use a secret, "innovative" decision to interpret its limits out of existence. We do not accept ignorance of the law as an excuse for bad behavior. Ignorance of technology is no excuse for bad policy. One way to avoid such ignorance is for national security lawyers to make sure they are asking the right people about what magic is possible.

The White House Office of Science and Technology Policy can play a critical role in ensuring that national security officials understand the state of the art. Ed Felten, a Princeton computer scientist, served in the Obama White House from 2015 to 2017 as the deputy in that office—during the time the NSA was implementing the Freedom Act. In 2014 Felten gave a talk at a San Francisco security conference describing how the NSA could redesign its bulk collection programs to protect privacy, based in part on Seny Kamara's work. President Obama included the director of the Office of Science and Technology Policy as one of the "regular attendees" at meetings of the National Security Council. President Trump took a step backward by failing to include the Office of Science and Technology Policy in his January and April 2017 orders to reorganize the NSC.[23]

The innovations that cryptography makes possible could be used to support a range of NSA programs that pose privacy concerns, not just bulk collection of metadata or other types of encrypted search on data at rest. Encrypted search could provide a solution to the problem of immaculate collection for programs like the NSA's upstream collection of the content of communications from the internet backbone under section 702 of FISA. Privacy advocates and the government have long fought over whether a device that scans data in motion should be regarded as searching all of the data that transit the device or only the data that the device is programmed to obtain. While there are special problems with applying encrypted search techniques to data in motion, methods for "private stream search" were outlined in 2007, a full decade before the debate over section 702 in Congress in 2017.[24]

For privacy, the holy grail might be fully homomorphic encryption—a technique that permits meaningful calculations on encrypted data without decrypting them first. As the purpose of encryption is to transform the data into indecipherable gibberish, this would seem to be impossible. Still, Rivest and other pioneers of modern cryptography have long thought there was a chance that there could be a scheme for fully homomorphic encryption that would actually work. At a security conference in San Francisco, Anna introduced me to the man who proved them right, Craig Gentry, one of the most brilliant of her brilliant group of friends.[25] If you search for research funded by the IARPA program, you will find scores of papers by Craig Gentry and many others in Anna's tight-knit research community that include seemingly impossible technical guarantees of privacy.[26] While Gentry's system requires too much computational time to be practical, more efficient approaches are likely to emerge with time. If efficient, fully homomorphic encryption could be used as a building block with other cryptographic technologies to make more technological magic possible.

FOR MANY TECHNICALLY SAVVY PEOPLE, encrypting communications and data seemed like the best response to the NSA revelations. Bruce Schneier, the popular security expert, urged his readers in 2013 to put their trust in math, not law or institutions like the NSA.[27] "Trust math, not law" was a popular message after Snowden. However, cryptographic techniques can do more than render data impenetrable to eavesdroppers. It can also help the eavesdroppers do their job with less damage to privacy. It is the rigor of the West Coast Code's definition of privacy that makes these techniques so useful. When a lawyer or a judge must decide whether East Coast Code protects the privacy of data—such as by determining whether NSA surveillance involves an "unreasonable search"—the choice all too often pits security against civil liberties. Technology offers us another option: you can collect the data you need, but only if you can provide a rigorous technical proof that offers guarantees for the privacy of the data you do not need.

Lawyers have been dominating debates in the United States at least since the days of Alexis de Tocqueville, and the debate over the NSA has been no different.[28] This needs to change. The law has proved to be a less than ideal guardian of our privacy. As we have seen, a 1979 Supreme Court decision from the era of analog telephones tells us that metadata lack protection under the Fourth Amendment. Courts have recognized a host of exceptions to the warrant requirement. Reforming surveillance requires innovative thinking, but it is technologists, not lawyers, who should be coming up with the innovations. Despite stunning advances in the state of the art, few institutions, public or private, make use of the privacy-enhancing techniques that Anna and her friends have devoted their lives to creating.

In making national security decisions, the president's advisers should work as closely with technologists as they do with lawyers. The government should continue to fund research into privacy-preserving cryptography, and intelligence agencies should start deploying some of these promising techniques in the real world. The NSA could start by trying out Seny Kamara's privacy-preserving metadata scheme and by piloting the use of private stream search in its upstream collection program under section 702 of FISA.

More magic is coming, if the lawyers would be quiet for once and listen to the scientists. As Anna can tell you, lawyers like to talk a lot. Dominating conversations is a bad habit. A marriage works only if both partners listen. While law has its place, the best strategy for protecting privacy in the digital age would join legal and technical methods to protect privacy—a marriage of East Coast Code and West Coast Code.

9

THE VIRTUES OF HYPOCRISY

THE STATUES AT THE PALACE OF WESTMINSTER WERE COVERED IN TRANSPARENT plastic to protect them from ongoing restoration work. It somehow seemed fitting. On May 14, 2014, I was the featured guest at an event organized by Big Brother Watch, a civil liberties organization dedicated to transparency about surveillance, for a discussion with activists and members of Parliament. The Obama administration's transparency and other surveillance reforms were designed in significant part to restore its reputation abroad. By the time I crossed the pond about a year after the Snowden revelations began, the international image of both countries was in need of serious repair when it came to privacy.

The United Kingdom is the oldest ally the United States has in signals intelligence. The partnership grew out of World War II and the Cold War. The U.K.'s Government Communications Headquarters (GCHQ) is one of the NSA's closest partners. Reporters for a British news organization, *The Guardian,* had disclosed many of GCHQ's most sensitive and intrusive programs by working with the Snowden documents. Big Brother Watch, Privacy International, and other human rights organizations were challenging the GCHQ's mass surveillance practices in court, as well as its cozy relationship with the Americans.

"We are spying in a transparent world," I told the crowd that had gathered in a cramped committee room to hear my remarks.[1] I continued with a defense of the U.S. administration's surveillance reforms. Congress had held hearings on the surveillance conducted by the National Security Agency. President Obama had made a thoughtful speech about surveillance and privacy. He had just issued Presidential Policy Directive 28, extending privacy protections to foreign data. The rules themselves were limited in practice, but I made the case that they were a major step as a statement of principle. Obama's directive affirmed this principle in ringing language. "All persons should be treated with dignity and respect," the directive declared, "regardless of their nationality or wherever they might reside, and all persons have legitimate privacy interests in the handling of their personal information."[2] The United States was saying that foreign privacy matters in signals intelligence operations, and not just because of the impact of those operations on the privacy of Americans.

I expected the advocates to point out the limits of these modest steps and grill me about the NSA's sweeping surveillance programs. While I received one tough question about the use of metadata to support drone strikes—a few days earlier, former NSA and CIA director Michael Hayden had said bluntly, "We kill people based on metadata"[3]—the sharpest words were reserved for the British government. Where were the U.K.'s reforms? Why had Parliament failed to hold oversight hearings? Why had the prime minister, David Cameron, failed even to give a speech about the surveillance controversy as Obama had done? I had come to London in part because I wanted to learn more about what the United Kingdom had done to reform surveillance in the wake of the Snowden revelations. Not much, apparently.

The event included members of Parliament from three political parties: David Davis of the Conservative Party, Chi Onwurah of the Labour Party, and Julian Huppert of the Liberal Democrats. Working across political parties had been second nature to me since my days as an American Civil Liberties Union activist, when liberal Democrats had to work with conservative Republicans to rein in the Patriot Act. Yet Emma Carr of Big Brother Watch told me that this sort of cross-party event was still an unusual occurrence in the United Kingdom. Because the prime minister must command a majority in the House of Commons, there is normally no need for members to work across the aisle. As a result, the United Kingdom lacks the strong American tradition of bipartisanship. At the time, the U.K.'s Liberal Democrats were in an uneasy coalition with the Conservatives, so at least these two parties had to work together.

The British system makes effective intelligence oversight more challenging. Parliament does have an Intelligence and Security Committee, established in the 1990s to oversee the security agencies. Like all committees, it is in the hands of whatever party or coalition is in power. David Davis, the Conservative member at the Big Brother event, observed that it typically avoided stirring up controversy. Surveillance reform was rarely a priority. The public did not seem to mind. According to Davis, the British were simply "far too relaxed" about surveillance. Julian Huppert, the MP for Cambridge, vividly described just how relaxed that attitude was. Huppert is a Liberal Democrat. It is not much of an exaggeration to say that his small centrist party invented civil liberties. It is the successor to the Liberal Party, whose origins lie in the centuries-long struggle to limit the power of the Crown. As a member of Parliament's home affairs select committee, Huppert had recently had an opportunity to hear testimony from Sir Mark Waller, the intelligence services commissioner. Waller's job was to oversee not only GCHQ but also the U.K.'s other intelligence services—the Security Service (MI5) and the Secret Intelligence Service (MI6). Waller's job was a part-time one. At the time, he had only one staff member. (This put into perspective my occasional complaints about the resources available to the ODNI's civil liberties and privacy office, I thought.)

Sir Mark Waller had told Huppert and other members that when the Snowden disclosures began, he worried that GCHQ had been hiding something from him. The disclosures raised the issue of "reverse targeting"—the question of whether GCHQ might try to get around the restrictions that British law placed on spying on U.K. nationals by accessing data collected by the NSA. The commissioner said he met with the deputy head of GCHQ to sort things out. As Huppert recounted Waller's testimony, the chummy meeting was eerily reminiscent of a scene from the satirical British television series *Yes, Prime Minister.*

This was the exchange between the chair of the home affairs select committee and the intelligence services commissioner about the commissioner's post-Snowden review:[4]

Q. And how did you satisfy yourself? It seems from your comment that you had a discussion with them.

A. Certainly.

Q. You heard what they had to say.

A. Certainly.

Q. And you accepted what they had to say?

A. Certainly.

Q. Is that it?

A. Certainly.

Q. Just a discussion?

A. Certainly.

Q. And that's the way you were satisfied that there was no circumventing U.K. law. You went down, you went to see them, you sat round the table, you had a chat?

A. You've got to remember that I've done a whole period—a year and a half's inspection. I have got a very good idea as to what the ethos of this agency is. They know perfectly well that they have had to make out their case and the legality of their case, etc., and I have absolutely, clearly, accepted it.

Julian Huppert is no longer able to raise tough questions about how government officials do (or do not) protect privacy. In 2015 the voters in Cambridge punished his party for its alliance with the Conservatives. Huppert was defeated, and the Conservatives won an outright majority. The government no longer had to share power with the likes of Huppert, heirs of the Whigs and the radicals.

Over the next few years, I stayed in touch with Big Brother Watch and other privacy activists in London. When I had first met them in the spring of 2014, they were on the offensive against GCHQ surveillance, seeking allies to ask the government tough questions and filing legal challenges. In 2015 the U.K.'s Investigatory Powers Tribunal ruled against the government for the first time in its history. The tribunal said that it had been illegal for GCHQ to obtain data from the NSA's Prism and upstream collection programs without publicly explaining how it was protecting the privacy of U.K. citizens.[5] By 2016 the privacy activists were on defense, facing a major fight over new surveillance legislation. In March the U.K.'s home secretary, Theresa May, introduced the latest version of the Investigatory Powers Bill. The bill expressly authorized many of the practices disclosed by *The Guardian* and other news outlets as a result of the Snowden disclosures. Opponents labeled the bill a "snooper's charter" and mounted an aggressive campaign against it. By the end of the year, May was prime minister and the "snooper's charter" was law. Human rights activists were aghast. "The UK now has a surveillance law that is more suited to a dictatorship than a democracy," one said.[6]

What is now the Investigatory Powers Act authorizes bulk collection of personal data sets, mass surveillance by the GCHQ of international communications, government hacking into computers and communications equipment (for both targeted and bulk collection), and the issuance of legal orders that can force companies to undermine encryption if it is "technically feasible" for them to do so. Perhaps the law's most far-reaching provision empowers the government to require service providers to retain "internet connection records" that include technical details that reveal what websites users visit, what apps they are using on smart phones, and how much data they are downloading. "Soon, a record will be kept of every website you ever go to," Julian Huppert lamented in a tweet.[7]

The new surveillance powers are "subject to strict safeguards and world-leading oversight," said Amber Rudd, the U.K.'s home secretary in November 2016. Rudd argued that the law strengthens the U.K.'s intelligence oversight system.[8] There is a powerful new Investigatory Powers Commission that replaces smaller oversight offices, including the intelligence services commissioner, the office held by Sir Mark Waller. The law also requires judicial review of intelligence surveillance, a significant step for reform. Previously, British intelligence services could target citizens for surveillance without any judge's involvement, using a "ministerial warrant"—an order signed by a secretary of state. Now these surveillance orders and many of the law's other powers will require the concurrence of a judicial officer. Supporters call this requirement a "double lock." Opponents argue that because the scope of review is limited, the double lock may be little more than a rubber stamp.

Whether all of this is really a big change for privacy in the United Kingdom remains to be seen. For years the GCHQ and other U.K. intelligence services have engaged in mass surveillance and other aggressive spying practices with limited oversight and without specific authority from Parliament. While critics describe these practices as illegal, the United Kingdom has no written constitution or bill of rights, and therefore no Fourth Amendment to restrain the intelligence agencies. When the powers of the GCHQ and other British intelligence services were unclear and in the dark, there was some doubt about their legality. The "snooper's charter" removes that doubt, at least under British law. Still, the truth is that even now, Amber Rudd is probably right when she says that the U.K.'s system of surveillance oversight is "world-leading," if only because many other governments have little or no oversight at all.[9]

"The UK has just legalized the most extreme surveillance in the history of western democracy," Snowden warned his followers in a tweet.[10] When Snowden leaked classified files on surveillance to respected foreign news outlets including *The Guardian*, he was hoping to start a debate on mass surveillance that would go well beyond the United States. *Guardian* reporters wrote story after story exposing what they saw as the misdeeds of the GCHQ and the impact of its operations on privacy and human rights. Neither Snowden nor those reporters seem to have considered that as a result of the "far too relaxed" British attitude toward surveillance, they might not win the debate they started.

WHILE THE UNITED KINGDOM DECIDED to leave the European Union in 2016, it remains part of the larger group of nations that are members of the European Convention on Human Rights. The European Convention established a court, which sits in Strasbourg, France, to hear complaints of violations by its members. Big Brother Watch and other human rights groups challenged the U.K.'s mass surveillance activities before the Strasbourg court in a series of cases beginning in 2013.[11] The United Kingdom remains subject to this highly respected international court's jurisdiction quite apart from its decision to leave the EU, and its government must continue to defend the GCHQ's collection of signals intelligence and its cooperation with the NSA before the Strasbourg court. The decisions of the European Court of Human Rights interpreting the right to privacy set a standard that the intelligence services of all of the world's democracies will at least have to consider seriously, if the rhetoric of the governments they serve about human rights is to have any meaning.

Today an array of international organizations is devoted to human rights protection, including ten separate treaty bodies in the United Nations system and regional human rights courts in Europe, the Americas, and Africa. Unlike the rights to protection against torture, racial discrimination, or discrimination against women, there is no separate treaty body or mechanism for privacy and surveillance.

Privacy is something of a late bloomer among human rights. While the Universal Declaration of Human Rights, adopted in 1948, includes a right to privacy, it was not until Snowden told the world about mass surveillance that the United Nations appointed a "special rapporteur"—a dedicated official—specifically devoted to privacy. The special rapporteur presented his first report in 2016.[12] As the process of giving content to the human right of privacy has been comparatively slow, the norms for government surveillance remain uncertain. What kinds of surveillance are allowed, for what reasons, and with what safeguards? May countries adopt different rules for domestic and foreign surveillance? Must surveillance always be targeted, or is bulk collection permitted, and if so, under what circumstances? Basic questions remain unresolved.

The International Covenant on Civil and Political Rights sets forth the right in general terms: "No one shall be subjected to arbitrary or unlawful interference with his privacy, family, home or correspondence."[13] A key question, of course, is what counts as "arbitrary or unlawful interference." The European Convention on Human Rights also protects privacy in rather similar language. It permits interference only when "necessary in a democratic society" for national security or other important reasons. Surveillance must also be "in accordance with the law." In a series of cases beginning in 1978, the Strasbourg court has given life to the right to privacy. According to this jurisprudence, "in accordance with the law" means a clear, detailed law, passed by a legislature, that gives fair notice to the public of what surveillance is permitted. "Necessary in a democratic society" means that a government's safeguards for surveillance must be effective; the discretion given to intelligence services must be checked by a court or some other independent institution. Surveillance must be justified by a legitimate aim, and the degree of interference with privacy must be "proportionate" to the government's objectives.[14]

The decisions of the European Court of Human Rights have prompted significant intelligence reforms, including in the United Kingdom. GCHQ and other security services used to base their authority on unwritten executive powers that belong to the Crown; these powers are now authorized by Parliament and are controlled by law. Nevertheless, it will be an uphill battle to convince the European Court of Human Rights to uphold the bulk collection of signals intelligence by GCHQ and the NSA that Parliament has now explicitly sanctioned under precedents that appear to require individualized suspicion for surveillance.[15] If the United Kingdom loses in Strasbourg, it will face pressure to reform its practices. The court's decisions are binding on the parties as a matter of international law. Still, countries sometimes ignore them. Russia, a party to the convention since 1996, has a relationship with the court that one scholar observes has been "under almost permanent strain."[16]

The United States will also have to live with any reforms required by the European Court of Human Rights in joint operations of the NSA and GCHQ, if the British government chooses not to take the Russian route of defiance. The United States may also come under more direct pressure to conform its own mass surveillance practices to human rights norms. While the United States is not a member of the European Convention, it is a party to the International Covenant on Civil and Political Rights and the American Convention on Human Rights, both of which protect the right to privacy. Although successive administrations have taken the position that human rights treaties do not apply to U.S. conduct outside its own territory, this position is both controversial and unpopular.[17] The United States does needless damage to its global image by attempting to evade international accountability for its collection of signals intelligence. American intelligence officials should welcome such scrutiny. The U.S. government can persuasively argue in international human rights forums that it has taken strong steps—stronger than those of virtually any other nation—to subject its surveillance practices to the rule of law. Owing to the robust oversight mechanisms that apply to the NSA and other agencies, the United States has a more respectable argument than many other countries that its signals intelligence operations are necessary, proportionate, and lawful.

AMONG MANY IN EUROPE, THE idea that the NSA or other U.S. intelligence agencies have any respect for privacy is a cause not just for skepticism but for laughter. In 2016 I ran into Austrian lawyer Max Schrems at a privacy conference in Brussels. The Computers, Privacy and Data Protection conference is held in a converted market hall each year in late January. Despite the invariably gloomy winter weather and decidedly unpretentious venue, the conference attracts lawyers and government officials from all over the world. Schrems was in a very good mood. The highest court in the European Union had just ruled in his favor in a major privacy case Schrems had dubbed "Europe v. Facebook." The reason for his victory was continuing European distrust of both the NSA and American technology companies as a result of the Snowden revelations.

Schrems once told a reporter he is "not a big privacy person."[18] Yet as a result of a case he initiated as a twenty-four-year-old law student—mainly because he thought it would be an interesting project—his name has become synonymous with the post-Snowden clash between the United States and Europe over privacy and surveillance. Schrems launched his quixotic challenge in 2011 while he was studying law at Santa Clara University, in California's Silicon Valley. One of Facebook's lawyers had given a talk about privacy in a class Schrems was taking. The lawyer was dismissive about European privacy law. Schrems was shocked by his cavalier attitude and decided it would be fun to challenge Facebook in court.[19]

Schrems argued that Facebook was breaking European law by transferring his personal data to the United States because the data could then be accessed by U.S. intelligence agencies through secret orders of the Foreign Intelligence Surveillance Court, including orders under section 702 of FISA. If this were happening, Facebook would have no way to notify him or to ensure any of the other rights that Europe's rules on privacy and data protection grant him. Snowden's disclosure of the NSA's Prism program in 2013 seemed to prove Schrems's fears right. At the end of 2015, the Court of Justice of the European Union ruled that European officials who had agreed to allow transfers of personal data to the United States had not properly addressed whether U.S. laws governing surveillance were adequate to protect privacy.[20]

When the EU's highest court decided *Schrems v. Data Protection Commissioner*, it struck down a pillar of transatlantic commerce, the "safe harbor" agreement that allowed routine transfers of personal data from Europe to the United States. On both sides of the Atlantic, businesses scrambled to react. The impact of the *Schrems* decision went far beyond Facebook and other U.S. technology giants, which are often the targets of privacy activists in Europe and elsewhere.[21] The safe harbor provision had been in place since 2000 and affected more than 4,000 companies. In an age of big data, it was unthinkable that companies in the United States and Europe could do business without routine transfers of personal data. A young lawyer named Max Schrems had managed to put all of that at risk.

The European understanding of privacy as a fundamental human right is intertwined with its commitment to data protection and digital privacy. The EU's rules on data protection, first adopted in 1995 and significantly strengthened in 2016, set forth detailed obligations for public and private institutions and provide data subjects with enforcement rights to access and correct their records. As a result, EU institutions play a major role in defining and enforcing the right to privacy in the digital age, as Google, Facebook, and other American technology giants have been learning, painfully. In addition, the EU's Treaty of Lisbon includes a Charter of Fundamental Rights, which applies to EU institutions. The EU charter provides not only a right to privacy but also a separate, explicit right to "the protection of personal data."

European law prohibits transfers of personal data to countries outside the EU unless those countries offer an "adequate level of protection" for privacy. The safe harbor scheme, administered by the U.S. Department of Commerce, was intended to satisfy this standard. Companies agreed to follow required privacy principles by signing up to the scheme. Although signing up was voluntary, the promises, once made, were enforced by the Federal Trade Commission (FTC). Against companies, these protections were more than theoretical—the FTC took many enforcement actions under the safe harbor scheme.[22]

According to the EU's Court of Justice, the safe harbor agreement that allowed Facebook to transfer Max Schrems's data to the United States was invalid because the European officials who approved it had failed to consider the impact of U.S. surveillance practices on the right to privacy and the right to data protection. The Snowden revelations had highlighted a weakness in the safe harbor agreement. While anyone could bring a case before the FTC, there was no meaningful recourse if a company like Facebook was compelled to give personal data to the NSA or other intelligence agencies. The agreement simply did not apply to data that companies provide to the government in accordance with surveillance laws. The European judges decided this failure doomed the safe harbor agreement because EU officials had not considered the impact of U.S. surveillance law on the privacy of EU citizens. According to the opinion, U.S. law allowed "access on a generalised basis to the content of electronic communications"—in other words, mass surveillance. The court said such surveillance "must be regarded as compromising the essence of the fundamental right to respect for private life."[23]

Many U.S. officials find the *Schrems* decision maddening. In the winter of 2016, some of those with whom I had worked in government descended in force on Brussels, arguing that the Court of Justice decision was simply wrong and that the EU should give safe harbor or something like it another chance. Peter Swire, a member of Obama's review group on surveillance, argued the point in a debate with Max Schrems himself at the privacy conference where Schrems was taking his victory lap. Swire said that the European court simply misunderstood the law, basing its conclusions on press reports instead of on what U.S. law actually permitted. The court's opinion conflated Prism, a program that permits surveillance of (an admittedly very large number of) specific targets, with separate NSA programs involving bulk collection of metadata. Section 702 of FISA, which governs Prism, does not authorize bulk collection of content. Section 702 requires the NSA to identify specific targets through the use of strong selectors, such as a telephone number or e-mail address.[24] Swire had a point, but the lawyers and activists in the packed hall were clearly skeptical. Swire had a better time of it than my old boss Bob Litt, the general counsel of the Office of the Director of National Intelligence, who had gone to Brussels in an effort to promote the surveillance reforms implemented since 2013. As he argued that Europeans had nothing to fear from the NSA because it was subject to strong oversight, the European lawyers and activists seated next to me laughed out loud in disbelief. Bob later told me he could hear the snickering.

Another of my former colleagues was even more pointed. Cameron Kerry, who was the general counsel of the U.S. Department of Commerce when I was at the White House, argued that the Europeans were not only wrong about section 702 of FISA, they were hypocritical. Kerry argued that the Europeans were applying a double standard when it came to surveillance and privacy and that they were doing so to protect their own companies from competition. U.S. law already met the test of the Court of Justice: its privacy protections were "essentially equivalent" to those of most EU member states, if not superior.[25] If the EU insisted as a prerequisite to digital commerce that the United States follow stricter standards than its own member states, it was violating a basic principle that governs international trade: equal treatment.

While Kerry's words were pointed, it is hard to understate the hypocrisy of European complaints about American surveillance laws. Very few countries in the world employ the safeguards the United States requires for intelligence surveillance, even for domestic surveillance against their own citizens. In 2013 the Center for Democracy and Technology, a civil liberties organization, conducted a survey of standards for government access to digital data, including communications. Only one of the four European countries included in the CDT study, Italy, then required any kind of court order for national security surveillance. France, Germany, and the United Kingdom did not. Since that time, France has expanded its surveillance laws; Germany reformed them without requiring a court order for surveillance; and the United Kingdom greatly expanded its laws while adding a limited form of judicial oversight for some forms of surveillance. In any event, Kerry had good reason in 2016 to complain that EU officials were hypocritically holding U.S. surveillance laws to an unfairly high standard.

It turned out that Max Schrems was lurking in the dark hall as Kerry was making his case. From the audience, Schrems shot back at Kerry. By focusing on double standards, U.S. officials were missing the point. Schrems was not trying to defend European companies and he had no love for the surveillance practices of European governments. Schrems did not care if U.S. law was just as good (or, as he put it, just as bad) as the law of any European country. His strategy was to push the EU to use its Charter of Fundamental Rights to set a higher standard for digital privacy for everyone. It was only common sense to start with the United States, with its dominant position in internet services. After all, that is where most of the world's data are.

In February 2016—a month after the showdown between Schrems and U.S. officials in Brussels—the United States and the EU finalized an agreement to replace the safe harbor, the so-called Privacy Shield. The goal of both U.S. and EU negotiators was to strike a deal that would not require either side to change any laws. Their hope was that the European Court of Justice's concerns would be addressed with a few cosmetic changes and with a better explanation of U.S. surveillance law. While I understand why officials on both sides of the Atlantic found it tempting to side-step most of the tough decisions on surveillance and privacy, I do not believe that papering over the problem will solve it in the long run. The Privacy Shield does offer a nod to concerns about government surveillance by designating a U.S. government official as an "ombudsman" to hear European complaints about intelligence surveillance. I doubt this will be enough. The Privacy Shield will have to withstand scrutiny in the European courts, and it is very unlikely that it will unless Congress reforms section 702 of FISA to provide more protections to foreign citizens.

While Max Schrems became a privacy activist almost accidentally, his strategy proved brilliant. Countries that ignore human rights decisions may be subject to international embarrassment and criticism, but they rarely suffer more tangible consequences. The Court of Justice of the European Union, however, is not a human rights tribunal; it is the supreme judicial authority of a unique supranational organization with real commercial power. The Court of Justice serves as a guardian for the rules that allow access to the European common market in goods and services. In 2014 trade between the United States and the European Union was more than one trillion dollars.[26] The EU's Court of Justice is uniquely positioned to put pressure on Europe's trading partners, including the United States, to adopt surveillance reforms.

The European approach to privacy and data protection is controversial. In the eyes of privacy activists, the EU is showing the world how to ensure personal autonomy in the digital age, giving real teeth to the human right of privacy through strict and detailed protections for personal data. For critics of the EU, its peculiar approach to privacy and data protection is just one more bureaucratic obstacle to innovation that it has no right to impose on other countries in the name of human rights, and its official post-Snowden complaints about surveillance are nothing more than hypocritical posturing. There is certainly reason to be skeptical of Europe's claims to privacy leadership. For one thing, the entire premise of the *Schrems* decision—that data can be protected by keeping them away from the United States—is a highly questionable one. Under Executive Order 12,333, the NSA has broad authority to collect data overseas and from satellites, subject to fewer protections than data collected inside the United States under section 702 of FISA. In one of the many ironies of *Schrems,* if Europeans succeed in keeping data outside the United States, perhaps by pressuring Facebook and other U.S. companies to locate more data centers in Europe, the NSA will be able to collect those data with far fewer legal restrictions and without the court review required by FISA.

More fundamentally, the U.S. complaint about double standards is an inevitable by-product of the EU's structure. International privacy lawyers have noted that "data protection authorities in Europe have very little power" over the surveillance laws of their own countries but "have much more power over non-E.U. countries because they can theoretically block data transfers."[27] The reason for this is that the power of the EU over its member states on issues of defense and intelligence is limited by treaty. The EU's Lisbon Treaty reaffirmed that "national security remains the sole responsibility of each Member State."[28] The EU's Court of Justice was able to consider whether the surveillance laws of the United States were consistent with the rights guaranteed by the EU Charter of Fundamental Rights only because it was reviewing the decision of an EU institution on an issue involving digital trade—the safe harbor agreement with the United States. Whether the European Court of Justice can find a way to review the rules for surveillance by its members' own intelligence services is far less clear. Any effort by the Court of Justice or other EU institutions to limit the surveillance practices of EU member states would provoke fierce protests that Brussels was overstepping its bounds.

It would hardly be the first time. In 2016 voters in the United Kingdom decided they were fed up with Brussels. On taking office, Prime Minister Theresa May vowed there would be no backsliding on the U.K.'s choice to leave the EU, declaring tautologically that "Brexit means Brexit." Whatever else "Brexit" may mean, the decision of the United Kingdom to leave the EU also means that the U.S. intelligence community has lost a vital friend and partner inside that organization. While the United States shares intelligence with many countries, the relationship between the U.S. and British intelligence communities is truly a special one. The United Kingdom was the only member of Five Eyes that was also a member of the EU. With the United Kingdom leaving the EU by 2019, it no longer enjoys influence over how the EU addresses issues of data protection and privacy. The United Kingdom has always served as a bridge between America and Europe, but Brexit will make it a less effective one.

In the summer of 2016, May put David Davis—the conservative member of Parliament who told me that the British were "far too relaxed" about surveillance—in charge of a new cabinet office responsible for negotiating Brexit. Privacy will be an important issue for Davis. The United Kingdom will need a green light from Brussels that its laws on privacy meet EU standards in order for its companies to store the personal data of European citizens on British soil. Whatever agreement the United Kingdom manages to reach on the issue will have to withstand review by the European Court of Justice, which will surely take a close look at U.K. surveillance laws, including the Investigatory Powers Act. The United Kingdom will no longer benefit from the provision of the Lisbon Treaty that reserves "national security" matters to EU member states. Instead, the United Kingdom will be in the same position as the United States was in the *Schrems* case. It is ironic but apparently true that a vote by the British public to "take back control" from Brussels will make it easier, not harder, for EU officials to scrutinize the practices of the U.K. intelligence services.

The U.K.'s awkward situation demonstrates once again the brilliance of Max Schrems's strategy. While it may well be that the EU's Court of Justice is subjecting government surveillance to a double standard, its decision to subject surveillance laws to scrutiny offers a unique reform opportunity. Nations outside Europe will need to meet the court's standards for surveillance if they wish to provide digital services to the more than 500 million citizens of the EU. The EU's double standards may do more than annoy American, British, and other officials who are subject to them; they may build real global momentum for reform. In time, the members of the EU will be forced to confront their hypocrisy. Despite the Lisbon Treaty, the logic of calling data protection a fundamental human right creates expectations that are hard to limit. Whatever rules the Court of Justice uses in judging the surveillance laws of others could eventually be applied by judges to the member states of the EU.

DESPITE ITS STATUS AS the unofficial "capital of Europe," Brussels is refreshingly free of self-importance. After seeing my old colleagues from the Obama administration face off against Max Schrems and other European privacy activists, I made sure to see what few sights the city has to offer. Its most famous symbol is a diminutive statue of a naked boy peeing into a fountain. There are many stories about what the centuries-old fountain commemorates. One is that the statue was erected in honor of a boy who saved the city from a bomb by urinating on its fuse.

If only it were so easy to stop today's bombs. In the winter of 2016, the atmosphere in Brussels was tense. It had nothing to do with the spirited discussions I had witnessed of contrasting American and European visions on issues of privacy. In the Belgian capital's streets and bars, there were heavily armed counterterrorism police. Only a few months earlier in Paris, terrorists associated with ISIS had murdered more than a hundred people. Many of the attackers, including the ringleader, had lived in the Molenbeek neighborhood of Brussels. Despite the increased police presence, the city suffered its own coordinated terrorist attacks in March. The failure of European security agencies to stop these and other attacks resulted mainly from failures in intelligence sharing and coordination, not from any lack of surveillance. The problem is not unlike what the United States faced after 9/11, although solving Europe's problems of information sharing and getting its agencies to work more closely together will be even more difficult. It is harder for nations to compromise on sovereignty than for bureaucracies to give up turf.

I have argued that Europe needs a high-level, cross-border commission to review its counterterrorism efforts. It should be modeled on the 9/11 Commission that led to reforms of the U.S. intelligence community, including the creation of the director of national intelligence. Instead, governments in France and elsewhere have offered the easy answer of new powers for the security agencies, including even broader surveillance powers.[29] The far right offers the even easier answer of demonizing Europe's Muslims. It is an abiding political reality that you cannot beat something, even a bad something, with nothing. A counterterrorism commission could give Europeans a policy agenda they can be *for*, keeping both the surveillance state and the far right from setting the agenda.

The NSA and other U.S. intelligence agencies work closely with their European counterparts in the struggle against international terrorism and other serious security threats. Indeed, most of the more than fifty terrorist plots and activities that the Privacy and Civil Liberties Oversight Board said were disrupted by intelligence obtained under section 702 of FISA involved attacks that would have taken place outside the United States; almost half of these—twenty-five—were in Europe.[30] Yet the NSA's surveillance operations are not very popular with ordinary people abroad, even among American allies. That is not because the global public is against surveillance in general but because it regards the NSA with understandable distrust, seeing the agency not as an ally against terrorism but as serving the narrow interests of the U.S. government. In 2014 the Pew Research Center asked almost 50,000 people in forty-four countries what they thought of NSA surveillance. Unsurprisingly, most strongly opposed surveillance by the United States of their own country's citizens and leaders. Eighty-one percent found monitoring of their country's citizens unacceptable, while 73 percent objected to monitoring their country's leaders. Most also objected (by a smaller margin) to the surveillance of U.S. citizens, with 62 percent opposed. However, if U.S. surveillance operations were limited to suspected terrorists, 64 percent of foreign respondents—a majority—were willing to support them.[31] Apparently there is still some trust in the United States among the world's citizens. It is hard to imagine similar support for Russian or Chinese spying operations, even if they were ostensibly directed at terrorists.

The United States, the United Kingdom, and other Five Eyes nations have tacitly agreed to give up spying on each other in order to pool their surveillance resources against common global threats. Following the Snowden revelations, some suggested expanding the Five Eyes to include other American allies. A more realistic proposal might be to create a new "no political spying" pact, a commitment by a select group of democratic nations to pool their intelligence resources while refraining from using their advanced surveillance capabilities against each other for anything other than genuine security threats. Democratic nations must answer to their own citizens. They are more likely to support surveillance if there is a meaningful commitment that the purpose of such surveillance is to keep them safe. A starting point for such a pact could be the six national security threats that permit use of signals intelligence collected in bulk under Presidential Policy Directive 28. They are espionage, terrorism, proliferation of weapons of mass destruction, cybersecurity threats, threats to military forces, and transnational crime.[32]

Of course, there are costs if the United States chooses to give up the use of signals intelligence for general foreign affairs purposes, even if only when spying on friends. Such surveillance provides real value, especially as it may aid in combating international corruption, enforcing economic sanctions, and policing trade agreements.[33] Agreeing to such a pact on surveillance might be seen as naïve. Should we really trust other governments, even democratic ones, to honor it? There is no need for blind trust. Any agreement should be conditioned on the adoption of meaningful and enforceable surveillance reforms, such as review of intelligence programs by an independent court. As we will see in the next chapter, Germany's post-Snowden reforms offer an intriguing model.

Snowden and his supporters have argued there should be a universal agreement among nations to ban mass surveillance practices and limit intelligence collection. Such a "Snowden Treaty" is both unrealistic and undesirable.[34] Unlike an arrangement limited to nations that are both democratic and have strong intelligence oversight mechanisms, a universal treaty would be unenforceable. It would also be destabilizing. Russia, China, Iran, and other adversaries of the United States cannot be trusted to limit their intelligence capabilities. It would be foolish for the United States and its allies to do so based on what could only be an empty promise.

The Snowden revelations unleashed an avalanche of hypocrisy. The French aristocrat François de la Rochefoucauld once said that "hypocrisy is the tribute that vice pays to virtue." If so, in the past few years foreign criticism has done much to pay homage to the NSA.[35] As surveillance faces increased scrutiny from international courts and institutions, hypocrisy on surveillance no longer appears to be a sustainable strategy. Political scientists Henry Farrell and Martha Finnemore note that a major effect of the Snowden leaks has been to "undermine Washington's ability to act hypocritically and get away with it."[36] One could make the same point about many other governments. When demonstrators from Berlin to San Francisco carry signs with Snowden's picture and reading "End Mass Surveillance!," the message is that the NSA is the world's chief threat to privacy. They should look at their own governments much harder.

Despite the failure of many governments to live up to values of privacy, human rights, and data protection, these values are plainly a force for good. In an age of global mass surveillance, we have to protect everyone's privacy if we want to protect our own. If Americans argue that the rest of the world should not point out the specks in our eyes because they have logs in their own, none of us may ever get around to seeing more clearly. Max Schrems may be a latter-day de la Rochefoucauld, but that does not make him wrong. As a strategy to reform mass surveillance, hypocrisy has its virtues.

10

LISTENING TO ALLIES

IT WAS A BEAUTIFUL FALL MORNING, ALMOST FIFTEEN YEARS TO THE DAY SINCE the attacks of 9/11. On September 8, 2016, I found myself again standing on the street outside a national parliament, preparing to discuss issues of privacy and surveillance with lawmakers. An inquiry committee of the federal parliament of Germany, the Bundestag, would shortly hear from me and other American experts about surveillance reform. German lawmakers were considering legislation outlining specific controls for the collection of information by the BND. The BND is Germany's external spy agency, the Federal Intelligence Service (Bundesnachrichtendienst). The Bundestag was also considering a draft law enhancing the oversight system that reviews the activities of all of Germany's intelligence services.[1]

On arriving in Berlin, I had taken a walk around the city to catch some sunlight and get myself on German time. Berlin's monuments and museums are constant reminders of the dangers of totalitarianism. Although the Berlin Wall has been gone for almost three decades, its route is still marked by signs and on maps. One of the city's museums is a former prison where "enemies of the people" were interrogated by the Stasi, the East German secret police. Another museum preserves daily life in the German Democratic Republic, in existence from 1949 to 1990; it was probably the world's most advanced surveillance state. By contrast, Article 10 of the basic law of the Federal Republic of Germany protects the right to privacy. In the late 1960s, the Federal Republic adopted the G10 Act to control domestic intelligence gathering. The communications of a German citizen or anyone in Germany cannot be monitored without a decision by a special oversight body of the parliament, the G10 Commission, composed of members chosen by both government and opposition parties, formed to prevent abuse of surveillance powers.

In front of the Reichstag, I paused to snap a selfie. The building is perhaps best known for a fire in 1933 that gave Adolf Hitler the excuse to abolish civil liberties and seize complete power. During the Cold War, the battered Reichstag suffered decades of neglect. It is now at the heart of a gleaming, modern complex that houses the German parliament. As a reminder of the Reichstag's fraught history, its restoration intentionally preserved the scars of war. The building is topped by a new glass dome, a symbol of transparency and hope, built after the unification of Germany in 1990. Above it, I spied both the tricolor of Germany and the blue flag of the European Union fluttering in the breeze. In the very seat of German sovereignty, the two flags are given essentially equal status. The highly educated Germans I met all regarded their European citizenship as a badge of honor. For all its faults, they saw the European Union as standing for human rights and the rule of law, and regarded Germany's membership in the EU as a rejection of bigotry and narrow nationalism.

As I was preparing for the trip, I learned that Germans described the controversy about surveillance that Snowden started as the "Snowden affair," in contrast to the more neutral "Snowden revelations." It was a subtle but telling difference. The signals intelligence operations of one of Germany's closest allies were being treated not as a policy issue with implications for privacy but as a full-blown scandal. Since 2013 revelations about the NSA's alleged activities in Germany had been appearing in the German press at a steady clip. The German newsmagazine *Der Spiegel*, famous for its investigative reporting, had published well over 100 Snowden documents—many more than its English-language competitors such as the *New York Times*, the *Washington Post*, and Britain's *The Guardian* had published.

Der Spiegel's biggest scoop was its sensational story in October 2013 revealing American eavesdropping on the mobile phone of Angela Merkel, the German chancellor. Merkel grew up in East Germany and took part in the popular movement that led to its abolition. She was deeply angered by the surveillance, and publicly scolded Obama. "Spying between friends, that's just not done," she said sternly.[2] Stung by the criticism, Obama apologized to Merkel. "We're not leaving it to Jim Clapper anymore," said one official. Not everyone thought this was such a good idea. The White House was looking for "immaculate collection," Clapper complained, borrowing my quip to make a different point.[3]

While Obama's apology helped mollify Merkel, the German parliament was not satisfied. In March 2014 the Bundestag launched an investigation into American spying, and any German cooperation with the Americans, convening a special committee known as a PUA (Parlamentarischer Untersuchungsausschuss). This PUA soon became known as the "NSA Committee," although its mandate was actually broader; it encompassed German signals intelligence operations by the BND and was charged with recommending reforms to German law. According to the invitation I received, the purpose of such a special inquiry committee is to "clarify the facts of a certain case"; under German law, a PUA has the power to take evidence "in a way similar to courts." The inquiry committee was embroiled in controversy from the start, after it invited Edward Snowden to appear as a witness. The United States had requested that allies, including Germany, arrest Snowden if he left Russia. The Merkel government refused to give assurances that Snowden would not be arrested if he came to Berlin to testify. Some members of the Bundestag argued this decision was obstructing the inquiry and challenged the government in court. The inquiry committee also sought information about the specific selectors that the BND had used in intelligence operations to obtain communications and data that were transiting German territory. The Merkel government rejected this request as well, and members again took the government to court.[4]

Under these circumstances, my old colleagues in the intelligence community had expressed misgivings to me about engaging with the inquiry committee. While they did not tell me in so many words to refuse the invitation, they did urge caution. The committee had shown an insatiable appetite for obtaining classified information and leaking it to the press, my colleagues warned. I understood their concerns. Along with my invitation, staff for the committee had forwarded to me a detailed, five-page list of questions it was investigating about the NSA, the BND, and any relationship between the two services. It was obvious that a complete answer to the committee's questions would require access to classified information. I resolved to be even more cautious than usual and limit what I would say to information that had been declassified as part of the Obama administration's transparency efforts. I was not interested in helping a foreign parliament, even the parliament of a close American ally, compromise American national security.

The inquiry committee was scheduled to meet at 11:30 a.m. in the Paul-Löbe-Haus, a strikingly modern building in the Bundestag complex. Four other American experts had made the trip, all dedicated civil liberties activists I knew well: Ashley Gorski and Chris Soghoian of the American Civil Liberties Union, internet freedom activist Amie Stepanovich, and Mort Halperin, the civil liberties veteran who had been a victim of Nixon's wiretapping. As we waited for the hearing to start, we spent some time comparing notes. It was soon clear that I was the only witness who would be making a strong case for Obama's surveillance reforms. This was no surprise. My fellow experts were all prominent critics of the NSA. They regarded the reforms with suspicion. Although the inquiry committee had invited others with experience in the American intelligence community who could have taken a more positive view, I had apparently been the only one who said yes.

After a brief delay, we were called to order. The committee chair, Patrick Sensburg, a member of Merkel's Christian Democratic Union, warned us we could be liable under German law if we did not tell the truth. We donned our headphones for the simultaneous translation. I began with a point I thought was necessary, although it was also one I knew was causing some in the Obama administration to squirm.

"Before a crowd of tens of thousands in Berlin in the summer of 2008, a young senator from Illinois and candidate for President, Barack Obama, drew cheers when he promised a more cooperative relationship with the world," I said. In that speech, Obama had "made the case for 'allies who will listen to each other, who will learn from each other—who will, above all, trust each other.'" Acknowledging the betrayal Germans felt when they read press reports of alleged American spying practices, I said it was natural that the German people "were not happy when they found out just how President Obama's intelligence community had been listening."

Still, I tried to make the case that in the past three years the United States had made sincere efforts to regain the trust of its allies, including Germany, with meaningful reforms of its surveillance practices. There was new transparency around surveillance. There were new rules to protect the privacy of foreigners as a result of Presidential Policy Directive 28. Congress had passed the Freedom Act, ending bulk collection of metadata inside the United States. The world was entering a "new reform era for intelligence surveillance," I argued, but "there is much more to do."[5]

For the next five hours, we discussed the legal and technical aspects of mass surveillance. Quite unlike most hearings in Congress I have ever attended, all members were present for the entire afternoon. As I had been warned, their questions were probing. The committee wanted to know just how many selectors the NSA and BND were using in collecting foreign signals intelligence, information that has not been declassified as part of the transparency efforts of the Office of the Director of National Intelligence (ODNI) concerning FISA surveillance. Committee chair Patrick Sensburg asked whether any of us might help him obtain some of these selectors for review. "I guess this is probably a good opportunity to say," I told him, "since you warned me of the criminal penalties of lying to this committee, that I am under potential criminal penalties if I told you specific selectors that the NSA has under surveillance. And luckily I don't have that information anyway."

Most of the committee's questions were less personally hazardous, but no less challenging. What would it mean, as a practical matter, to apply human rights principles of proportionality and necessity to modern programs of mass surveillance? What protections should apply to foreigners who were outside German territory? How could the German and American publics be assured that any privacy protections were really effective, if the rules that applied to the NSA protected only Americans and the rules for the BND protected only Germans? Germany's old rules against domestic spying had not accounted for this.

As Mort Halperin observed, the committee had learned that "there is not a single country that has clean hands on this subject"— certainly not Germany.[6] The inquiry committee was spending most of its time considering the activities not of the NSA but of its own BND. As an external intelligence service, the BND's activities were largely unconstrained by Germany's strict controls for domestic spying, designed to enforce the right to privacy protected by Article 10 of the basic law of the Federal Republic of Germany. The G10 Commission did not have review of these operations unless a German citizen or a person in Germany was being targeted.

The G10 Commission functions much like the U.S. Foreign Intelligence Surveillance Court and, like the FISA court, has been criticized for being a rubber stamp. More fundamentally, the G10 Commission did not review the BND's surveillance of foreign targets outside Germany.[7] As in the United States, Germany's domestic controls simply did not address the questions raised by transnational surveillance operations in the digital age. Germany's intelligence reform laws were designed to correct this. Germany serves as an internet hub between Europe and the Middle East, making the data that transit German territory of immense intelligence value. As authority for its transnational surveillance activities, the BND was relying only on the general authority to collect intelligence contained in its organic statute. There were no specific rules for collection of data on foreigners abroad, as there were for surveillance operations targeting German citizens. The German equivalent of the NSA's "upstream collection" and Prism programs, which in the United States are conducted under directives reviewed by the FISA court, did not require any independent review. The reports that had gripped Germany that said that Merkel's phone was being monitored had painted quite a misleading picture, portraying Germany mainly as a victim of surveillance. In reality, Germany, like the United States, was engaged in broad programs of mass surveillance. The question was what to do about it.

One member thought the answer was clear. "This fundamental question has already been resolved in Germany," declared Konstantin von Notz, a member of the opposition Green Party. "There existed for many decades two Germanys: one Germany in which private communications were groundlessly read on a massive scale, and one in which this was not the case"—the Federal Republic of Germany, with its constitutional protection for the right to privacy in Article 10, reflected in institutions like the G10 Commission. "In 1990, we were fortunately able to dissolve the former state, as we found it utterly disgraceful that the sphere of privacy be 'snuffed out' on such a massive scale and without provocation." The issue before the Bundestag was not whether Germany should engage in mass surveillance—that was forbidden—but how to update the law to prevent mass surveillance of the internet while permitting legitimate surveillance. "Now it is our task to find a way whereby we can render these fundamental rights into the digital era," von Notz concluded.[8]

Von Notz's ringing denunciation of mass surveillance was both inspiring and characteristic of the general distrust of surveillance I encountered among most Germans. Still, one might take some issue with his historical analysis. The BND's transnational surveillance operations, however intrusive, have nothing to do with the intelligence operations of the Stasi and other defenders of East Germany's totalitarian state. In fact, the opposite is the case: it was the BND's mission to fight the Stasi. The BND's operations have always been bound by the liberal principles embodied in the constitution of the Federal Republic of Germany. Modern Germany was facing the same problem the United States was facing; its laws had offered strong protections against domestic spying but until now had done little to restrain transnational mass surveillance practices that were directed at everyone else and were increasingly affecting the privacy of Germans themselves.

German lawmakers were beginning to understand that they could not protect the privacy of their own citizens without offering some protection for everyone's privacy. As Mort Halperin noted at the hearing, there was now "agreement in principle that this is something that democratic countries need to do." While it was still the case that no democratic country had yet "committed itself in its enacted laws to protect the privacy of citizens of other countries who are not in their own territory," Germany was well positioned to lead that effort.[9] In PPD-28, the United States had articulated a policy that everyone's privacy was entitled to dignity and respect, but this was not reflected in any statute. Germany, prodded by the "Snowden affair" and its obligations under EU law, was on the verge of passing a BND reform law that would provide just such protection.

In October 2016 the Bundestag passed its surveillance reform laws. When I had a chance to study them in detail, I experienced a sense of déjà vu. The new BND law was designed to provide programmatic review somewhat similar to that required by section 702 of FISA. It created a new independent panel of judges to oversee the BND's collection of data in its operations targeting foreigners abroad.[10] The new BND law, however, went further in some respects than U.S. surveillance law did in regulating transnational surveillance. The new law covered all signals intelligence activities, not just those that collected data on domestic soil. It also included restraints to protect the privacy of foreign targets. While FISA requires judicial review of the NSA's collection of data inside the United States even when the NSA is targeting a foreigner abroad, the review is designed to protect the privacy of Americans who may be in touch with the NSA's targets, not the privacy of those targets themselves.

Obama's reforms protecting the privacy of foreigners were embodied in a policy document, Presidential Policy Directive 28, not a law, and they are not enforceable by the FISA court. Germany, by contrast, had provided privacy protections for foreign targets in its enacted laws and had created a new judicial panel to enforce them.

The problems confronting the BND were remarkably similar to the problems I had been helping the NSA navigate for over a decade, inside and outside the government. The words were different but the concepts were the same. Some of the reforms mirrored those adopted by the United States after 2013, including an explicit ban on economic espionage.[11] The German reform law also prohibits the use of joint operations with any foreign intelligence service to circumvent national restrictions protecting citizens of either country. The law restricts the "circular exchange" of information, an idea described as *Ringtausch*, to ensure that the BND may not ask a foreign intelligence service for information it may not collect directly. It is an intelligence oversight principle with which I was familiar because the same rule appears in Executive Order 12,333 as a ban on "indirect participation" in actions that are otherwise forbidden.[12] As discussed in the previous chapter, Britain's GCHQ made a similar public commitment in the course of defending its cooperation with the NSA against a legal challenge by human rights organizations. Of course, Germany's reforms offered stronger protection simply by virtue of being laws, and they go further in other ways. For example, systematic cooperation with foreign intelligence partners now requires a written agreement, to be shared with the German parliament's standing oversight committee.

The most far-reaching reform, however, showed that Germany was determined to provide an example of democratic leadership for the European Union. The German reform law gives EU governments, institutions, and citizens new privacy protections, with a higher bar for surveillance than for other foreigners abroad. The independent panel of judges created to review the BND's transnational surveillance enforces these new rules. While the independent panel does not review every case like the G10 commission, it has power to audit specific selectors.[13] Embodying Merkel's insistence that spying on friends "is just not done," the law's explanatory memorandum described its requirement that the use of all selectors "must be consistent with the foreign and security policy interests of Germany" as carrying the implication that "as a matter of principle, no keywords may be used that will lead to the targeted gathering of traffic of heads of state with which Germany has close relations and a good partnership."[14]

Whatever its faults, it was clear to me that the parliamentary inquiry committee's main focus was not on scolding the Americans, but on pressuring Angela Merkel for surveillance reform. I decided I had done the right thing by engaging with German lawmakers. While the inquiry committee was causing the Merkel government undeniable headaches, I thought that in the long run, the Bundestag's debate about the "NSA affair" was providing an immensely valuable service that Germany's intelligence agencies would eventually come to recognize. The German public had debated sensitive issues of intelligence cooperation before, during the Iraq War and in the context of controversial counterterrorism operations, but these debates had not focused on mass surveillance, privacy, and the internet. For the first time, there was a public debate in Germany about the implications of transnational surveillance for human rights and other liberal values that modern Germany professed to honor. Just as the NSA had emerged stronger as a result of the post-Snowden reforms, the BND and other German intelligence agencies will find themselves enjoying greater legitimacy because of reform.

Some lawmakers were disappointed in Germany's surveillance reform efforts. One member, Martina Renner, argued that the new law "effectively legalizes the BND's notorious breaches of the law." She objected that the BND had shown no "repentance," but instead was "being given a free pass to continue mass surveillance."[15]

Renner's frustration was understandable. Germany's surveillance reform laws were not a product of the inquiry committee's investigation, although the committee had certainly created pressure for reform. Instead, these laws had been drafted by a few senior politicians, in consultation with the Merkel government and Germany's national security establishment. There were doubts about the powers of the independent panel established to review the BND's external surveillance operations, among other criticisms. I encountered a similar attitude among many Germans concerned about privacy when I visited again in early 2017. They dismissed Germany's surveillance reform efforts as a tepid response to the "Snowden affair" by mainstream politicians.

There was some irony in Renner's criticism. Renner belongs to the Left party. The Left is now a fully democratic party, but it is a descendant of East Germany's ruling Socialist Unity Party—the party that once ran the Stasi. The Left party grew in popularity as the mainstream Social Democrats made compromises in 2005 and 2013 to join a grand coalition with Merkel's Christian Democrats. As a result of Germany's surveillance reforms, members of all parties will have more opportunity to question the BND and other intelligence services. A permanent commissioner, answerable to parliament and not to the chancellor, will coordinate and strengthen existing oversight of

German intelligence agencies. Every year the heads of the BND and other agencies will be required to appear to answer questions from members of the parliamentary oversight committee at a public hearing.[16] The intelligence chiefs will soon find themselves being cross-examined in public on secret programs, just as Jim Clapper was by Ron Wyden, navigating the tensions between keeping secrets and telling the truth.

Members of the Bundestag should continue to ask tough questions about Germany's role in mass surveillance. They should look beyond the BND and other intelligence agencies. At the hearing in September 2016, Chris Soghoian, the ACLU's chief technologist, was particularly tough on German companies that sold surveillance devices to authoritarian governments. "When it comes to surveillance, Germany is not innocent; you have a lot of blood on your hands," he said. "You are enabling surveillance by some of the worst regimes in the world."[17] Soghoian's harsh words supplied the headline for the German press's coverage of the hearing, although he had spent more time warning members of their own vulnerability to surveillance. Soghoian urged them to take special care to protect their data and communications against any number of well-resourced foreign intelligence services. His warning should not have been news to a parliament that sits in Berlin, a capital immortalized both in popular culture and in reality as the city of spies.

For both the German and American governments, the new transparency about surveillance has been painful, and it has not been without cost. On December 1, 2016, WikiLeaks released more than 2,000 internal documents from the inquiry committee, consisting of 90 gigabytes of information. The release was accompanied by a statement from Julian Assange accusing the committee of being a whitewash, saying it had been "too cowardly" to fight hard enough to allow Snowden to testify. It seemed at first that Germany's NSA committee had its own Snowden, frustrated with the pace of German surveillance reform. While the unauthorized disclosures may appear to prove that both the German and American governments were right to regard the inquiry committee with mistrust, that impression may prove misleading. The committee itself may have been a victim of espionage. Committee chair Patrick Sensburg maintains the documents may have been obtained through hacking by Russian intelligence.[18]

It is a plausible theory. Disrupting the Bundestag's investigation into the NSA and the BND serves the Russian government's strategy of discrediting democratic institutions. Less than a week after the disclosures, the head of Germany's BfV—its domestic intelligence agency, the Federal Office for the Protection of the Constitution (Bundesamt für Verfassungsschutz)—issued a statement accusing Russia of a campaign to "destabilize" Germany ahead of the 2017 elections. The BfV director said Russia had launched "aggressive and increased cyberspying and cyberoperations that could potentially endanger German government officials, members of parliament, and employees of democratic parties." The statement noted a "striking increase" in attacks by Fancy Bear, the hacking group responsible for the successful penetration of the Democratic National Committee in 2016.[19] Plainly, German parliamentarians should have heeded Soghoian's warnings about their vulnerability to spying.

For years, German lawmakers and the Merkel government had been fighting over how to reconcile mass surveillance with Germany's commitment to privacy and human rights, with both the NSA and BND looking on nervously. The inquiry committee's Green Party member, Konstantin von Notz, had argued that Germany's unification as a democratic state within the liberal European order meant that the debate about mass surveillance had been resolved, and the question now was only about how to translate the right of privacy into the digital age. Historical quibbles aside, von Notz's statement is a fair description of the challenge faced not only by Germany but by every democratic country that engages in modern programs of signals intelligence. By the end of 2016, however, liberal principles were being tested as they had not been for decades.

During the inquiry committee's hearing, Chris Soghoian had cautioned members of the German parliament that the panel of American experts it had assembled "is definitely not representative of the American society." For one thing, he noted, all of us were white, and "if this panel represented all of America it would look very different."[20] Our lack of diversity was not limited to race. We were all highly educated professionals who had chosen to specialize in technology or technology-relevant fields. Wherever we came down on surveillance reform, we had little to fear and much to gain from a global economy that was producing enormous wealth for people like us. In my stroll through Berlin in early September amid the relics of the German past, I had also seen a glimpse of the future, and it was an unsettling one. Berlin was holding an election later that month, and the political placards were everywhere. The smiling faces of mainstream politicians in business suits, promising good government, were overwhelmed by bolder messages. The Left party promised to challenge a timid Social Democratic establishment that had failed the working class. The signs for Germany's far right parties warned of the dangers of "Islamization" and said they were the only ones who could be trusted to safeguard the public against a horde of Muslim refugees. In Merkel's home state, her traditional conservative party had just narrowly lost to a fast-growing new party, Alternative für Deutschland (AfD), which was hostile to immigration and skeptical of the European Union. A few weeks later Berliners gave the mainstream parties another kicking, and AfD entered the Berlin state parliament for the first time.

The debate civil liberties activists and national security experts thought we had been having ever since 2013—on both sides of the Atlantic—was the one described by von Notz. How can we hold modern programs of advanced surveillance to the standards of liberal democracy in an age of globalization and the internet? It was a conversation driven by the cosmopolitan concerns of mainstream politicians, technology companies, privacy and human rights activists, computer scientists, and the civil servants that run surveillance agencies. Perhaps, I thought, the narrow outlook of those who were engaged in that conversation had resulted in a failure of imagination. We were ignoring the signs of a more ominous future—signs that were everywhere, if only we chose to look.

According to von Notz, Germany's debate over mass surveillance had ended (or should have ended) with the demise of East Germany, a process that began with the fall of the Berlin Wall. On November 9, 1989, an East German official made a surprise announcement that his government would no longer enforce travel restrictions between East and West Germany. Thousands took to the streets. By evening, crowds of Berliners were dancing on the hated concrete barrier. In

2016, in the early morning hours of another November 9, confirmation that Donald Trump had won the U.S. presidential election proved almost as surprising. Trump's most memorable promise was a featured chant at his campaign rallies, and it had become a potent slogan for the so-called alt-right, the far right fringe empowered by the internet: "Build that wall!"

Germany's struggle to reform its surveillance practices offers a hopeful example if its democratic allies are willing to listen, but the process is a fragile one. With the rise of populist nationalism amid the continuing threat of terrorism, values that many of us have taken for granted for decades are now at risk.

11

LIBERTARIAN PANIC

THE DAY AFTER DONALD TRUMP'S ELECTION AS PRESIDENT, A LARGE CROWD OF students chanting "Not my president!" marched by my house on the campus of Brown University. It was one of many spontaneous protests across the country. The reaction was unprecedented in modern history. "One would have to go back to Abraham Lincoln's election in 1860 to see these types of widespread demonstrations in response to the election of a president," said Douglas G. Brinkley, a history professor at Rice University.[1] Within days, the Leadership Conference on Civil and Human Rights held a meeting of more than fifty progressive organizations to mobilize against the threats to basic freedoms that many were sure a Trump presidency would pose. Among the people I knew in the American Civil Liberties Union and other privacy and civil liberties organizations, only those who had been part of the hastily assembled coalition to defend freedom after 9/11—the movement that fought the Patriot Act and other Bush policies in the "war on terror"—could remember anything like it.

While political campaigns can often be divisive, the atmosphere of crisis might seem odd. It was, after all, an election the nation had just experienced, not a terrorist attack. Yet if such a reaction to the choosing of a new president appears strange, it was stranger still that my old friends from my ACLU days were joined in their fear of Trump by many of my newer friends: my colleagues who had served in the intelligence community or in other national security positions during the Bush and Obama years. Jack Goldsmith, a former Justice Department official in the Bush administration, noted the frightened reaction of the normally sober writers of *Lawfare*, the national security blog he cofounded. (I am a contributing editor for *Lawfare*.) The website "serves as a kind of bulletin board" for the national security establishment, as *New York Times* reporter Emily Bazelon has noted. It counts among its writers many veterans of Republican administrations who might have been expected to welcome a Republican president, especially after eight years in the political wilderness.[2] Many, instead, were profoundly worried about what President Trump might do to basic constitutional principles.

The rift between Trump and the national security establishment developed long before the controversy over Russian interference in the 2016 presidential election and the FBI's investigation of possible coordination between Russian intelligence officers and Trump campaign officials. The tensions arose in significant part because of Trump's campaign rhetoric, and especially his endorsement of policies at odds with civil liberties. In the summer of 2016, an impressive roster of national security experts who had served in Republican administrations signed a statement denouncing Trump as "dangerous" and pledging never to serve in a Trump administration. They included several former cabinet members from the George W. Bush administration, among them John Negroponte, the first director of national intelligence and the man who led that office when I joined it ten years earlier. Trump "appears to lack basic knowledge about and belief in the U.S. Constitution, U.S. laws, and U.S. institutions, including religious tolerance, freedom of the press, and an independent judiciary," they wrote.

Of course, these were just the sort of issues that had put the signatories at odds with civil liberties and human rights advocates. Many were lawyers, including some with whom I had fought at the ACLU, later worked with in government, and often disagreed with, such as

Kenneth Wainstein, a Justice Department official who had played a crucial role in defending Bush's National Security Agency programs, including warrantless wiretapping.[3] For the civil liberties community, one silver lining to the panic over Trump was that the lawyers and officials they had argued against for so long looked like they might be seeing the light. One ACLU lawyer wrote after the election that he was "heartened" to see his newfound allies in the national security establishment finally "appreciating the dangers in a too-powerful executive branch."[4]

During his campaign in 2015 and 2016, Donald Trump openly promised his administration would engage in abuses of civil liberties and human rights. Trump said that to fight terrorism he would use tactics that went further than those of his Republican predecessor, George W. Bush. Trump promised to bring back waterboarding "and a hell of a lot worse." Trump brushed aside the issue of whether such tactics amounted to torture, arguing, against all evidence, that "torture works." He sneered at what he termed a "politically correct" emphasis on avoiding civilian casualties in strikes against terrorist targets, urging the military to "take out their families." After an outcry, Trump's campaign put out a statement saying he would not order the military to violate international law. Nevertheless, Trump explained that he wanted to "expand the law" to allow waterboarding and other tactics, and promised to "work on it with the generals." Retired four-star general Michael Hayden, who led the NSA and CIA during the George W. Bush administration, said that CIA operatives had learned to be wary of going along with such policies, knowing that they would be the ones to suffer the blowback while the politicians who had pushed the policies escaped any responsibility. If Trump wanted to bring back waterboarding, Hayden said, "he better bring his own bucket, because CIA officers aren't going to do it."[5]

On surveillance, Trump's campaign promises drew less attention but were just as alarming. Following the terrorist attacks in Paris in November 2015, Trump said bluntly, "I want surveillance," explaining that he would not let "political correctness" get in the way. "You're going to have to watch and study the mosques," he said. Trump was referring to a program the New York Police Department had instituted after 9/11 to infiltrate Muslim communities without any factual predicate. The program resulted in multiple civil rights lawsuits, including from the ACLU. After more than a decade in operation, the NYPD's so-called Demographics Unit had not produced a single lead in any terrorism cases. In 2014 New York's new police commissioner, William Bratton, finally abandoned the program. Trump argued that because of the growing threat of ISIS, that had been a mistake. "Under the old regime we had tremendous surveillance going around and in the mosques in New York City," he said, neglecting to note that the main reason the NYPD's surveillance had ended was that it, like the NSA's telephone records program, had proved ineffective.[6]

When a reporter from Yahoo News asked Trump if his counterterrorism strategy might include "warrantless searches of Muslims," he agreed, saying that "while some people are going to be upset about it," the terrorist attacks in Europe were a sign that drastic measures were needed. He warned that his surveillance policies would include "things that were frankly unthinkable a year ago." Trump's comments on warrantless searches were overshadowed by hints of even more drastic authoritarian policies. When the reporter asked Trump if he favored a special identification card or database for Muslims, he coyly refused to rule out either option. Amid the ensuing firestorm, Trump eventually repudiated the idea of a "Muslim registry." Trump's endorsement of warrantless searches went largely unnoticed.[7]

While Trump's promised policies on surveillance were worrying if somewhat vague, his support for conspiracy theories and his dismissal of basic facts were chilling. My friends in the national security community regarded Trump's Muslim-baiting as especially dangerous. Many had worked for years to build bridges with the Muslim community in the United States and around the world. This strategy began almost immediately after the 9/11 attacks. "Islam is peace," President Bush said in a visit to a mosque in Washington, D.C., on September 17, 2001. "The face of terror is not the true faith of Islam."[8] Bush often went out of his way to emphasize that what he called the "war on terror" should not be seen as a clash of civilizations. By the time I began working in the Bush administration in 2006, national security officials were careful to avoid describing terrorists as "Islamic," referring instead to "extremists," "terrorists," or simply "killers." This messaging strategy was continued by the Obama administration. It had nothing to do with sensitivity or political correctness. It was a pragmatic decision based on advice from intelligence analysts who wanted to avoid playing into narrative promoted by al-Qaeda, ISIS, and other terrorist organizations. Trump's message could not have been more different. During the campaign, Trump insisted that as he "watched the World Trade Center go down" on 9/11, there were "thousands of people" in the Muslim community in New Jersey who "were cheering that the building was coming down." In addition to being preposterous on its face, the rumor had been repeatedly debunked.[9] For counterterrorism professionals, this was worse than a lie; it was a mistake that was sure to be exploited by terrorist organizations to radicalize new recruits.

Perhaps Trump's talk was campaign rhetoric, not to be taken literally. A writer for *The Atlantic*, Salena Zito, famously summed up better than anyone else the difference in the way Trump's supporters and the media experienced Trump's way of speaking. "When he makes claims like this, the press takes him literally, but not seriously; his supporters take him seriously, but not literally."[10] It seemed a perfect way to explain Trump's election to the majority of Americans who had voted against him and had a hard time understanding those who had supported him. A few days after the 2016 presidential election, one of the Republican officials who had signed the statement opposing Trump and refusing to serve in his administration, former State Department official Eliot Cohen, appeared to have second thoughts. Cohen wrote, "Trump may be better than we think," arguing that his lack of fixed principles might make him more open to persuasion by his advisers. While Cohen professed no interest in a job for himself, he penned a hopeful essay to an unnamed "anxious friend" making the case for serving in a Trump administration. Cohen wrote that military, intelligence, and diplomatic officials must remember that their oath is to the Constitution and not to the president. Prospective appointees should say yes if Trump asked them to join his national security team, but only if they could be sure they were doing so "out of a sense of duty rather than mere careerism," and only if "they keep a signed but undated letter of resignation in their office desk (as I did when I was in government), and that they not recant a word of what they have said thus far."[11]

As I read Cohen's words, I could not help but think of my own decision to join the intelligence community during the Bush years, at a time when the administration's counterterrorism policies had engendered deep distrust in the civil liberties community and the broader public. Looking back, I realized that I had done just what Cohen advised. I had told my new colleagues I had no interest in recanting the criticism I had leveled against Bush's terrorism policies as an ACLU lawyer, and they had always respected my position. My resignation letter was not a physical one, but in my mind it was always there. When I learned of the NSA's programs of bulk collection and other intrusive programs, it was never far from my thoughts. As these programs were gradually brought under court review and I helped devise new safeguards and oversight mechanisms, I mentally put my resignation letter back in my desk drawer, ready to retrieve it if necessary. Most of my ACLU friends—though not all—had supported my decision to try to make a difference on the inside, and I have never regretted it.

Cohen's musings were part of an unprecedented debate during the Trump transition among national security professionals, who typically take pride in any opportunity to serve the commander in chief regardless of politics, about whether it was ethical to work for President Trump. Despite Cohen's initial advice, he quickly changed his mind. After an angry telephone call with Trump's transition team, Cohen said he would tell his friends to stay away from Trump, "at least during the early phase of the administration," arguing they "would probably have to make excuses for things that are inexcusable and defend people who are indefensible."[12]

During the initial months of the Trump presidency, marked by a chaotic and abrupt ban on travelers from several majority-Muslim countries, Cohen's warning was prescient. The Trump White House was marked both by inexcusable policies and indefensible people.

Among the more indefensible people who decided to join Trump's team was retired general Michael Flynn. Flynn was briefly Trump's national security adviser before he was forced to resign in February 2017 over his failure to disclose conversations he had had with Russia's ambassador to the United States, Sergey Kislyak, during the presidential transition. This was not the first time Flynn had been fired. Flynn had been dismissed from his job as head of the Defense Intelligence Agency by my old boss's boss, Director of National Intelligence Jim Clapper, after clashes with both subordinates and superiors. During his time at the DIA, Flynn became known for peddling conspiracy theories popular with the alt-right, and would refuse to change his mind when others tried to point out they were false. It was a saying inside the agency that there were facts, and then there were "Flynn facts," such as the idea that Sharia law was spreading inside the United States. In Trump, Flynn found a kindred spirit. After his dismissal by Clapper in 2014, Flynn became a harsh critic of the Obama administration's terrorism policies, eventually joining the Trump campaign as a self-confessed advocate of Islamophobia. "Fear of Muslims is RATIONAL," Flynn wrote in a tweet in 2016.[13]

My friends in the national security community were relieved by Flynn's dismissal from the White House after less than a month in his job. They were delighted after President Trump named a respected military strategist, Lieutenant General H. R. McMaster, to replace Flynn as national security adviser. In McMaster's first meeting with the staff of the National Security Council, he pointedly rejected the term "radical Islamic terrorism," saying that it was more effective to refer to terrorists as "un-Islamic."[14] McMaster was voicing the mainstream view of most military officers and counterterrorism professionals, but he was also repudiating the preferred language of his own commander in chief. Only one month earlier, President Trump had vowed on the steps of the United States Capitol to "unite the civilized world against Radical Islamic Terrorism, which we will eradicate completely from the face of the Earth." (The phrase is capitalized in the official White House transcript.)[15]

Trump's dystopian inaugural address was written by Stephen K. Bannon, his counselor and chief strategist. President Trump's initial memorandum organizing the National Security Council made clear that Bannon was invited to all meetings and made him a regular member of the council's "principals committee"—"the Cabinet-level senior interagency forum for considering policy issues that affect the national security of the United States."[16] Most of my friends in the national security community were stunned at this development, as I was. While the advice of political aides may be helpful in communicating policy decisions, previous administrations have taken great care to ensure that the professionals are in charge.

In April 2017 the national security community took comfort in

Trump's decision, at McMaster's request, to remove Bannon from this role, for which he was plainly unqualified. Bannon is the former chair of Breitbart News, a provocative website that Bannon himself once described as "the platform for the alt-right."[17] He embraces the idea of a "clash of civilizations" between Islam and the West that both Bush and Obama strived to avoid. As a Hollywood filmmaker, Bannon once proposed a documentary warning of "enablers among us" who were helping radical Muslims in their quest to remake the country into the "Islamic States of America."[18] Bannon's views on the dangers of radical Islam are shared by Sebastian Gorka, a former national security editor for Breitbart who joined the White House as a member of Bannon's Strategic Initiatives Group. Gorka has written a bestselling book in which he faults President Bush for showing excessive sensitivity in his positive statements about Islam, an approach he argues "reached outlandish and surreal proportions under President Barack Obama." On the night of Trump's inauguration, Gorka created a stir by appearing on Fox News in a traditional black jacket favored by Hungarian nationalists, which he said he did to honor his family's Hungarian heritage. Gorka told the host, Sean Hannity, that Trump's speech marked the defeat of "political correctness" in national security policy. "When he used those three words today— radical Islamic terrorism—he put the marker down for the whole national security establishment." Trump had sent a message, Gorka said: "The alpha males are back."[19]

In his book, Gorka argues that the Muslim Brotherhood, a global political movement of conservative Sunni Muslims, should be designated a terrorist organization. This view is not shared by the intelligence professionals I worked with in government. While the brotherhood shares some ideas in common with terrorist organizations, such as support for a strict application of Sharia law, intelligence analysts are careful to distinguish peaceful supporters of political Islam from violent terrorists. Labeling the Muslim Brotherhood a terrorist organization would have serious consequences for the civil liberties of many American Muslims. For years a number of mainstream American Muslim organizations have had to contend with claims that they are linked to the Muslim Brotherhood and represent a foreign threat to American democracy.

The worst surveillance abuses in American history—the wiretapping of Dr. Martin Luther King Jr. and the widespread monitoring of civil rights and antiwar movements in the 1960s and early 1970s— have resulted from presidents and other officials who looked for intelligence agencies to confirm "facts" that simply are not true. In that era, Presidents Johnson and Nixon were convinced the antiwar and other protest groups were secretly funded by Moscow. They would not accept the truth that these movements were a genuine reaction of many Americans to their own mistakes, demanding instead that the FBI, NSA, and CIA expand their surveillance of Americans to find the evidence they were sure would prove them right.[20] This experience shows that when the president and top officials demand information that proves links to foreign threats that are not there, the response of the intelligence agencies has too often been not to refuse but to look harder, to intensify surveillance in a vain effort to satisfy their customers.

Trump has showed a similar disdain for facts. In early 2017 Trump fought with the intelligence community over its report that Russian president Vladimir Putin had deliberately intervened in the election in order to help Trump.[21] Eventually, he accepted the reality that the Russian government was indeed behind the successful hacking of the Democratic National Committee and Hillary Clinton's campaign director, John Podesta. Nevertheless, he soon deepened his feud with his own intelligence agencies when he falsely accused President Obama of wiretapping his phone during the 2016 election, a claim that resulted in a frantic search by the Trump White House to find evidence of abusive surveillance by the Obama administration. The controversy demonstrated that Trump views facts as malleable, to be judged primarily for how they might affect him. The intelligence community is not well positioned to advise a president or a White House staff that believes in what Kellyanne Conway, counselor to the president, infamously called "alternative facts."

WAS THE OUTSIZED FEAR THAT was uniting the national security and civil liberties communities at the beginning of the Trump era rational? Jack Goldsmith did not think so. He termed the reaction "the flip side of the more familiar 'security panic,' which is essentially a sharp reaction and possibly overreaction to a security event (like a terrorist attack) that leads to actions later deemed excessive or oppressive." The opposite of this, Goldsmith argued, was "libertarian panic," which he defined as a "sharp reaction and possibly overreaction to perceived or anticipated security measures that are believed to represent unjustified attempts to violate the law or curtail civil liberties."[22]

Goldsmith pointed to a host of constraints on executive power, including bureaucracy, transparency, and new oversight bodies, such as the privacy office at the Office of the Director of National Intelligence (ODNI), where I had once worked. Goldsmith's thesis about executive power is more fully developed in *Power and Constraint*, his book about how the Bush and Obama administrations, despite their greatly expanded theoretical authority in the arena of national security, were in practice hemmed in by a host of smaller checks and balances—and about how those restraints actually empowered the national security community to keep the country safe.[23] According to Goldsmith, the panic over Trump was "misplaced." Nevertheless, Goldsmith argues that the overreaction to Trump was "useful, indeed vital, even if misplaced," because the "libertarian panic" would ensure that those with the power to check the executive branch from without and within—lawyers, journalists, and activists—would be especially vigilant, putting the Trump administration on a short leash.

Goldsmith's point about bureaucracy is well taken. Changing government policy is much easier in theory than in practice. The president of the United States exercises vast powers under Article II of the Constitution, including power over surveillance, that can in theory be unleashed with the stroke of a pen. In reality, executive orders, presidential directives, and agency guidelines are deeply embedded in the culture of the intelligence community. Trump's national security team may, of course, recommend that he revoke or change reforms adopted by Obama, such as Presidential Policy Directive 28 that protects the privacy of foreigners, but the bureaucracy will resist changing rules they have become accustomed to obeying. The rules offer the intelligence community valuable protection against pressure by top officials to "look harder" in ways that professionals know will backfire, and they are useful in deflecting criticism—from the press,

Congress, communications providers, and European governments, to name just a few.[24] The Justice Department's Office of Legal Counsel has made clear that both executive orders and presidential directives "remain effective until subsequent presidential action is taken."[25] If zealous White House officials argue they need not obey surveillance limits embodied in executive orders or because they stem not from the law but from the president's powers, intelligence officials can tell them confidently that they are wrong.

As I learned during my time in the White House, real power often resides far from 1600 Pennsylvania Avenue, in the departments and agencies that actually run the government. By March 2017 Trump had rounded out his administration with two retired Marine generals, Secretary of Defense James Mattis and Secretary of Homeland Security John Kelly; a former energy company executive, Secretary of State Rex Tillerson; and three Republican politicians who had served in Congress, Attorney General Jeff Sessions, CIA director Mike Pompeo, and Director of National Intelligence Dan Coats. Quite unlike Bannon, Gorka, or Flynn, who did not require Senate confirmation, these were all highly conventional choices for a Republican president, although some (like Sessions) had quite troubling views on civil liberties issues.

The last of these cabinet officials to be confirmed, Dan Coats, offered some reassurance. Coats is a former Republican senator from Indiana who served on the Senate Select Committee on Intelligence. With Coats as director of national intelligence, I thought there was hope that Obama's surveillance reforms could survive the Trump years, mostly because of his experience outside Congress. From 2001 to 2005, Dan Coats served as ambassador to Germany, where he had to navigate the tensions between the Bush administration and Europe in the initial phase of the "war on terror." When Coats returned to Washington, he became a lobbyist, representing Sprint during the debate in Congress over the FISA Amendments Act, which renewed section 702 of FISA and provided immunity to telecommunications companies that participated in Stellar Wind. In answers to questions from the Senate Select Committee on Intelligence prior to his confirmation, Coats wrote approvingly of Presidential Policy Directive 28. Coats agreed that the policy had "reassured" Europeans and had made possible continued data transfers between the United States and the European Union.[26]

When Coats became the head of the intelligence community in March 2017, two influential and powerful constituencies whose reputation had been damaged by questionable NSA surveillance—friendly foreign governments and U.S. communications providers—gained a sympathetic ear.

NEVERTHELESS, DESPITE MY FAITH IN the civil servants in the three-letter agencies and my belief in the value of transparency, judges, oversight officials, and all the rest, I could not shake a lingering sense of libertarian panic. On election night, a former contestant on Trump's reality show who had become one of Trump's campaign aides, Omarosa Manigault, ominously warned Trump's "enemies" that he "has a long memory and we're keeping a list."[27] Manigault later joined the White House. Still, I did not worry that Trump would be able to unleash the full power of the surveillance state on an "enemies list" of his political opponents, as Richard Nixon did. I had no doubt that the NSA, CIA, FBI, and other three-letter agencies would refuse a direct order to engage in political surveillance, and they could point to laws such as FISA as a reason that such surveillance would be illegal.

My fears did not stem from any lack of faith in the intelligence community's commitment to the law. Surveillance abuses were far more likely to result not from outright violations of the law but from what Jack Goldsmith described to me as "impulsive, ill-informed lawful presidential discretion." In the wrong hands, such discretion can do a great deal of damage. Some of Trump's supporters have hinted at dark conspiracies involving their political rivals that might provide a legal pretext for surveillance. During the 2016 presidential campaign, Representative Sean Duffy, a Republican from Wisconsin, accused Hillary Clinton's top aide Huma Abedin of having "ties to the Muslim Brotherhood" and of having been the "editor for a Sharia newspaper." The accusations had no factual basis—they are a prime example of how "fake news" shared on social media had an impact on mainstream debate in 2016. The "Sharia newspaper" claim was based on the fact that Abedin was listed as the assistant editor of a scholarly journal specializing in articles about Muslim communities that live as minorities in non-Muslim countries.[28]

Nevertheless, an aggressive lawyer might argue that such accusations were alarming enough that they required some action. After 9/11, the attorney general's investigative guidelines for the FBI were loosened to reflect a more preventative approach to national security cases. Assessments, the lowest form of investigative activity, "require an authorized purpose but not any particular factual predication." If the Trump White House were to push for a probe of Abedin or others who work with Muslim groups they believed "have ties" to the Muslim Brotherhood—as I once did at the ACLU—the FBI might find it difficult to say no.

Of course, surveillance targeting an American requires an order of the FISA court, based on probable cause. However, the FBI is allowed to access records from other federal agencies in a threat assessment.[29] As we have seen, the FBI and other intelligence agencies have for years been routinely querying incidentally collected information about Americans collected through the NSA's Prism and upstream collection programs under section 702 of FISA. In January 2017 the Obama administration finally got around to issuing long-awaited procedures for sharing raw data the NSA collects overseas and from satellites, which is content and metadata that have not been examined by NSA analysts and may contain information about U.S. persons. Other agencies may use NSA data only for national security purposes, and the agencies must follow equivalent protections to the safeguards NSA analysts themselves apply.[30] Still, the NSA's culture is quite different from that of other agencies. They may use their newfound access to raw signals intelligence databases to query U.S. person information in more aggressive ways than the NSA's analysts would, if they think this is what they must do to give the White House what it wants.

When I worked as a lawyer in the intelligence community, my colleagues were fond of saying that we should take care to ensure we did not take what the law permits "to the darkest corner of the room." Because it is not clear whether Trump's lawyers will feel the same sense of restraint, I have just done so. Surveillance law is complex. A clever lawyer can exploit its complexities. Even without violating the law, a zealous or partisan official in the right position can do quite serious damage, given the loopholes available to him or her.

WHEN I JOINED THE GOVERNMENT, I swore an oath to support the Constitution, including the Bill of Rights, just as every other official does. Those who serve in the executive branch are obliged to protect civil liberties, regardless of whether their actions are ever reviewed by Congress or the courts. The familiar arguments over the "dangers of a too-powerful executive branch" are not about whether the executive must respect the Bill of Rights, but about how much deference Congress and the courts should show the executive branch as it interprets those rights in matters of national security. These arguments take for granted that all three branches are committed in principle to following the Constitution. While deference poses risks to civil liberties, there is not a straight line between deference to the executive and abuse of civil liberties. Perhaps the best example of this is the NSA's Stellar Wind program. The program posed a serious threat to the separation of powers. It prompted a crisis when executive branch officials, including Goldsmith and Comey, decided that part of it was illegal. Still, according to a joint inspector general review, it was not used for political surveillance or other plainly improper purposes during the entire time it was in operation from 2001 to 2007.[31]

George W. Bush and his team had shown an ideological commitment to expanding the president's powers under Article II, or, as Dick Cheney had argued, restoring the president's powers following their erosion by the post-Watergate reforms to the intelligence community. By contrast, Obama and his team strongly emphasized the separation of powers, to the point that they sometimes overlooked individual rights issues. With Trump, something quite different was happening, or so it seemed to me. Trump and his most fervent advisers were not interested in arcane debates about Article II. Instead they took aim directly at the freedoms protected by the Bill of Rights—"religious tolerance, freedom of the press, and an independent judiciary," as the statement signed by Republican national security officials put it. Trump was no national security conservative, determined to defend a strong executive within the Constitution's system of checks and balances. Trump was a right-wing nationalist and a populist; his election had been part of a global rejection of mainstream politics and liberal principles.

In his inaugural address, Trump described his "oath of office" as "an oath of allegiance to all Americans"—an unusual formulation in a republic whose chief executive swears to "preserve, protect and defend the Constitution of the United States."[32] Trump was instead claiming a direct connection between the people and their leader, unmediated by traditional institutions. This was a difference in kind, not in degree, and it was a difference that appeared to justify my panic about civil liberties in 2017 perhaps even more than in 2001.

A host of unwritten rules keeps the national security community in bounds, but there is a weakness in these constraints. Transparency, internal oversight, the judiciary, and even whistleblowing depend on shame to make them effective. For example, in 2004 the Justice Department concluded that part of the NSA's Stellar Wind program was illegal, provoking the "hospital crisis." When Jim Comey, then deputy attorney general, decided to stand up to the White House, his colleagues supported him with threats of resignation. At that time, President Bush decided against pushing the crisis any further, showing respect for institutional norms by seeking court approval for surveillance. In May 2017 President Trump abruptly fired Comey from his job as director of the FBI even as the FBI was investigating contacts between Trump campaign officials and Russian intelligence, ostensibly because of Comey's mistreatment of Hillary Clinton during the FBI's investigation of her use of a private e-mail server. Trump's firing of Comey was more evidence of his utter lack of shame.

A major terrorist attack could empower a President Trump to further erode institutional norms. If President Trump were to exploit the threat of terrorism to abuse civil liberties without shame, policies that were once unthinkable could become normalized. There would be resistance, of course, from inside and outside the government. Would the resistance succeed? In the wake of a deadly attack, with the president of the United States inciting fear among the public and cheering on the abuse, it is at least an open question.

PARADOXICALLY, THE BIGGEST DANGER TO civil liberties may stem not from Trump's strongman tendencies but from his weaknesses: his isolation, his insecurity, and especially his paranoia about leaks. In February 2017 Jack Goldsmith argued that the "main danger in a Trump presidency is not that it will be too strong, but that it will be too weak."[33] At the time, the *New York Times* had just reported that intelligence intercepts showed contacts between senior Russian intelligence officials and several Trump campaign aides. Trump supporters pushed back by arguing that permanent national security officials were part of a "deep state"—a term ordinarily associated with authoritarian governments—and that they were out to get Trump.[34]

On March 4 President Trump said in a series of tweets that former president Barack Obama ordered a wiretap on his phones in Trump Tower. "Terrible! Just found out that Obama had my 'wires tapped' in Trump Tower just before the victory. Nothing found. This is McCarthyism!" In defending his accusation that Obama had wiretapped him during 2016, Trump insisted that he should be taken seriously, but not literally. "Wiretap covers a lot of different things," he told Tucker Carlson of Fox News in an interview on March 15, 2017. "I think you're going to find some very interesting items coming to the forefront over the next two weeks."

As the White House scrambled to justify Trump's accusation, staff searched through classified intercepts of foreign targets in which members of the Trump transition team had been incidentally overheard trying to make the case that the Obama administration had misused foreign surveillance for political purposes. In a press briefing on March 16, White House Press Secretary Sean Spicer defended his boss by taking surveillance under the Obama administration to the darkest corner of the room. As reporters pressed Spicer to defend Trump's false tweets, Spicer argued that Trump "had 'wiretapping' in quotes; he was referring to broad surveillance." Spicer provided no evidence of improper surveillance, but instead repeated press speculation about how intelligence agencies might have engaged in surveillance of the Trump campaign at the behest of Obama administration officials.

Ironically, Spicer's defense of the indefensible made an excellent case for the continuing risks of "broad surveillance" to civil liberties. In doing so, Spicer unwittingly raised the specter of a laundry list of loopholes in surveillance law that could be exploited by an administration intent on abuse. These included claims of abuse of the new information-sharing rules for NSA's raw signals intelligence issued in January 2017; alleged FISA monitoring of either content or metadata involving a computer server belonging to the Trump organization that was apparently in communication with Russian banks; alleged mishandling of U.S. person information involving Michael Flynn and other Trump officials that had been incidentally collected while monitoring valid foreign targets; and possible misuse of intelligence sharing with foreign governments to evade intelligence oversight rules.

In making the last claim, Spicer repeated speculation by a Fox News commentator that Obama had asked Britain's GCHQ for help in surveillance of Trump, damaging one of the NSA's closest partnerships. The British agency issued a rare public rebuke, calling the claims "ridiculous" and prompting a White House apology.[35] On March 20 Jim Comey, the director of the FBI, and Admiral Mike Rogers, the director of the NSA, firmly rejected Trump's claims of wiretapping in testimony before the House Permanent Select Committee on Intelligence. Comey also confirmed that the FBI was engaged in a counterintelligence investigation of Russian interference with the 2016 election, including whether there was coordination between Russian officials and the Trump campaign. At the hearing, Republican members focused most of their attention on leaks.[36] Later that week, Devin Nunes, the chair of the committee, publicly accused Obama administration officials of improperly handling U.S. person information in intercepted communications involving Trump transition officials. Nunes cited classified intercepts that later turned out to have been supplied to him by the Trump White House. Officials there later accused Obama's national security adviser, Susan Rice, of improperly requesting the "unmasking" of Trump officials overheard in those intercepts. In the ensuing controversy, Nunes was forced to step down from his role investigating Russian interference in the election.[37]

While it was tempting for critics of Trump to cheer on the leakers, I thought it was disturbing that both Trump's critics and Trump officials were disclosing the contents of intercepted communications so casually. While it is legal for the government to listen to the calls of Americans who are talking with valid intelligence targets, the Constitution permits this invasion of privacy only when the government uses the information for national security purposes. The NSA and other agencies had been given broad surveillance powers after 9/11. President Obama had expanded them. The leaks of classified intercepts about the Trump campaign and its alleged ties to Russia were the most consequential political use of such surveillance information in decades. For now, they were damaging Trump, but the normalization of what amounted to a form of surveillance abuse could easily backfire. "My message to the resistance is that you have to be careful," I told a columnist on March 17. J. Edgar Hoover and Nixon had both been prolific leakers of information derived from surveillance, I noted. "These laws exist to protect all of us and our constitutional rights, and there is a difference between leaking the contents of surveillance transcripts and whistle blowing involving questionable government policy."[38] Even if there was no illegal surveillance or improper handling of U.S. person information by the Obama administration, it was surely an abuse to leak information in a manner that could smear Trump campaign officials who may turn out to have done nothing wrong.

Nevertheless, the cure for leaks could be worse than the disease. "Must find leaker now!" Trump said in a tweet on March 20. Paranoia about leakers could well prompt Trump, like Nixon, to engage in illegal or abusive surveillance.[39] Of course, leaks may also serve to prevent civil liberties abuses. Jack Goldsmith had predicted that "national security leaking, already widespread" would become even more prevalent in the Trump administration. The permanent bureaucracy was "on edge to ensure that Trump does not violate the law," he noted, and "it will leak at the slightest hint of illegal action."

IN DECEMBER 2016 THE CATO INSTITUTE, a libertarian think tank, invited me to speak at its annual conference on surveillance on a panel addressing the topic of intelligence in the Trump administration. I argued that we were fooling ourselves if we believed that existing checks and balances, despite all the surveillance reforms adopted after 2013, had made the NSA tyrant-proof. I was seated next to Carrie Cordero, a former Justice Department lawyer and colleague from my days at the ODNI, and Susan Hennessey, a former NSA lawyer who was now the managing editor of *Lawfare*. Cordero and Hennessey were both highly critical of Trump, but they disagreed with my conclusion. They thought the constraints that applied to NSA surveillance would prevent political spying or otherwise abusive surveillance by the new administration.

Joining us that morning was Matthew G. Olsen, who had served as an official in the Justice Department in the Bush administration, as general counsel of the NSA, and in other top national security positions. Olsen had also served President Obama for three years as director of the National Counterterrorism Center, the cross-agency intelligence analysis center that is part of the ODNI. The National Counterterrorism Center is the agency that connects the dots and ensures the government stays one step ahead of emerging terrorist threats. It was the principal solution to the problem the 9/11 Commission said was at the heart of the government's inability to prevent those attacks: the intelligence community's failure of imagination.[40]

For as long as I have known him, Matt Olsen has been an advocate of stronger surveillance powers. I remembered that it had been Matt who had briefed President Obama in the Oval Office on the NSA's bulk collection and other programs when he first took office. After Matt had explained the programs, Obama had decided to keep them without much change. When Yahoo challenged the law that allowed collection of information on its foreign customers in the FISA courts, it had been Matt Olsen's signature on many of the government's filings, including its threat to impose fines of $250,000 a day if Yahoo refused to hand over e-mails belonging to the NSA's foreign targets.

Given Matt's experience, I thought I knew what he would say as we shared a stage at a Washington think tank on that frigid winter morning. Matt would make the case that the rules governing surveillance are already good enough to keep any president in bounds, and that my fears were overblown. While we have known each other for many years, Matt can still surprise me. "Tim and I have argued a lot on these issues," Matt said, but now "I am finding myself drawn into his perspective a bit." Matt spoke quietly and calmly, but I could see he was troubled by the possibility that the surveillance powers he had long defended as necessary might be abused. "I fought hard," he said, "for increased information sharing, breaking down barriers within domestic agencies, and for the modernization of FISA," referring to section 702 of FISA, the law that allows for the domestic collection of data from American technology companies and the internet backbone. "But," the former top lawyer for the NSA went on, "as I fought for these changes, I did not bargain on a President Trump. That was beyond my ability to imagine."[41]

12

BEYOND SNOWDEN

ON A SPRING MORNING A FEW YEARS AFTER THE WORLD BEGAN TO LEARN OF THE NSA's mass surveillance programs, visitors to a Brooklyn park discovered a new statue. Activists had affixed a four-foot-tall, 100-pound bust of Edward Snowden to the top of a granite column honoring patriots who had died as prisoners of war in the American Revolution. It was a dramatic way to pay tribute to the man who had become a symbol of a global movement to protect privacy, civil liberties, and human rights in the digital age. Police removed the unauthorized addition the same day.

It has been harder for the U.S. government to knock Snowden off the virtual pedestal he continues to occupy. By exposing the NSA's secret programs of mass surveillance, Snowden sparked a global conversation about digital privacy. Snowden is the subject of multiple books, an Oscar-winning documentary, and a feature film by Oliver Stone. He is even the subject of a musical composition, featured at a festival I attended in Scotland a few summers after I left government. The composer, Matthew Collings, explained that his "Requiem for Edward Snowden" is a piece that mourns the "death of the excitement of the Internet" and the "death of privacy." The title of Collings's work also reflects the extreme distrust felt around the world for the NSA and other U.S. intelligence agencies. While Collings was writing his requiem for Snowden, he was "convinced" that Snowden "would shortly be dead," adding that it was "interesting that he isn't."[1]

"Change will not come if we wait for some other person or some other time," Barack Obama once said. "We are the change that we seek." While working in the White House during Obama's first term, I drew inspiration from these words. During my time in government, I worked with lawyers and privacy officials to bring about change for the better. We helped ensure the NSA obeyed the laws it was given, brought its transnational surveillance programs under court review, and devised new oversight mechanisms.

Snowden was also inspired by Obama's words, he has said. During the second term of Barack Obama's presidency, Snowden made a far more reckless and more consequential decision to "be the change" he wanted to see in the world. Snowden took this step after waiting in vain for deeper surveillance reforms than my colleagues and I had managed to achieve by working in the shadows. As a result of Snowden's choice, Obama's second term was marked by the most significant reforms to surveillance that have been made since those of the Church Committee in the mid-1970s. Engineers and technologists designed more secure communications systems. The NSA's program of bulk collection of American telephone records was ended by Congress. The debate over section 702 of FISA, the authority for the Prism program and upstream collection, became more informed. International courts began to weigh whether mass surveillance can ever be consistent with human rights principles. New rules were adopted to protect the privacy of foreigners. In short, the NSA became more transparent, more accountable, and more protective of privacy—and, as we have seen, reforms have also made the NSA more effective.

Snowden has said his decision to steal a trove of highly classified documents, give them to reporters, and seek asylum in Russia was motivated by the same kind of patriotism that the monument in Brooklyn was meant to honor.[2] Snowden's detractors scoff at this idea, arguing his actions have more in common with Benedict Arnold and other famous traitors. Snowden's more thoughtful critics, including Jack Goldsmith and Geoffrey Stone (the law professor who served on Obama's review group in 2013), concede that his leak of the NSA's bulk collection of telephone records might be seen in a patriotic light, as an act of whistleblowing that was motivated by concern for the privacy of Americans. Nevertheless, they condemn Snowden because of his disclosure of other NSA programs involving foreign collection. Stone says, "No changes were generally made in those programs, and Americans don't really care."[3]

With respect, Stone is wrong on both counts. Americans do (or at least should) care, and the reforms that have been made to address foreign privacy—at the recommendation of the review group of which Stone was a part—are also needed to protect the privacy of Americans. Distinctions in the law between data collected inside the United States and data collected abroad are relics from the analog era. If Snowden and the journalists who worked with him had revealed only the NSA's bulk collection of American telephone records, the public would simply have no inkling of the scale of the problems posed by the NSA's transnational and foreign programs, including incidental collection of U.S. person information and the weakening of computer and internet security. The Snowden disclosures made stark as nothing else could the risks to Americans' privacy posed by the NSA's collect-it-all approach.

Like me, Snowden took an oath to support and defend the U.S. Constitution, not the internet or some ideal of global ethics. The Supreme Court has said that the Fourth Amendment does not apply to foreigners outside the United States. Still, the privacy of foreign citizens should also count for something. The Constitution provides that "all Treaties made . . . under the Authority of the United States, shall be the supreme Law of the Land." The United States has ratified the International Covenant on Civil and Political Rights, which guarantees the right against "arbitrary or unlawful interference" with anyone's "privacy, family, home or correspondence." Whatever specific legal obligations this and other human rights treaties impose on the NSA's mass surveillance programs, at a minimum they mean that respect for the right of every human being to privacy need not be seen as some cosmopolitan concern that is at odds with devotion to this country.[4]

Because of Snowden, it is now a matter of principle for the U.S. government that everyone "should be treated with dignity and respect, regardless of their nationality or wherever they might reside" when it comes to mass surveillance programs.[5] This change is more important in the long run than ending one NSA program of bulk collection of American telephone records. By taking this stand for global privacy, the United States not only raises the bar for its own intelligence agencies, it also sets a standard for its friends and allies, and it has greater standing to criticize its adversaries.

Surveillance reform had already strengthened intelligence collection. If we have learned anything from the Snowden revelations, it is that effective intelligence programs depend on support from many outside the U.S. government, including the general public, technology companies, and foreign governments. Surveillance programs are more effective when they are legitimate and seen to be legitimate: grounded in law, subject to multiple layers of oversight, and as transparent as possible. In the words of former NSA and CIA director Michael Hayden, "although the public cannot be briefed on everything" that intelligence agencies do, "there has to be enough out there so that the majority of the population believe what they are doing is acceptable."[6]

This is true not just for the public in the United States but also for the global public. *New York Times* reporter Charlie Savage has noted that judging "whether Snowden's disclosures served the public interest—whether they did more harm than good—turns in part on who counts as 'the public.'" The problem with defining "the public" in nationalist terms, as Snowden's critics do, is not just that it ignores the impact of foreign programs on American privacy and disparages the privacy rights of foreigners.[7] Ignoring the concerns of the global public is also self-defeating for the NSA. The U.S. intelligence community does not have the luxury of defining the public in exclusively nationalist terms. It has critical partnerships with some of the world's most robust democracies. Our most important allies share our democratic values and must answer to their own citizens.

Intelligence officials may be tempted to say that reform has gone far enough, or even to go back to old habits. That would be a mistake. The experience of reforming surveillance has demonstrated that transparency, accountability, and meaningful protections for privacy and human rights in intelligence collection are not merely good government values; they are essential to national security. Although this round of surveillance reform has moved the NSA and other surveillance agencies in the right direction, many weak points remain in the checks and balances that apply to intelligence agencies. Transparency reforms are too fragile and too dependent on the good faith of officials in the executive branch. Members of Congress and other oversight institutions have an incentive to pass the buck instead of doing their job. The Foreign Intelligence Surveillance Court is too dependent on the intelligence agencies and the Justice Department, and is underresourced for its new role in reviewing entire programs of surveillance instead of individual surveillance orders. The NSA and other agencies have yet to take advantage of extraordinary advances in privacy-enhancing technology. The global debate about mass surveillance has lasted much longer than anyone could have expected when the first stories based on the Snowden leaks began in June 2013, yet the United States and its allies have barely begun to reconcile their transnational surveillance programs with fundamental human rights principles of privacy.

Snowden and his supporters remain skeptical of surveillance reform. If the result of Snowden's actions "is only measured by legal and legislative reforms and by the extent to which the NSA's activities are now effectively regulated by American courts and Congress, then, sadly, he probably should have stayed in Hawaii," said Christopher Soghoian, chief technologist for the American Civil Liberties Union, in his remarks to the German parliament in September 2016.[8] I do not agree. It is true that if what Snowden and his supporters were seeking was an end to the NSA's mass surveillance, then they have not succeeded. The reason is straightforward: the public simply has not seen the issues raised by mass surveillance in the same black-and-white terms that Snowden and some of his supporters do. One danger of being a privileged insider is the casual assumption that the public would agree with you if only it had the same access to information as you do. The national security community has often fallen victim to this myopic assumption, but it does not seem to have occurred to Snowden or his supporters that they too might be vulnerable to such thinking.

The idea of a shadow government, operating outside the law and the ordinary structures of democratic accountability, strikes a powerful chord in the imagination, as does the image of the lone hero with the courage to confront that shadow government when it goes astray. Snowden's story fits this narrative so well that his supporters regarded as self-evident that the surveillance programs he revealed were established with malicious intent. "Taken in its entirety, the Snowden archive led to an ultimately simple conclusion," Glenn Greenwald argues. "The US government had built a system that has as its goal the complete elimination of electronic privacy worldwide."[9] If Greenwald is right, there is no hope for reform because the government will never obey the rules it is given. Thankfully, he is not.

It is easier to shout slogans than to reform surveillance. One side puts Edward Snowden on a pedestal (literally). Another calls for his execution as a traitor—as Mike Pompeo did while in Congress, before he became the director of the CIA in the Trump administration.[10] Even the less extreme voices in the surveillance debate far too often talk past each other. My goal in these pages has been not only to go beyond Snowden but to go beyond the familiar arguments offered by both the national security establishment and civil libertarians. I have sought instead to draw on values that both communities should in principle embrace, such as the need for greater transparency, the value of oversight and judicial review, the importance of privacy protection, the need for international cooperation, and the importance of standing by liberal democratic principles.

In each of these areas, I have offered recommendations for changes in law, policy, institutional culture, technical capabilities, and foreign relations. They are not meant to be exclusive; it was simply not possible to cover every possible issue in a book of this kind. My failure to address some of these in detail, such as proposals to strengthen protection for whistleblowers in the intelligence community or specific reforms suggested by civil liberties and privacy advocates to section 702 of FISA, should not be taken to imply I do not think they are important. The reforms I have offered are not meant as a short-term action plan for Congress or the intelligence community. Surveillance reform will be a long-term effort.

A serious surveillance reform agenda would work toward these goals by building on the progress that has been made since 2013. This book has offered many concrete ideas for doing so:

- The time has come for legislative and judicial controls on the NSA's overseas and satellite collection. These activities should be brought within the Foreign Intelligence Surveillance Act (FISA).

- The federal courts should reconsider outdated legal doctrines that undermine the Fourth Amendment in an era of bulk collection and transnational mass surveillance. Collection of metadata and surveillance of foreign targets affect the constitutional rights of Americans, and the federal courts must devise rules that protect these rights in the digital age.

- Intelligence agencies should do more about overclassification. It is a basic security principle that a system should be designed to minimize as far as possible the number of secrets you need to keep. Today, intelligence agencies often do the opposite.

- Legal doctrines such as the state secrets privilege and the mosaic theory also need reform. Secrecy should be about protecting national security, not winning lawsuits.

- Congress should do its homework. Members should not vote for surveillance powers unless they are willing to oversee them, and that means attending classified briefings, however frustrating those briefings may be.

- The president should strengthen oversight inside the executive branch, in particular by giving full support to the Privacy and Civil Liberties Oversight Board. From 2013 to 2016 this tiny independent agency inside the executive branch did more to spur accountability for the effectiveness of surveillance programs than Congress had for years.

- The Supreme Court should reform the legal doctrine of standing to make it easier for the ordinary federal courts to hear constitutional challenges to surveillance.

- The judges of the Foreign Intelligence Surveillance Court need more help. Having outside lawyers in the FISA court to contest the government's legal arguments is a good first step, but if judges are to be effective in overseeing today's complex mass surveillance programs, they could use more assistance, including the assistance of technical experts and magistrates. The process for selecting judges should be changed so that the Chief Justice of the United States does not have the power to stack the court.

- The intelligence community should continue asking computer scientists for advice on how technology can provide alternatives to bulk collection and other mass surveillance practices. Federal agencies should also fund more research into cryptography. The field has already created amazing capabilities. More magic is on the horizon.

- The intelligence community should deploy some real-world privacy-preserving collection programs. Existing encrypted search technology offers less intrusive alternatives to bulk collection of metadata and for programs such as upstream collection.

- The United States should champion reforms that protect the privacy of ordinary citizens in foreign countries (such as PPD-28) and should embody such protections in laws such as FISA. Without stronger reforms to address foreign privacy, including reform of section 702 of FISA, it is likely that European courts will continue to strike down agreements that permit commercial data transfers that are vital to transatlantic commerce, such as the Privacy Shield.

- The United States, United Kingdom, and other nations with advanced mass surveillance capabilities should engage with the international human rights community. Britain's GCHQ should take advantage of challenges before the European Court of Human Rights to make reforms.

- Democratic countries that are willing to commit to reform of transnational and foreign mass surveillance programs should agree to refrain from using their most advanced surveillance capabilities against each other's citizens for anything but genuine security threats, and should enforce those commitments through such mechanisms as judicial review.

- Finally, those who work in the NSA or other agencies in the intelligence community must hold strong to American values, regardless of who occupies the White House or which party controls Congress.

The rise of nationalist populism in the United States and around the world is testing our commitment to the basic liberal values that are the foundation of privacy and civil liberties. The press, public, advocacy groups, and overseers must keep a careful watch for abuse and should refrain from using abusive tactics such as leaking surveillance information. The NSA and other intelligence agencies have vast surveillance powers. Despite reform, they are not tyrant-proof. Civil liberties advocates should not be afraid to embrace unlikely allies they have fought in the past. The national security community and the civil liberties community disagree on many policies, but on basic values they agree more often than they realize.

The struggle to reform mass surveillance is far from over. If the NSA, other U.S. intelligence agencies, and their partner services in allied countries want to earn the trust of ordinary people in this country and around the world, there is a lot more to do.

AND WHAT DO I THINK about Edward Snowden? It is a question I have been asked countless times since 2013. When people ask the Snowden question—traitor or whistleblower?—it is rarely because they have any genuine interest in what should happen to Snowden himself. They want to know whether you side with the surveillance state or with its discontents. A poster for Oliver Stone's feature film about Snowden reads, "You don't have to pick a side. But you will." It was effective marketing, but the notion could not have been more wrong. In Barack Obama's first inaugural address, he challenged the nation to "reject as false the choice between our safety and our ideals."

The Snowden question seemed to demand just such a choice. For more than three years I avoided giving my opinion on what to do about Snowden precisely because the purpose of the question was to force me to choose between two communities that I love—the privacy and civil liberties movement and the national security community. They are more than my professional colleagues; they include some of my closest friends.

In the fall of 2016, my friends at the ACLU asked me to add my name to a letter urging President Obama to pardon Edward Snowden. After considerable soul-searching, I signed it. As it was an unpopular position with my former colleagues in the national security community, I decided to explain my reasoning more fully in an article for *Lawfare*. It sparked a lively debate.[11]

As should by now be clear, I did not view Snowden simply as a heroic whistleblower, which was how the ACLU letter I signed had portrayed him. I acknowledged that his disclosures caused "great damage to national security." Nor did I view the NSA as the enemy. Instead, I wrote that the status quo was harming the interests of the United States. It made no sense for the U.S. government to continue to pursue Snowden "like a digital age Inspector Javert" while benefiting from the reforms his disclosures made possible. Snowden had become a potent symbol for privacy and civil liberties, human rights, and an open internet in which surveillance operations are controlled by law. His presence in Moscow was a gift to Vladimir Putin, allowing the Russian leader to cynically pose as a defender of digital human rights. Every time Snowden made a virtual appearance before his admirers, the unspoken message was that he had been forced to seek asylum (in Russia!) because the United States opposes privacy and internet freedom. The message was no less effective for being false and unfair.

Letting Snowden off the hook would incentivize future leakers, my former colleagues protested. Snowden's actions were criminal and he deserved to be punished. While I sympathized, I thought their concerns pointed in the opposite direction. The only way Snowden would ever be punished was if the government lured him back to the United States with a generous plea agreement that would violate the Justice Department's long-standing (and sensible) policy of never negotiating with fugitives. An unreviewable act of presidential clemency was a better answer. Pardons are exceedingly rare. A pardon sets no precedent and so creates no incentives. Future leakers could not count on one.

A pardon for Snowden would signal presidential approval of his actions, some argued. I did not agree. Throughout history, presidents have pardoned people whose actions obviously deserved censure, because doing so was in the broader interests of the nation. In addition to the more familiar examples of Ford's pardon of Nixon and Carter's pardon of Vietnam War–era draft evaders, I pointed to the example of George Washington, who was the first president ever to use the pardon power. Constitutional scholar Akhil Amar notes that Washington's example enjoys "special authority on a wide range of issues, especially those concerning presidential power."[12] So how did Washington choose to use the pardon power? He pardoned traitors. Washington is still the only president to have personally led troops into battle. He did so to suppress a rebellion by farmers in western Pennsylvania over a tax on whisky. Still, Washington pardoned the very rebels he fought on the battlefield, including convicted traitors who were sentenced to hang. This did not mean Washington agreed with the rebels or that he approved of treason. Washington had the judgment to know that the national interest was more important than punishment.

At bottom, I argued, Snowden's disclosures were neither the actions of a traitor nor were they the actions of a traditional whistleblower who seeks to expose plainly illegal conduct by the government. Snowden argued that the surveillance he disclosed was both illegal and unconstitutional. Yet by 2013 the real problem for privacy was that global mass surveillance was not illegal, yet it still was not sufficiently controlled. As we have seen, some of the most controversial programs that Snowden leaked, including bulk metadata collection and the NSA's programs of transnational surveillance under section 702 of FISA, were based on laws that had been approved by Congress on multiple occasions and had been found by federal judges (in secret) to be both lawful and constitutional. To me, Snowden's actions were best described as neither treason nor whistleblowing but as a rash act of rebellion in an effort to save the internet—with collateral damage to legitimate intelligence operations. A pardon for Snowden would have been an olive branch from the surveillance state to its severest critics in this war over internet freedom, I argued, and a powerful statement to the world that the United States had learned from its mistakes.[13] I do not know if my arguments changed any minds about Snowden. Of course, the ACLU's campaign to pardon Snowden failed to convince Barack Obama, who was the only person whose opinion really mattered. For good or for ill, Snowden is likely to remain in Russia for the foreseeable future.

It is time to move beyond Snowden. The battle over Snowden has obscured the fact that the NSA and its critics generally agree much more than they realize. Among both intelligence officials and civil libertarians, there is or at least ought to be common call in service of a future that reconciles the need for surveillance programs that respect such values as internet freedom, privacy, and human rights. Now more than ever, reforms to protect privacy and civil liberties in intelligence surveillance is a calling worth fighting for, not only for the surveillance state's discontents but for the surveillance state itself.

Appendix A

NATIONAL SECURITY SURVEILLANCE TIMELINE

1952: President Harry Truman creates the National Security Agency by top secret directive.

1975: Senator Frank Church heads an investigation of intelligence agencies that uncovers abusive domestic surveillance.

1978: Congress passes the Foreign Intelligence Surveillance Act, creating a special court to review national security wiretapping but leaving most NSA programs unregulated.

1981: President Ronald Reagan issues Executive Order 12,333, authorizing intelligence programs but requiring rules to protect the privacy of United States persons.

2001: On September 11, terrorists kill thousands in coordinated attacks on New York City and Washington, D.C. Congress passes the USA Patriot Act expanding surveillance powers. In secret, President George W. Bush authorizes Stellar Wind, an NSA program of warrantless wiretapping and bulk collection of telephone records and other communications metadata.

2004: Justice Department attorneys conclude that some aspects of Stellar Wind are illegal. The Bush administration obtains the FISA court's approval for these activities under the Patriot Act. Congress creates the Office of the Director of National Intelligence.

2005: The *New York Times* reveals the NSA's warrantless wiretapping program.

2006: Congress renews the expiring provisions of the USA Patriot Act. *USA Today* reveals the NSA's bulk collection of telephone records.

2007: The Bush administration reveals that the FISA court has rejected collection of international communications. Congress passes the Protect America Act, authorizing such collection under a new section 702 of FISA.

2008: Congress passes the FISA Amendments Act, renewing section 702 of FISA while adding new safeguards. Senator Barack Obama votes for the law, disappointing many of his supporters.

2009: President Obama is informed of serious compliance issues in several NSA programs but decides to continue them. Later that year, Congress again renews the expiring provisions of the USA Patriot Act, following briefings on the NSA's use of these provisions for bulk collection.

2011: Congress reauthorizes the expiring provisions of the USA Patriot Act for the third time.

2012: Congress reauthorizes section 702 of FISA. At a conference in Las Vegas, NSA director Keith Alexander says it is not true that the NSA has "a file on everyone."

2013: The Supreme Court rejects a challenge to the NSA's surveillance under section 702 of FISA, saying the challengers' fears are too speculative. In testimony before Congress, Director of National Intelligence Jim Clapper says it is not true that the NSA intentionally collects data on "millions or hundreds of millions of Americans." In Hong Kong, former NSA contractor Edward Snowden provides documents to journalists that prove this statement false and gives details on a host of other programs. Snowden is charged with disclosing classified communications intelligence; he receives asylum in Russia. Clapper launches a transparency drive, declassifying thousands of pages of documents about NSA programs. A review group appointed by Obama recommends reforms.

2014: President Obama issues Presidential Policy Directive 28 (PPD-28), providing protections for the personal information of foreigners and limiting the use of signals intelligence collected in bulk. An independent privacy board issues a report finding no unique value in the NSA's bulk collection of telephone records. A second report by the same board finds that section 702 of FISA has been valuable but requires reform to protect privacy.

2015: Congress enacts the USA FREEDOM Act, ending domestic bulk collection and reforming the FISA court by encouraging the appointment of outside lawyers. A sympathetic documentary about Edward Snowden wins an Oscar. The Court of Justice of the European Union invalidates commercial transfers of personal data to the United States, citing fears of surveillance by the NSA.

2016: The United States and the European Union reach agreement on a "Privacy Shield" agreement allowing commercial transfers of personal data. Congress holds hearings on section 702 of FISA, which expires at the end of 2017. An unsuccessful campaign is launched to encourage Obama to pardon Edward Snowden.

2017: Donald Trump becomes president of the United States, vowing to fight "radical Islamic terrorism" and having promised "I want surveillance" during his campaign. The FBI says it is investigating possible coordination between Trump campaign officials and Russian intelligence. Without evidence, Trump accuses the Obama administration of illegally wiretapping him during the 2016 campaign.

Appendix B

MASS SURVEILLANCE: A GUIDE FOR THE PERPLEXED

Following are a few key concepts to keep in mind as you read this book.

Foreign intelligence. The National Security Agency (NSA) collects foreign intelligence, which is information about foreign security threats such as terrorism, as well as broader information about foreign governments and foreign affairs. The NSA may collect this information outside and inside the United States, using different legal authorities. The NSA does not engage in law enforcement surveillance, which is governed by different rules.

Executive Order 12,333. Most of the NSA's surveillance programs— which the agency calls "signals intelligence collection"—involve collection of communications and data from outside the United States or from satellites. These programs are authorized not by a law passed by Congress but by the president, and they are governed by Executive Order 12,333. They require no court review.

United States person. A U.S. person is a U.S. citizen, a lawful permanent resident, a U.S. corporation, or an unincorporated association composed substantially of U.S. persons.

U.S. person rules. The NSA's "U.S. person rules" are its privacy rules for how it handles U.S. person information. These rules limit collection, retention, and dissemination of such information and are set forth in United States Signals Intelligence Directive 18 (USSID 18). Presidential Policy Directive 28 (PPD-28) extends some of these retention and dissemination protections to foreign persons.

Foreign Intelligence Surveillance Act (FISA). FISA governs the NSA's collection of information inside the United States, or any collection that intentionally targets a U.S. person. FISA collection must be authorized by a special federal court that meets in secret, the Foreign Intelligence Surveillance Court (FISC or FISA court).

Content and metadata. The NSA collects both content and metadata. Content collection means listening to telephone calls or reading e-mails or other internet communications. Metadata collection means obtaining telephone numbers, e-mail addresses, or other routing information.

Bulk collection. When the NSA uses a discriminant, such as an e-mail address, to filter data at the point of collection, it describes this collection as targeted. When it collects everything, it describes this collection as bulk. Presidential Policy Directive 28 (PPD-28) limits the use of signals intelligence collected in bulk.

Stellar Wind. From 2001 to 2007 the NSA collected information inside the United States without the court orders required by FISA, under a legal theory that President Bush had the power to do so in the "war on terror." The program involved targeted collection of content and bulk collection of metadata.

Section 702 of FISA. Section 702 of FISA allows the collection of information inside the United States associated with targets who are foreigners outside the United States. Under section 702, the FISA court issues a single order each year for tens of thousands of foreign targets.

- The targets must be "reasonably believed" to be foreigners outside the United States, based on procedures approved by the court.

- The FISA court also issues minimization rules to protect the privacy of U.S. persons who may be in contact with foreign targets.

Section 702 of FISA was first created by the Protect America Act of 2007. It was reauthorized with additional safeguards in the FISA Amendments Act of 2008. The NSA uses section 702 of FISA for two kinds of collection inside the United States, "upstream collection" and Prism collection.

- *Upstream collection.* In upstream collection, the NSA uses a court order under section 702 of FISA to obtain international communications that transit the facilities of major communications providers. Communications are obtained from the internet backbone if they match selectors, such as an e-mail address, that are associated with a foreign target.

- *Prism.* The Prism program refers to the NSA's collection under section 702 of FISA of the contents of e-mails and other internet communications of foreign targets that have accounts with technology companies in the United States.

USA PATRIOT Act. The USA PATRIOT Act (Patriot Act) was adopted by Congress shortly after the terrorist attacks of September 11, 2001. From 2006 to 2015 the NSA used a secret interpretation of the "business records" provision of the Patriot Act, section 215, to obtain orders from the FISA court authorizing the domestic bulk collection of both international and domestic telephone records.

- NSA analysts were permitted to search the bulk database only if they started with a "seed number," that is, a telephone number or other identifier associated with an international terrorist suspect, based on a standard of *reasonable, articulable suspicion.*

- NSA analysts were then permitted to look up any number in contact with the seed number. For telephone records, NSA analysts could search up to three "hops" until 2013, and up to two "hops" thereafter.

The NSA used a different provision of the Patriot Act for domestic bulk collection of internet metadata, in a similar program that ended in 2011.

USA FREEDOM Act. The USA FREEDOM Act (Freedom Act) was passed by Congress in 2015. It ended the NSA's ability to obtain FISA court orders for domestic bulk collection of metadata. It authorized a new kind of FISA court order that allows NSA analysts to query records held by communications providers (based on a seed number, out to two "hops").

AUTHOR'S NOTE

THIS BOOK GREW OUT OF A MORE AMBITIOUS PROJECT I BEGAN IN THE FALL OF 2013. My plan was to put the debate about Edward Snowden in perspective by writing a condensed history of intelligence surveillance and privacy in the United States, concluding with Obama's surveillance reforms. I soon found myself getting lost in past surveillance controversies. While the stories were fascinating and often illuminating, it seemed that my goal of writing a book that could contribute to the dialogue on privacy was only getting further away.

At the beginning of 2016, I asked my friend and *Lawfare* colleague, Jack Goldsmith, for advice on what to do. He suggested that I put the history project on hold and instead write a book about the contemporary surveillance reform debate. Jack's advice proved excellent and this book is the result.

I have many others to thank for their help in making this book a reality. My editor at Brookings Institution Press, Bill Finan, has held my hand throughout the process and his revisions could not have been more helpful. I am also deeply indebted to Siobhan Gorman, formerly of the *Wall Street Journal*, and Stephen Kinzer, my colleague at the Watson Institute. In the summer of 2016, Siobhan and Stephen helped me organize my ideas on how to reform surveillance into a much more coherent, more personal, and more effective narrative.

The book benefited from critical comments from a number of friends and former colleagues with differing perspectives, including past and present government officials, civil liberties activists, and outside observers. I am grateful to Alex Joel, Bob Litt, Chris Inglis, and David Kris for providing critical feedback. I am also obliged to my former ACLU colleagues, Greg Nojeim and Jameel Jaffer, for offering me detailed notes. Equally valuable were the comments of Charlie Savage, Marc Zwillinger, Ben Wittes, Jennifer Daskal, Paul Rosenzweig, and Jeffrey Kosseff.

Several chapters have benefited greatly from the expertise of others who have been generous with their time. I thank Seny Kamara for helping make sure that chapter 8 reflects the state of the art on technical approaches to protecting privacy. I also thank Bobby Chesney for inviting me to the transatlantic dialogue that introduced me to the German debate on surveillance reflected in chapter 10. Thorsten Wetzling of the Berlin-based Stiftung Neue Verantwortung offered me helpful comments on this chapter.

Brown University has given me a home throughout the project. The Watson Institute for International and Public Affairs, the Department of Computer Science, and the School of Professional Studies have all provided valuable support. Carina Cournoyer of the Brown University Library was always cheerful and helpful. Thanks to my former student, Cassandra Carothers, for some help with translating sources in chapter 10. All my student research assistants worked tirelessly and provided valuable insights—many, many thanks to Meredith Angueira, Madeleine Matsui, Ezra Kagan, Grace Alzaibak, Alexia Ramirez, and Daniel Duhaime.

My family has provided me with unwavering support. For the extraordinary opportunities and privileges I have enjoyed in my life and career, I thank my parents, Clem and Tina Edgar, for believing in me, for teaching me the value of quiet patriotism, and for sending me to college and law school. For standing by me during my time at the ACLU and in my decision to join the government, I thank Koraly Perez-Edgar. Although our marriage ended in 2010, her support during those years was steadfast, as was her love and friendship. Our two children, Gabriel and Elisa, remain a source of joy and delight.

This book is dedicated to the love of my life, Anna Lysyanskaya, who chose to marry me in January 2013. While I am thankful for her comments on drafts and for countless conversations about surveillance and privacy, I am mostly grateful to her for her boundless optimism. Our first child, Marie, was born in August 2013, just after I left the government. Marie has now been joined by Arthur, born in May 2017, just before this book went to press. Throughout all these changes, Anna's positive outlook has been a constant source of strength. Without her encouragement, this book could never have been written.

NOTES

1. I joined the Office of the Director of National Intelligence (ODNI) in June 2006, the same month Edward Snowden was hired as a CIA contractor by BAE Systems. Snowden converted from contractor to permanent CIA employee in August. House Permanent Select Committee on Intelligence, *Review of the Unauthorized Disclosures of Former National Security Agency Contractor Edward Snowden*, September 15, 2016 (http://intelligence.house.gov/uploaded-files/hpsci_snowden_review_declassified.pdf), p. 3.

2. For example, in my testimony during oversight hearings on the information-sharing provisions of the USA PATRIOT Act in 2005, I speculated that information obtained by the FBI during raids on several American Muslim organizations might now be shared with intelligence agencies and with foreign governments. *Implementation of the USA PATRIOT Act: Effect of Sections 203(b) and (d) on Information Sharing: Hearing Before the Subcommittee on Crime, Terrorism and Homeland Security of the House Judiciary Committee*, 109th Cong., 1st sess. (Government Printing Office, April 29, 2005), pp. 23–24.

3. "Statistical Transparency Report Regarding the Use of National Security Authorities for Calendar Year 2016," *IC on the Record*, April 2017 (https://icon therecord.tumblr.com/transparency/odni_transparencyreport_cy2016).

4. Laura Poitras and Glenn Greenwald, "NSA Whistleblower Edward Snowden: 'I Don't Want to Live in a Society That Does These Sort of Things,'" *The Guardian* (video), June 9, 2013 (www.theguardian.com/world/video/2013/jun/09/nsa-whistleblower-edward-snowden-interview-video).

5. *American Civil Liberties Union v. Clapper*, 785 F.3d 787 (2d Cir. 2015).

6. Uniting and Strengthening America By Fulfilling Rights and Ensuring Effective Discipline Over Monitoring Act (USA FREEDOM Act) of 2015, Pub. L. No. 114-23, 129 Stat. 268 (June 2, 2015).

7. Section 401 of the Freedom Act sets forth the process for appointment of amici curiae to the courts established by the Foreign Intelligence Surveillance Act. The Foreign Intelligence Surveillance Court announced its list of amici in November 2015. See Cody M. Poplin, "Amici Curiae for FISC Announced," *Lawfare*, December 1, 2015 (www.lawfareblog.com/amici-curiae-fisc-announced).

8. White House, "Presidential Policy Directive—Signals Intelligence Activities (Presidential Policy Directive 28/PPD-28)," news release, January 17, 2014 (obamawhitehouse.archives.gov/the-press-office/2014/01/17/presidential-policy-directive-signals-intelligence-activities); Office of the Director of National Intelligence, "Signals Intelligence Reform: 2015 Anniversary Report," *IC on the Record* (icontherecord.tumblr.com/ppd-28/2015/privacy-civil-liberties#ppd-28).

9. The law that authorizes Prism and upstream collection is section 702 of the Foreign Intelligence Surveillance Act, 50 U.S.C. § 1881(a), which was added by the FISA Amendments Act of 2008, Pub. L. No. 110-261, 122 Stat. 2436 (July 20, 2008). Section 702 was reauthorized in 2012. See FISA Amendments Act Reauthorization Act of 2012, Pub. L. No. 112-238, 126 Stat. 1631 (December 30, 2012).

10. Privacy and Civil Liberties Oversight Board, *Report on the Surveillance Program Operated Pursuant to Section 702 of the Foreign Intelligence Surveillance Act*, July 2, 2014 (www.pclob.gov/library/702-Report.pdf), pp. 137–40 (recommending limits on U.S. person queries); Privacy and Civil Liberties Oversight Board, *Recommendations Assessment Report*, February 5, 2016 (www.hsdl.org/?view&did=790166), pp. 16–18 (reporting the implementation of limits on U.S. person queries).

11. Jack Goldsmith, "Three Years Later: How Snowden Helped the U.S. Intelligence Community," *Lawfare*, June 6, 2016 (www.lawfareblog.com/three-years-later-how-snowden-helped-us-intelligence-community).

12. Glenn Gerstell, "New National Security Tool Activated at Challenging Time," *Lawfare*, January 7, 2016 (www.lawfareblog.com/new-national-security-tool-activated-challenging-time). See also "Statistical Transparency Report Regarding the Use of National Security Authorities for Calendar Year 2016."

13. Matthew Jaffe, "Eric Holder Says Edward Snowden Performed a 'Public Service,'" *The Axe Files* (podcast), May 31, 2016 (www.cnn.com/2016/05/30/politics/axe-files-axelrod-eric-holder/index.html).

14. Edward Jay Epstein makes the case that Snowden was acting for the Russians in *How America Lost Its Secrets: Edward Snowden, the Man and the Theft* (New York: Alfred A. Knopf, 2017). It is a theory that some of my former col-

leagues in the intelligence community would like to believe, but the facts supporting it are thin. Charlie Savage argues that Epstein's "indulgence in speculation, his treatment of questionable claims as established facts, and his misunderstanding of surveillance combine to undermine his book's credibility." "Was Snowden a Russian Agent?," *New York Review of Books*, February 9, 2017.

15. Poitras and Greenwald, "NSA Whistleblower Edward Snowden."

16. A national security blog sponsored by the Brookings Institution has cataloged these revelations involving many programs directed at legitimate targets. "Snowden Revelations," *Lawfare* (https://lawfareblog.com/snowden-revelations).

17. Geoffrey R. Stone, "What I Told the NSA," *Huffington Post*, March 31, 2014 (www.huffingtonpost.com/geoffrey-r-stone/what-i-told-the-nsa_b_5065447 .html).

18. The Stasi's devastating impact on human dignity was captured brilliantly in *The Lives of Others*, a German film that won an Oscar in 2007. See generally John O. Koehler, *Stasi: The Untold Story of the East German Secret Police* (Boulder, Colo.: Westview Press, 1999), pp. 8–9, 20.

19. Glenn Greenwald, *No Place to Hide: Edward Snowden, the NSA, and the U.S. Surveillance State* (New York: Henry Holt, 2014), pp. 90–169. For two views on this question, see Andrew Curry, "No, the NSA Isn't Like the Stasi—and Comparing Them Is Treacherous," *Wired*, January 14, 2015 (www.wired .com/2015/01/nsa-stasi-comparison/), and Thomas Coombes, "Lessons from the Stasi," *The European*, April 1, 2015 (www.theeuropean-magazine.com/thomas-coombes/9982-the-stasi-legacy-and-its-impact-on-modern-surveillance).

20. Greenwald, *No Place to Hide*, p. 94.

21. In an interview on November 19, 2015, Hunter Walker of *Yahoo News* asked Donald Trump about the French government's response to terrorist attacks in Paris. Here is Walker's exchange with Trump on the issue of "warrantless searches":

Walker: "France declared this state of emergency, where they closed the borders, and they established some degree of warrantless searches. I know how you feel about the borders, but do you think there's some kind of state of emergency here, and do we need warrantless searches of Muslims?"

Trump: "Well, we're going to have to do things that we never did before. And some people are going to be upset about it, but I think now that everybody is feeling that security is going to rule, and certain things will be done that we never thought would happen in this country in terms of information and learning about the enemy. And so we're going to have to do certain things that were frankly unthinkable a year ago, when you look at what's happening."

Walker's next question to Trump was whether, in order to "pull off the kind of tracking we need," Trump thought "we might need to register Muslims in some type of database, or note their religion on their I.D.?" Trump replied,

"Well, we're going to have to look at a lot of things very closely. We're going to have to look at the mosques." The fact that Trump had not rejected the idea of a registry or special identification card based on religion, with its echoes of Nazi Germany, created a firestorm. Lauren Carroll, "In Context: Donald Trump's Comments on a Database of American Muslims," *PolitiFact*, November 24, 2015 (www.politifact.com/truth-o-meter/article/2015/nov/24/donald-trumps-comments-database-american-muslims/).

While Walker's story accurately described his exchange with Trump, the Trump campaign insisted that Trump's comments were being distorted. In response, Walker posted a recording of his interview on a social media site. See Hunter Walker, "The Ticket," *Yahoo Politics*, November 20, 2015 (https://theticket.tumblr.com/post/133614895582/here-is-the-excerpt-of-yahoo-news-interview-with). For Walker's original article, see "Donald Trump Has Big Plans for 'Radical Islamic' Terrorists, 2016, and 'That Communist' Bernie Sanders," November 19, 2015, *Yahoo News* (www.yahoo.com/news/donald-trump-has-big-plans-1303117537878070.html).

22. Poitras and Greenwald, "NSA Whistleblower Edward Snowden."

CHAPTER 2

1. During this critical week, a writer for *Rolling Stone* shadowed the director of the ACLU Washington office, Laura Murphy, and recounted the experience in a sympathetic article. Robert Dreyfuss, "John Ashcroft's Midnight Raid," *Rolling Stone*, November 22, 2001, p. 47.

2. For example, scattered reports of celebrations among American Muslims proved completely unfounded (although there were a few celebrations in foreign countries). Serge F. Kovaleski and Fredrick Kunkle, "Northern New Jersey Draws Probers' Eyes," *Washington Post*, September 18, 2001. In the 2016 election campaign, Donald Trump claimed without evidence that he had witnessed the cheering personally. Glenn Kessler, "Fact Checker: Trump's Outrageous Claim That 'Thousands' of New Jersey Muslims Celebrated the 9/11 Attacks," *Washington Post*, November 22, 2015.

3. Philip Shenon and Neil A. Lewis, "A Nation Challenged: Safety and Liberty; Groups Fault Plan to Listen, Search and Seize," *New York Times*, September 21, 2001; ACLU Media Advisory, "In Defense of Freedom: Broad New Coalition Calls for Reasoned Debate to Protect National Security and Crucial American Freedoms," September 19, 2001 (www.aclu.org/news/broad-new-coalition-calls-reasoned-debate-protect-national-security-and-crucial-american).

4. *Final Report of the Senate Select Committee to Study Governmental Operations with Respect to Intelligence Activities,* Senate Report No. 94-755 (Government Printing Office, 1976) ("Church Committee report"), book 3, p. 324.

5. David S. Kris and J. Douglas Wilson, *National Security Investigations and Prosecutions,* 2nd ed. (Eagan, Minn.: West, 2012), vol. 1, §§ 3.6–3.9, pp. 102–13.

6. This provision replaced the word "the" in a part of the Foreign Intelligence Surveillance Act governing orders to intercept communications. It requires the government to attest that "the purpose of the surveillance" is collecting foreign intelligence. After the Patriot Act was passed, the government would only be required to say that collecting foreign intelligence was "a significant purpose." See Uniting and Strengthening America By Providing Appropriate Tools Required to Intercept and Obstruct Terrorism Act (USA PATRIOT Act) of 2001, at § 218, Pub. L. No. 107-56, 115 Stat. 252 (October 26, 2001). The Foreign Intelligence Surveillance Court of Review later said that both the lower federal courts and the Justice Department had been too restrictive in their interpretation of the law, even before the Patriot Act. See *In re Sealed Case*, 310 F.3d 717 (2002).

7. Patriot Act § 215, amending 50 U.S.C. §§ 1861–63. The original business records provision, enacted only three years earlier, was a narrow one. It applied only to records belonging to "a common carrier, public accommodation facility, physical storage facility, or vehicle rental facility." It required "specific and articulable facts giving reason to believe that the person to whom the records pertain is a foreign power or an agent of a foreign power." See Intelligence Authorization Act for Fiscal Year 1999 at § 602, Pub. L. No. 105-272, 112 Stat. 2396 (October 20, 1998), adding a new Title V to the Foreign Intelligence Surveillance Act of 1978, codified at 50 U.S.C. §§ 1861–63.

8. Senate Roll Call Vote No. 302, *Congressional Record* S10604 (daily ed. October 11, 2001).

9. House Roll Call Vote No. 386, *Congressional Record* H6775–76 (daily ed. October 12, 2001).

10. House Roll Call Vote No. 398, *Congressional Record* H7224 (daily ed. October 24, 2001).

11. Patriot Act § 224 (providing that certain provisions expire on December 31, 2005).

12. That letter remains on the ACLU website: "Letter to the House Urging Them to Vote 'No' on the Patriot Act" (www.aclu.org/letter/letter-house-urging-them-vote-no-patriot-act). Although the letter does not mention section 215, the provision did not go completely unnoticed. It is included in a detailed chart that was part of the ACLU's lobbying efforts and that was updated after the law passed. "Surveillance Powers: A Chart" (www.aclu.org/other/surveillance-powers-chart).

13. Indeed, the term "tangible things" includes things that are not tangible while excluding some things that are. It is a curious legal anomaly that data count as a "tangible thing" while clearly physical items, including contraband fish, do not. See *Yates v. United States*, 135 S. Ct. 1074 (2015). See also Timothy Edgar, "Fishing Expedition," *Lawfare*, February 27, 2015 (www.lawfareblog.com/fishing-expedition).

14. Robert D. McFadden, "F.B.I. in New York Asks Librarians' Aid in Reporting on Spies," *New York Times*, September 18, 1987. See also Herbert N.

Foerstel, *Surveillance in the Stacks: The FBI's Library Awareness Program* (New York: Greenwood Press, 1991), pp. 28, 133–50.

15. For example, a resolution adopted by a major library association in California includes this language. See Librarians Association of the University of California, "Resolution on the USA PATRIOT Act, the Homeland Security Act, and Related Measures That Infringe on the Rights of Library Users," May 30, 2003 (www.ala.org/offices/oif/ifissues/issuesrelatedlinks/usapatriotact).

16. *Department of Justice Oversight: Preserving Our Freedoms While Defending against Terrorisms: Hearings Before the Senate Committee on the Judiciary*, 107th Cong., 1st sess. (December 6, 2001) (testimony of Attorney General John Ashcroft).

17. John Ashcroft, "Memorandum for Director Robert S. Mueller," September 18, 2003; Dan Eggan, "Patriot Act Claims Dismissed: Government Has Not Tracked Bookstore or Library Activity, Ashcroft Says," *Washington Post*, September 19, 2003.

18. *USA PATRIOT Act: Hearing Before the Select Committee on Intelligence of the United States Senate*, S. Hrg. 109-341, 109th Cong., 1st sess. (April 19 and 27 and May 24, 2005) (prepared statement of Attorney General Alberto Gonzales and FBI Director Robert Mueller), p. 90.

19. The relevant language in the version of the Patriot Act passed in 2001 said that an order for business records or other tangible things

> "shall specify that the records concerned are sought for an authorized investigation conducted in accordance with subsection (a)(2) to obtain foreign intelligence information not concerning a United States person or to protect against international terrorism or clandestine intelligence activities."

USA PATRIOT Act § 215, codified at 50 U.S.C. 1861(b)(2).

20. *Illinois v. Gates*, 462 U.S. 213, 238-39 (1983) (probable cause); *United States v. R. Enterprises*, 498 U.S. 292, 300 (1991) (relevance). In *Terry v. Ohio*, 392 U.S. 1 (1968), the Supreme Court upheld the constitutionality of such a stop and frisk, based on a police officer's "specific reasonable inferences which he is entitled to draw from the facts in light of his experience" (p. 28).

21. Although Kate Martin did not remember the details of this specific conversation when I discussed it with her for this book, she remembered the issue. In testimony on the Total Information Awareness program before a public hearing of the House Intelligence Committee in 2003, she explained, "Oversight of the implementation of the Patriot Act is crucial" and called for the government to make public information about its plans for "data-mining and the creation of linked databases." Statement of Kate Martin, Director, Center for National Security Studies, before the House Permanent Select Committee on Intelligence, "Securing Freedom and the Nation: Collecting Intelligence Under the Law," April 9, 2003 (http://cnss.org/data/files/CongrTestimony/Martin_Testimony_House_Intel_-_Securing_Freedom_and_the_Nation_-_2003.pdf), pp. 5–6.

22. Congress suspended the program in January 2003 with the adoption of the Wyden amendment. See Adam Clymer, "Senate Rejects Privacy Project," *New York Times*, January 24, 2003. It was later defunded permanently. See Department of Defense Appropriations Act, 2004, Pub. L. No. 108–87, § 8131, 117 Stat. 1054, 1102 (2003). Years later, however, officials would not give an answer to Wyden's questions about whether parts of the program had been going on inside a classified research office. See Shane Harris, "TIA Lives On," *National Journal*, February 23, 2006; "Total Information Awareness Lives On inside the National Security Agency," *Democracy Now!*, February 27, 2006 (www.democracynow.org/2006/2/27/total_information_awareness_lives_on_inside).

23. The new language required an order under section 215 to include

"a statement of facts showing that there are reasonable grounds to believe that the tangible things sought are relevant to an authorized investigation (other than a threat assessment) conducted in accordance with subsection (a)(2) to obtain foreign intelligence information not concerning a United States person or to protect against international terrorism or clandestine intelligence activities, such things being presumptively relevant to an authorized investigation if the applicant shows in the statement of the facts that they pertain to–

"(i) a foreign power or an agent of a foreign power;

"(ii) the activities of a suspected agent of a foreign power who is the subject of such authorized investigation; or

"(iii) an individual in contact with, or known to, a suspected agent of a foreign power who is the subject of such authorized investigation. . . ."

USA PATRIOT Improvement and Reauthorization Act of 2005, Pub. L. No. 109-177, 120 Stat. 192 (March 9, 2006), at § 106, amending 50 U.S.C. § 1861(b)(2).

CHAPTER 3

1. *9/11 Commission Recommendations: Counterterrorism Analysis and Collection: The Requirement for Imagination and Creativity: Hearings Before the Permanent Select Committee on Intelligence,* 108th Cong., 2nd sess. (August 4, 2004) (statement of ACLU, testimony of Timothy H. Edgar, Legislative Counsel) (www.globalsecurity.org/intell/library/congress/2004_hr/040804-edgar.pdf). A video of the hearing is available at www.c-span.org/video/?182996-2/september-11-commission-report-afternoon (Edgar testimony begins at 11:39).

2. National Security Act of 1947, at § 103D, as amended by the Intelligence Reform and Terrorism Prevention Act of 2004, at § 1014, Pub. L. No. 108-458 118 Stat. 3638 (December 17, 2004), codified at 50 U.S.C. § 403-3d.

3. James Risen and Eric Lichtblau, "Bush Lets U.S. Spy on Callers without Courts," *New York Times*, December 16, 2005, p. A1.

4. Details about this program, including who had been granted clearance to review it, remained highly classified for many years. As discussed in chapter 4, Congress later mandated that the inspectors general of the agencies involved conduct an investigation of the program, which was completed in 2009. In 2015 the government declassified and released a redacted version of the joint report of all the agency inspectors general. "Joint IG Report of the PSP," *IC on the Record,* April 25, 2015 (https://icontherecord.tumblr.com/post/117330907753/the-department-of-justice-releases-inspectors).

The report of the inspector general of the Office of the Director of National Intelligence reveals that the general counsel for the ODNI was granted access to the program in January 2006, only after it was leaked, and that Alex Joel, the civil liberties protection officer, was not granted access until much later, in October 2006. The ODNI report is contained in "Annex to the Report on the President's Surveillance Program," vol. 2, pt. 3, July 10, 2009 (www.dni.gov/files/documents/424/2009 Joint IG Report on the PSP_Annex Vol. II-C.pdf). The report's discussion of program access is on p. 229 of volume 2 (p. 73 of the PDF file).

5. Jodie Tillman, "Ex-USF Professor Sami al-Arian Deported to Turkey," *Tampa Bay Times,* February 5, 2015.

6. "Declassified UKUSA Signals Intelligence Agreement Documents Available," NSA press release, June 24, 2010 (www.nsa.gov/news-features/press-room/press-releases/2010/ukusa.shtml).

7. "National Security Council Intelligence Directive No. 9," March 10, 1950, in *Foreign Relations of the United States, 1945–1950: Emergence of the Intelligence Establishment,* edited by C. Thomas Thorne and David S. Patterson (Government Printing Office, 1996), pp. 1124–35.

8. *Final Report of the Senate Select Committee to Study Governmental Operations with Respect to Intelligence Activities,* Senate Report No. 94-755 (Government Printing Office, 1976) ("Church Committee report"), book 3, p. 765.

9. Ed Pilkington, "Declassified NSA Files Show Agency Spied on Muhammad Ali and MLK," *The Guardian,* September 26, 2013; Matthew M. Aid and William Burr, "Secret Cold War Documents Reveal NSA Spied on Senators," *Foreign Policy* (September 25, 2013). For the declassified history that discussed some Minaret targets, see William Burr and Matthew M. Aid, "'Disreputable If Not Downright Illegal,'" *National Security Archive Electronic Brief Book No. 441,* September 25, 2015 (http://nsarchive.gwu.edu/NSAEBB/NSAEBB441/).

10. Sec. 101(f) of FISA, 50 U.S.C. § 1801(f).

11. Senate Report No. 95-604—Part 1, p. 34, reprinted in *United States Code Congressional and Administrative News* 4 (1978–30), p. 3935.

12. Even with a careful reading of FISA's definition of "electronic surveillance" in section 101(f), this point is not immediately apparent. Paragraph (f)(2) brings within FISA "the acquisition by an electronic, mechanical, or other surveillance device of the contents of any wire communication to or from a person in the United States, without the consent of any party thereto, if such acquisition

occurs in the United States," which would seem to exclude foreign-to-foreign communications. However, because there is no intent required in paragraph (f) (2)—in sharp contrast to paragraphs (1) and (3)—the government may acquire communications from a wire inside the United States only if it is confident the data it acquires are merely passing through U.S. territory. Modern forms of communication, especially over the internet, make it difficult for the government to know in advance of collection that all parties to a communication are foreigners outside the United States. For an excellent discussion of the overall issue, see Charlie Savage, *Power Wars: Inside Obama's Post-9/11 Presidency* (New York: Hachette Book Group, 2015), pp. 170–77.

13. After Executive Order 12,333 was issued in 1981, a young lawyer in the Reagan Justice Department, Theodore Olson, wrote what Senator Dianne Feinstein of California has described as a "seminal" legal opinion governing collection activities under the order. Senate Judiciary Committee, "Attorney General Nomination," January 28, 2015 (www.judiciary.senate.gov/meetings/attorney-general-nomination).

Olson later became a star among conservative lawyers. He argued the case for Bush in the Supreme Court concerning the disputed 2000 election and championed the cause of marriage equality. Tragically, Olson's wife died in the 9/11 attacks; she had been a passenger on American Airlines Flight 77, which hijackers crashed into the Pentagon.

14. In 2013 several versions of USSID 18 were released along with other NSA training materials, although this was not the first time these rules had been released. The key provisions have remained reasonably constant. "DNI Clapper Declassifies Additional Intelligence Community Documents Regarding Collection under Section 501 of the Foreign Intelligence Surveillance Act," *IC on the Record,* November 18, 2013 (https://icontherecord.tumblr.com/post/674199639 49/dni-clapper-declassifies-additional-intelligence).

15. USSID 18 at § 7.2(c) (January 25, 2011, version).

16. Orin Kerr, "The Surprisingly Weak Reasoning of Mohamud," *Lawfare,* December 23, 2016 (www.lawfareblog.com/surprisingly-weak-reasoning-moha mud). For a broader discussion, see Orin Kerr, "The Fourth Amendment and the Global Internet," *Stanford Law Review* 67 (2015), p. 285.

17. "Joint IG Report of the PSP," vol. 1, pp. 7–10, 16–21 (pp. 17–20, 26–31 of the PDF).

18. Leslie Cauley, "NSA Has Massive Database of Americans' Phone Calls," *USA Today,* May 22, 2006.

19. The only amendment to section 101(f) of FISA made during this period was a minor amendment to (f)(2) in the Patriot Act to harmonize the treatment of computer trespassers under FISA with their treatment under criminal wiretap laws. See 50 U.S.C. § 1801 note; USA PATRIOT Act, § 1003. For an excellent discussion of the e-mail issue, see David S. Kris and J. Douglas Wilson, *National Security Investigations and Prosecutions,* 2nd ed. (Eagan, Minn.: West 2012), vol. 1, § 16.6, pp. 560–65.

20. See, for example, Michael Chertoff, "NSA Surveillance Vital to Our Safety," *USA Today,* September 11, 2013.

21. Savage, *Power Wars,* pp. 182–83; Charlie Savage, *Takeover: The Return of the Imperial Presidency and the Subversion of American Democracy* (New York: Little, Brown, 2007), pp. 36–37.

22. "Joint IG Report of the PSP," vol. 1, pp. 6–21 (pp. 16–31 of the PDF).

23. Ibid., vol. 1, p. 14 (p. 24 of the PDF).

24. After the program leaked, the Justice Department issued a public memorandum arguing that Congress's authorization for the use of military force after 9/11 provided authority to ignore FISA if necessary to gather intelligence on the enemy. Department of Justice, "Legal Authorities Supporting the Activities of the National Security Agency Described by the President," January 19, 2006 (www.justice.gov/archive/opa/docs/whitepaperonnsalegalauthorities.pdf)

25. Charlie Savage offers the best account of this episode. Savage, *Power Wars,* pp. 190–94.

26. "Obama's FBI Pick: James Comey, Challenged Wiretapping by Bush White House," Associated Press, June 21, 2013. The vote was 93-1. *Congressional Record* S5997–6004 (daily ed. July 29, 2013).

27. "Senate Hearing on U.S. Attorney Firings" (transcript, part 2), *Washington Post,* May 15, 2007.

28. Jack Goldsmith, *The Terror Presidency: Law and Judgement Inside the Bush Administration* (New York: W. W. Norton, 2007), p. 181.

29. These cases involving bulk collection of metadata are discussed in more detail in chapter 4.

30. As a legal matter, the FISA court accomplished this by approving a single order for collection under title I of FISA based on a general finding of probable cause, and then requiring the NSA to apply individual probable cause determinations to its targeting decisions as part of the minimization procedures it used for this collection, which the court described as the "minimization probable cause standard." As probable cause is normally relevant to the initial acquisition of a communication and not to the handling of the information acquired, this was a highly unorthodox legal theory. Judge Malcolm Howard's January 10, 2007, "foreign order" was released in 2014. "The Department of Justice Releases Additional Documents," *IC on the Record,* December 12, 2014 (https://icontherecord.tumblr.com/post/105032620703/the-department-of-justice-releases-additional).

31. See Judge Roger Vinson's order and memorandum opinion of April 3, 2007, in "The Department of Justice Releases Additional Documents," pp. 14, 19–20. The government had described the FISA court's bulk collection theory as "ground breaking and innovative" in an earlier filing. Memorandum of Law in Support of Application for Certain Tangible Things for Investigations to Protect against International Terrorism, No. BR 06-05 (F.I.S.C. May 23, 2006), at p. 3.

32. "Joint IG Report of the PSP," vol. 1, p. 59 (p. 69 of the PDF).

33. Kris and Wilson, *National Security Investigations*, §§ 11:2–11:11, pp. 391–416.

34. The reporter decided to publish the interview in full. Chris Roberts, "Transcript: Debate on the Foreign Intelligence Surveillance Act," *El Paso Times*, August 22, 2007. It is no longer available from the newspaper's website, but the Electronic Frontier Foundation, a civil liberties organization, has archived a copy on its website (www.eff.org/files/filenode/att/elpasotimesmccon nelltranscript.pdf).

35. Roberts, "Transcript."

36. Greg Miller, "Spy Chief's Disclosures Stun Congress," *Los Angeles Times*, August 24, 2007.

37. The way Alex and I approached assessments under the Protect America Act was described in a letter we sent to the House Permanent Select Committee on Intelligence shortly after they began. The letter was released following a Freedom of Information Act request from the Electronic Frontier Foundation. Letter from Alex Joel to Rep. Silvestre Reyes, September 17, 2007, p. 42 of the PDF (www.dni.gov/files/documents/FOIA/EFF - FOIA.pdf).

38. USSID 18 § 1.1 (2011), in "DNI Clapper Declassifies Additional Intelligence Community Documents Regarding Collection under Section 501 of the Foreign Intelligence Surveillance Act."

CHAPTER 4

1. James Bamford, "The Most Wanted Man in the World," *Wired*, June 13, 2014 (www.wired.com/2014/08/edward-snowden/#ch-1).

2. Charlie Savage, *Power Wars: Inside Obama's Post-9/11 Presidency* (New York: Little, Brown, 2015), pp. 50–55.

3. "The Department of Justice Releases Inspectors General Reports Concerning Collection Activities Authorized by President George W. Bush after the Attacks of September 11, 2001," *IC on the Record*, April 25, 2015 (https://icontherecord.tumblr.com/post/117330907753/the-department-of-justice-releases-inspectors).

4. Protect America Act of 2007, Pub. L. No. 110-55, 121 Stat. 552 at § 2, adding a new section 105A to the Foreign Intelligence Act of 1978, codified at 50 U.S.C. § 1805a (repealed by the FISA Amendments Act of 2008).

5. *Congressional Record* H1748 (daily ed. March 14, 2008).

6. Barack Obama, "My Position on FISA," *Huffington Post*, July 11, 2008 (www.huffingtonpost.com/barack-obama/my-position-on-fisa_b_110789.html). In fact, Congress's intent in the 1978 law to make FISA exclusive had always been clear, not only from the text but also from the legislative history. The Senate report on the bill refers to a landmark case on separation of powers in which the Supreme Court had rejected President Truman's order to seize steel-manufacturing facilities without statutory authority during the Korean War. The reference to Justice Jackson's famous concurring opinion in that case makes clear that Congress intended to use all of its power under the Constitution to

forbid the president from acting unilaterally—as Bush did with Stellar Wind. Senate Report No. 95-604, Part 1 (November 1977), p. 16 n. 28, in *United States Code Congressional and Administrative News* 4 (1978-30), pp. 3917–18 (citing *Youngstown Sheet & Tube Co. v. Sawyer*, 343 U.S. 579 (1952)).

7. Ryan Lizza, "State of Deception: Why Won't the President Rein in the Intelligence Community?," *New Yorker*, December 16, 2013.

8. White House, "Remarks by the President on Securing Our Nation's Cyber Infrastructure," news release, May 29, 2009 (https://obamawhitehouse.archives .gov/the-press-office/remarks-president-securing-our-nations-cyber-infrastruc ture)

9. Much of the discussion below is based on documents released through *IC on the Record*, including opinions of the FISA court. While I had heard of the NSA's compliance problems from John DeLong and others, I was not involved in these proceedings.

10. Memorandum Opinion (Foreign Intelligence Surveillance Court, October 3, 2011) (Judge Bates), pp. 2, 48, in "DNI Declassifies Intelligence Community Documents Regarding Collection under Section 702," *IC on the Record*, August 21, 2013 (updated July 16, 2014) (https://icontherecord.tumblr.com/ post/58944252298/dni-declassifies-intelligence-community-documents).

11. In his October 2011 opinion, Judge Bates warned the government that its "revelations regarding the scope of NSA's upstream collection implicate 50 U.S.C. § 1809(a), which makes it a crime" to engage intentionally in unlawful surveillance or to disclose or use the fruits of unlawful surveillance. Bates Memorandum Opinion (October 2011), p. 17 n. 15.

In a separate opinion involving bulk collection of internet metadata, Judge Bates returned to this theme in a lengthy analysis of whether the NSA could use data it had already collected by mistake as part of its bulk metadata program, even though the data might include content. Judge Bates concluded that the NSA could not, because the intentional use of such data would be a criminal offense. Memorandum Opinion (Foreign Intelligence Surveillance Court, PR/TT 2 [date redacted]), pp. 100–16, in "DNI Clapper Declassifies Additional Intelligence Community Documents Regarding Collection under Section 501 of the Foreign Intelligence Surveillance Act," *IC on the Record*, November 18, 2013 (https:// icontherecord.tumblr.com/post/67419963949/dni-clapper-declassifies- additional-intelligence).

12. These problems with "upstream collection" are discussed at length in Judge Bates's October 2011 Memorandum Opinion, cited in note 10. The NSA failed to live up to the restrictions imposed by the FISA court. NSA analysts continued to query "upstream collection" data for information about U.S. persons, even though the court had prohibited the NSA from doing this. In April 2017 the NSA announced that as a result of these compliance problems, the agency had decided to end "about" collection altogether. Charlie Savage, "N.S.A. Halts Collection of Americans' Emails About Foreign Targets," *New York Times*, April 28, 2017.

13. *In re Production of Tangible Things from [Redacted]* (Foreign Intelli-

gence Surveillance Court, January 28, 2009) (Judge Walton), p. 4, in "DNI Clapper Declassifies Intelligence Community Documents Regarding Collection under Section 501 of the Foreign Intelligence Surveillance Act," *IC on the Record*, September 10, 2013 (https://icontherecord.tumblr.com/post/608675 60465/dni-clapper-declassifies-intelligence-community).

14. Memorandum Opinion (Foreign Intelligence Surveillance Court, PR/TT 2) (Judge Bates), p. 11 n. 13.

15. This often frustrating but essential process is outlined in Presidential Policy Directive 1 (PPD-1), "Organization of the National Security Council System," February 13, 2009. See also Alan G. Whittaker and others, *The National Security Policy Process: The National Security Council and the Interagency System* (Washington: National Defense University, 2011).

16. Lanny Davis, "Why I Resigned from the President's Privacy and Civil Liberties Oversight Board—and Where We Go from Here," *The Hill*, May 18, 2007.

17. This story is best told in a blog post written by a former ACLU colleague. Jay Stanley, "Small but Significant Privacy Oversight Institution Almost a Reality after a Pathetic Story of Delay," *ACLU Free Future Blog*, February 28, 2013 (www.aclu.org/blog/small-significant-privacy-oversight-institution-almost-reality-after-pathetic-story-delay).

18. Gregory J. Millman, "Compliance in Government: Q&A with John DeLong of the NSA," *Wall Street Journal*, January 23, 2014.

19. Barton Gellman, "NSA Broke Privacy Rules Thousands of Times per Year, Audit Finds," *Washington Post*, August 15, 2013.

20. Semiannual Assessment of Compliance for FISA § 702, June 1, 2012–November 30, 2012 reporting period (August 2013), pp. 7, 23.

21. About a year after the Snowden revelations began, a former Obama administration official argued in an op-ed that "Americans should be even more concerned about the collection and storage of their communications under Executive Order 12333" than they should be about the programs governed by the Foreign Intelligence Surveillance Court that were consuming more attention. John Napier Tye, "Meet Executive Order 12333: The Reagan Rule That Lets the NSA Spy on Americans," *Washington Post*, July 18, 2014.

22. Executive Order 12,333 § 1.1, *Federal Register* 40, no. 235 (December 8, 1981), as amended by Executive Order 13,470, *Federal Register* 73, no. 150 (July 30, 2008).

23. "Letter to Senator Charles E. Grassley from NSA Office of the Inspector General, dated September 11, 2013" (www.grassley.senate.gov/news/news-releases/nsa-inspector-general-responds-grassley-about-intentional-surveillance-americans).

24. Julian Hattem, "Google Chief on NSA: 'We're Going to End Up Breaking the Internet,'" *The Hill*, October 8, 2014.

25. *United States v. Verdugo-Urquidez*, 494 U.S. 259 (1989).

26. Amended Memorandum Opinion, *In re Application of the Federal Bureau of Investigation for an Order Requiring the Production of Tangible Things From*

[Redacted] (Foreign Intelligence Surveillance Court, July 19, 2013) (Judge Eagan), pp. 8–9, 17 n. 19 (discussing *Smith v. Maryland*, 442 U.S. 735 [1979]) (www.fisc. uscourts.gov/public-filings/amended-memorandum-opinion-and-primary-order). Judge Eagan's opinion was issued in July 2013. Surprisingly, the court did not analyze the constitutional issues involved in bulk collection of telephone metadata at the time the court approved the program in 2006. The court did so only after the telephone records program was leaked in 2013. However, Eagan cites the opinion issued by Judge Kollar-Kotelly many years earlier approving the collection of internet metadata, which takes the identical position. See Eagan opinion at 8, quoting Opinion and Order (Foreign Intelligence Surveillance Court, PR/TT 1 [date redacted]), pp. 62–63.

27. Lee Ferran, "Ex-NSA Chief: 'We Kill People Based on Metadata,'" *ABC News*, May 12, 2014 (http://abcnews.go.com/blogs/headlines/2014/05/ex-nsa-chief-we-kill-people-based-on-metadata/).

CHAPTER 5

1. Information Security Oversight Office (ISOO), National Archives and Records Administration, *2013 Report to the President*, June 2, 2014 (www .archives.gov/isoo/reports/annual-report-archive.html), pp. 4, 6.

2. *Report of the Commission on Protecting and Reducing Government Secrecy*, S. Doc. 105-2 (Government Printing Office, 1999), p. xxi.

3. ISOO, *2013 Report to the President*, p. 6.

4. *Office of the Director of National Intelligence Classification Guide, Version 2.1* ("*ODNI Guide*"), September 30, 2014 (approved for release March 3, 2016) (www.fas.org/sgp/othergov/intel/odni-cg.pdf). See also Steven Aftergood, "ODNI Classification Guide Released," *Secrecy News*, March 23, 2016 (fas. org/blogs/secrecy/2016/03/odni-class-guide/).

5. *ODNI Guide*, p. 27; Executive Order 13,526, at § 1.2 (December 29, 2009), *Federal Register* 75, no. 2 (January 5, 2010), p. 707; Executive Order 12,958 at § 1.3 (April 17, 1995), *Federal Register* 60, no. 76 (April 20, 1995), p. 19825.

6. "Exclusive: President Barack Obama on 'Fox News Sunday'" (transcript), Fox News, April 10, 2016 (www.foxnews.com/transcript/2016/04/10/exclusive-president-barack-obama-on-fox-news-sunday/).

7. *Department of State Classification Guide (DSCG 05-01)* (January 2005) (www.fas.org/sgp/othergov/dos-class.pdf), pp. 7–8, 14.

8. Michael Kinsley, "Gaffes to the Rescue," *Time*, February 8, 2007.

9. House Judiciary Committee, *Hearing on the Espionage Act and the Legal and Constitutional Implications of WikiLeaks* (December 16, 2010) (statement of Thomas Blanton, Director, National Security Archive, George Washington University) (http://nsarchive.gwu.edu/news/20101216/Blanton101216.pdf), pp. 8–10.

10. Glenn Greenwald, "NSA Collecting Phone Records of Millions of Verizon Customers Daily," *The Guardian*, June 6, 2013.

11. "DNI Statement on Recent Unauthorized Disclosures of Classified Information," *IC on the Record*, June 6, 2013 (https://icontherecord.tumblr.com/post/57722853436/dni-statement-on-recent-unauthorized-disclosures).

12. "Secret Spying: From Critic to Supporter," *CNN's Amanpour* (video), June 18, 2013 (http://amanpour.blogs.cnn.com/2013/06/18/secret-spying-from-critic-to-supporter/).

13. Senate Hearing 113-89, *Current and Projected National Security Threats to the United States: Hearing Before the Senate Select Committee on Intelligence* (March 12, 2013). See also Glenn Kessler, "James Clapper's 'Least Untruthful' Statement to the Senate," *Washington Post,* June 12, 2013.

14. Snowden said this in an interview with a German public radio station. "Snowden-Interview: Transcript," Norddeutscher Rundfunk, January 26, 2014 (www.ndr.de/nachrichten/netzwelt/snowden277_page-2.html).

15. Kessler, "James Clapper's 'Least Untruthful' Statement."

16. Matt Welch and Todd Krainin, "Rand Paul: 'I'd Put Clapper and Snowden in the Same Jail Cell,'" *Reason*, June 4, 2015 (http://reason.com/reasontv/2015/06/04/rand-paul-on-edward-snowden).

17. Kim Zetter, "NSA Chief Tells Hackers His Agency Doesn't Create Dossiers on All Americans," *Wired*, July 27, 2012 (www.wired.com/2012/07/nsa-chief-denies-dossiers/).

18. National Security Act of 1947 § 102A(i)(1), 50 U.S.C. § 403-1(i)(1). This duty was given to the director of central intelligence by Congress when the modern intelligence community was created. When Congress passed the Intelligence Reform and Terrorism Prevention Act of 2004, this responsibility was transferred to the director of national intelligence.

19. Senate Hearing 113-89.

20. "The National Security Agency and Fourth Amendment Rights, October 29 and November 6, 1975," *Hearings before the Select Committee to Study Governmental Operations with Respect to Intelligence Activities of the United States Senate* (Government Printing Office, 1976), vol. 5, p. 3.

21. *Harriet Ann Phillippi v. Central Intelligence Agency*, 546 F.2d 1009 (D.C. Cir. 1976).

22. Julia Barton, "Confirmed: The CIA's Most Famous Ship Headed for the Scrapyard," *PRI's The World,* September 7, 2015 (www.pri.org/stories/2015-09-07/ship-built-cias-most-audacious-cold-war-mission-now-headed-scrapyard).

23. House Judiciary Committee, *The Administration's Use of FISA Authorities*, Hearing No. 113-35 (Government Printing Office, July 17, 2013), p. 14. See also Charlie Savage, *Power Wars: Inside Obama's Post-9/11 Presidency* (New York: Little, Brown, 2015), p. 168.

24. See Bill Chappell, "Snowden Is a Whistle-Blower, Americans Say in Poll," *The Two-Way* (blog), National Public Radio, July 10, 2013 (www.npr.org/blogs/thetwo-way/2013/07/10/200878660/snowden-is-a-whistle-blower-americans-say-in-poll). Public opinion may have shifted on Snowden among Americans, but he remains popular overseas. Steven Nelson, "Edward Snowden Unpopular at Home, a Hero Abroad, Poll Finds," *U.S. News and World Report*,

April 21, 2015 (www.usnews.com/news/articles/2015/04/21/edward-snowden-unpopular-at-home-a-hero-abroad-poll-finds).

25. Andres Jauregui, "Yes We Scan: Shepard Fairey Likes Obama NSA Parodies, 'Pleased' with Subversive Symbolism," *Huffington Post,* June 23, 2013 (www.huffingtonpost.com/2013/06/28/yes-we-scan-shepard-fairey-obama-nsa_n_3517213.html).

26. Timothy H. Edgar, "Big Transparency for the NSA," *Wall Street Journal,* August 2, 2013.

27. Timothy H. Edgar, "The Good News about Spying: Obama, the NSA, and the Future of Intelligence," *Foreign Affairs* (April 13, 2015).

28. David Kravets, "Administration Cites State Secrets in Bid to Derail Spy Lawsuit," Associated Press, May 12, 2006.

29. *Jewel v. National Security Agency,* No. C 08-04373 JSW (N.D. Cal. July 8, 2013), at 10 (quoting *Al-Haramain v. Obama,* 507 F.3d at 1200).

30. *New York Times v. United States Dep't of Justice,* 752 F.3d 123, 140–41 (2d Cir. 2014). See also David McCraw, "FOIA Litigation Has Its Own Rules, But We Deserve Better," *Just Security,* March 15, 2016 (www.justsecurity.org/29974/foia-litigation-rules-deserve).

31. John Perry Barlow, "Decrypting the Puzzle Palace," *Communications of the ACM* 35, no. 7 (1992), p. 25.

32. Victor Marchetti and John D. Marks, *The CIA and the Cult of Intelligence,* with an introduction by Melvin Wulf (New York: Alfred A. Knopf, 1974), p. xxvi.

33. *United States v. Marchetti,* 466 F.2d at 1309, 1318 (4th Cir. 1972).

34. David E. Pozen, "Note: The Mosaic Theory, National Security, and the Freedom of Information Act," *Yale Law Journal* 115 (2005), pp. 638–39.

35. *New York Times Co. v. United States,* 403 U.S. 713, 729 (1971) (Stewart, J., concurring).

36. Steven Aftergood, Federation of American Scientists, "ODNI Rethinks Secrecy and Openness in Intelligence," *Secrecy News* (blog), FAS.com, March 20, 2014 (fas.org/blogs/secrecy/2014/03/litt-transparency/); "Snowden's Leaks Lead to More Disclosure from Feds," *NPR Morning Edition,* October 11, 2013 (www.npr.org/2013/10/11/231899987/snowdens-leaks-lead-to-more-disclosure-from-feds).

37. Foreign Intelligence Surveillance Act of 1978, as enacted, Pub. L. No. 95-511 at §§ 107, 108, 92 Stat. 1783, 1795–96 (1978). The annual reports to Congress from 1979 to 2014, and other information included in declassified opinions, are collected by the Federation of American Scientists (fas.org/irp/agency/doj/fisa/).

38. A simple comparison of the reports from the Justice Department, which continue to be released as required by law, and the more detailed transparency reports of the ODNI shows just how much has changed. Letter to Chairman Charles Grassley et al. from Peter J. Kadzik, assistant attorney general, April 20, 2015 (fas.org/irp/agency/doj/fisa/2014rept.pdf); ODNI Calendar Year 2014 Transparency Report, "Statistical Transparency Report Regarding Use of Na-

Notes to Pages 88–91   245

tional Security Authorities," *IC on the Record,* April 22, 2015 (icontherecord. tumblr.com/transparency/odni_transparencyreport_cy2014).

39. Jack Goldsmith, "Why President Obama Won't, and Shouldn't, Pardon Snowden," *Lawfare,* September 16, 2016 (www.lawfareblog.com/why-presi dent-obama-wont-and-shouldnt-pardon-snowden).

40. Sara Sorcher, "Insiders: The Value of Snowden's Disclosures Was Not Worth National Security Damage," *National Journal,* February 6, 2014 (www. nationaljournal.com/defense/2014/02/06/insiders-value-snowdens-disclosures-was-not-worth-national-security-damage).

41. A website sponsored by the Canadian Journalists for Free Expression with support from the University of Toronto and Queen's University maintains an archive of all the Snowden documents ever published. On March 23, 2017, the archive listed 1,182 documents, the most recent of which had been published on August 19, 2016. See "The Snowden Archive," CJFE.org (www.cjfe.org/ snowden). See also David Ignatius, "Edward Snowden Took Less Than Previously Thought, Says James Clapper," *Washington Post,* June 5, 2014.

42. "Reporter: Snowden Is 'the Classically Responsible Whistleblower,'" *The Lead with Jake Tapper* (blog), CNN.com, July 15, 2013 (thelead.blogs.cnn.com /2013/07/15/reporter-snowden-is-the-classically-responsible-whistleblower/).

43. David Meyer, "Edward Snowden Is Not Down with WikiLeaks' Methods," *Fortune,* July 29, 2016 (http://fortune.com/2016/07/29/snowden-criti cizes-wikileaks-clinton/).

44. "Last Week Tonight with John Oliver: Government Surveillance," *HBO* (video), April 5, 2015 (www.youtube.com/watch?v=XEVlyP4_11M).

45. Bruce Schneier, "China and Russia Almost Definitely Have the Snowden Docs," *Wired,* June 16, 2015 (www.wired.com/2015/06/course-china-russia-snowden-documents/); James Risen, "Snowden Says He Took No Secret Files to Russia," *New York Times,* October 17, 2013.

46. Shane Harris, "Congressmen Reveal Secret Report's Findings to Discredit Snowden," *Foreign Policy* (January 9, 2014) (foreignpolicy.com/2014/01/ 09/congressmen-reveal-secret-reports-findings-to-discredit-snowden/).

47. Jason Leopold, "Office Reports on the Damage Caused by Edward Snowden's Leaks Are Totally Redacted," *Vice News,* February 25, 2015 (news. vice.com/article/official-reports-on-the-damage-caused-by-edward-snowdens-leaks-are-totally-redacted).

48. House Permanent Select Committee on Intelligence, "Review of the Unauthorized Disclosures of Former National Security Agency Contractor Edward Snowden," September 15, 2016 (http://intelligence.house.gov/news/document single.aspx?DocumentID=743). The full report was released on December 22, 2016. Journalist Bart Gellman responded to an earlier summary report, pointing out a number of inaccuracies. Barton Gellman, "The House Intelligence Committee's Terrible, Horrible, Very Bad Snowden Report," *The Century Foundation,* September 16, 2016 (tcf.org/content/commentary/house-intelli gence-committees-terrible-horrible-bad-snowden-report/).

49. Jonathan Katz and Yehuda Lindell, *Introduction to Modern Cryptography*, 2nd ed. (Boca Raton, Fla.: CRC Press, 2015), pp. 7–8. See also Auguste Kerckhoffs, "La Cryptographie Militaire," *Journal des Sciences Militaires* 9 (January 1883), p. 12; David Kahn, *The Codebreakers: The Story of Secret Writing* (New York: Scribner's, 1996), p. 235.

50. ISOO, *2015 Report to the President*, July 15, 2016 (www.archives.gov/isoo/reports), pp. iii, 7.

CHAPTER 6

1. "New Details on the Scope of NSA Surveillance," *The Diane Rehm Show* (Steve Roberts, guest host), August 22, 2013 (thedianerehmshow.org/shows/2013-08-22/new-details-scope-nsa-surveillance).

2. *Report on the Telephone Records Program Conducted under Section 215 of the USA PATRIOT Act and on the Operations of the Foreign Intelligence Surveillance Court* (Washington: Privacy and Civil Liberties Oversight Board, 2014), p. 146.

3. Modern computer analysis has confirmed suspicions that Hamilton tried to take credit for more papers than he had actually written and that it was Madison who was the sole author of the twelve "disputed" essays, including number 51. Glenn Fung, "The Disputed Federalist Papers: SVM Feature Selection via Concave Minimization," *Journal of the ACM* 5 (2003), p. 1.

4. *Congressional Record* H3741–42 (daily ed. May 26, 2011).

5. Jim Sensenbrenner, "This Abuse of the Patriot Act Must End," *The Guardian*, June 9, 2013.

6. This history is described in detail in the ACLU's brief in its successful challenge of the bulk collection of telephone records before a federal appeals court in New York. *Brief for Plaintiffs-Appellants in American Civil Liberties Union v. Clapper*, No. 14-42 (March 6, 2014), pp. 26–29.

7. *Congressional Record* S3386–87 (daily ed. May 26, 2011). See also Ryan Lizza, "State of Deception: Why Won't the President Rein in the Intelligence Community?," *New Yorker*, December 16, 2013.

8. Peter Wallsten, "Lawmakers Say Administration's Lack of Candor on Surveillance Weakens Oversight," *Washington Post*, July 10, 2013.

9. For an example, see David Husband, "Skipping Classified Briefings: Why Not Attending Makes Sense from a Functional Perspective," *Privacy Rights Blog @epic.org* (blog), Epic.org, January 28, 2014 (epic.org/blog/2014/01/skipping-classified-briefings-why-not-attending-makes-sense-from-a-functional-perspective.html).

10. *Brief for Plaintiffs-Appellants in American Civil Liberties Union v. Clapper*.

11. House Roll Call Vote No. 412, *Congressional Record* H5028 (daily ed. July 24, 2013).

12. Timothy Edgar, "Big Transparency for the NSA," *Wall Street Journal*, August 2, 2013.

13. Glenn Greenwald, "Sen. Ron Wyden: NSA 'Repeatedly Deceived the American People,'" *The Guardian*, September 27, 2013.

14. There is no official published transcript of this hearing, but a video is available. Senate Select Committee on Intelligence, "Open Hearing: FISA Legislation," September 26, 2013 (www.intelligence.senate.gov/hearings/open-hear ing-fisa-legislation).

15. Dominic Rushe and Paul Lewis, "Tech Firms Push Back against White House Efforts to Divert NSA Meeting," *The Guardian*, December 17, 2013; Claire Cain Miller, "Revelations of N.S.A. Spying Cost U.S. Tech Companies," *New York Times*, March 21, 2014.

16. *Liberty and Security in a Changing World: Report and Recommendations of the President's Review Group on Intelligence and Communications Technologies*, December 12, 2013 (www.whitehouse.gov/sites/default/files/ docs/2013-12-12_rg_final_report.pdf).

17. For example, Ben Wittes, a scholar at the Brookings Institution with a reputation as a surveillance hawk, argued that the report was "a really awkward document for the Obama administration," full of recommendations its national security team were sure to reject. Benjamin Wittes, "The Very Awkward President Review Group Report," *Lawfare*, December 18, 2013 (www.lawfareblog .com/very-awkward-president-review-group-report).

18. White House, "Presidential Policy Directive—Signals Intelligence Activities (Presidential Policy Directive 28/PPD-28)," news release, January 17, 2014 (www.whitehouse.gov/the-press-office/2014/01/17/presidential-policy-dir ective-signals-intelligence-activities).

19. Carrie Cordero, "A Three-Post Reaction to the Surveillance Review Group Report," *Lawfare*, January 1, 2014 (www.lawfareblog.com/three-post-reaction-surveillance-review-group-report).

20. Privacy and Civil Liberties Oversight Board, *Report on the Surveillance Program Operated Pursuant to Section 702 of the Foreign Intelligence Surveillance Act*, July 2, 2014, p. 107.

21. Michael V. Hayden and Michael B. Mukasey, "NSA Reform That Only ISIS Could Love," *Wall Street Journal*, November 17, 2014. See also Philip Bump, "Jeb Bush's Foreign Policy Team Is Eerily Familiar, in One Venn Diagram," *Washington Post*, February 18, 2015.

22. *American Civil Liberties Union v. Clapper*, 785 F.3d 787 (2d Cir. 2015).

23. Senate Roll Call Vote No. 201, *Congressional Record* S3444 (daily ed. June 2, 2015).

24. Glenn Gerstell, "New National Security Tool Activated at Challenging Time," *Lawfare*, January 7, 2016 (www.lawfareblog.com/new-national-secur ity-tool-activated-challenging-time). See also "Statistical Transparency Report Regarding the Use of National Security Authorities for Calendar Year 2016," *IC on the Record*, April 2017 (https://icontherecord.tumblr.com/transparency/odni _transparencyreport_cy2016).

25. Senate Report Number 95-604—Part 1, p. 34 (November 15, 1977), in "Legislative History of the Foreign Intelligence Surveillance Act of 1978, Pub.

L. 95-511," *United States Code Congressional and Administrative News* 4 (1978), pp. 3935–36.

26. Barton Gellman and Ashkan Soltani, "NSA Collects Millions of E-Mail Address Books Globally," *Washington Post,* October 14, 2013.

27. Charlie Savage, "File Says N.S.A. Found Way to Replace Email Program," *New York Times,* November 19, 2015.

28. For a good discussion of this issue, see Jennifer C. Daskal, "The Un-Territoriality of Data," *Yale Law Journal* 125, no. 2 (2015), p. 326.

29. Axel Arnbak and Sharon Goldberg, "Loopholes for Circumventing the Constitution: Unrestrained Bulk Surveillance on Americans by Collecting Network Traffic Abroad," *Michigan Telecommunications & Technology Law Review* 21 (2015), p. 317.

30. The American Civil Liberties Union did not have to go very far to find someone with standing to challenge the NSA's bulk collection of telephone records. The ACLU was itself a customer of Verizon, the subject of the FISA court order that was disclosed in the very first story based on the Snowden documents. As discussed in chapter 5, Director of National Intelligence Jim Clapper almost immediately confirmed the order's authenticity. The Second Circuit found that because "the government's own orders demonstrate that [the ACLU's] call records are indeed among those collected as part of the telephone metadata program," the ACLU had standing to sue. *ACLU v. Clapper,* 785 F.3d 787, 801 (2d Cir. 2015).

These were extremely unusual circumstances, quite unlikely to be repeated. They depended both on the bulk nature of the telephone records program and on the government's own concession that Verizon was a participant in the program. Ordinarily, there is some doubt about whether challenged surveillance is actually taking place. Even so, the government argued that the ACLU lacked standing because it did not know if any of its records had been searched by NSA analysts. The Second Circuit rejected this argument.

31. Scalia set forth his philosophy on standing while still a judge of the United States Court of Appeals for the District of Columbia Circuit. Antonin Scalia, "The Doctrine of Standing as an Essential Element of the Separation of Powers," *Suffolk University Law Review* 42 (1983), p. 881. For an excellent discussion of how this philosophy influenced Scalia's approach to standing while a Supreme Court justice, see Cass Sunstein, "What's Standing after *Lujan*? Of Citizen Suits, 'Injuries,' and Article III," *Michigan Law Review* 91 (1992), p. 163.

32. *Clapper v. Amnesty International,* 568 U.S. __, No. 11-1025 (February 26, 2013).

33. See Charlie Savage, "Door May Open for Challenge to Secret Wiretaps," *New York Times,* October 16, 2013; Jameel Jaffer and Patrick C. Toomey, "The Solicitor General Should Correct the Record in Clapper," *Just Security,* October 18, 2013 (www.justsecurity.org/2219/solicitor-general-correct-record-clapper/).

34. *Spokeo v. Robins,* 578 U.S. __, No. 13-1339, pp. 7–10 (May 16, 2016) (internal quotation marks and citations omitted). Surprisingly, Alito cited a footnote in his opinion in *Clapper* to suggest that the Supreme Court could take

a more flexible approach to standing in a future case. "In some instances, we have found standing based on a 'substantial risk' that the harm will occur, which may prompt plaintiffs to reasonably incur costs to mitigate or avoid that harm." *Clapper*, 568 U.S. __, slip op., p. 15 n.5 (citations omitted).

35. "Transcript: Obama's Remarks on NSA Controversy," *Wall Street Journal*, June 7, 2013.

CHAPTER 7

1. Glenn Greenwald, "Fisa Court Oversight: A Look inside a Secret and Empty Process," *The Guardian*, June 18, 2013.

2. Watson Institute for International and Public Affairs, Brown University, "Bruce M. Selya: The View from Inside the FISA Courts," February 10, 2014 (webcast) (http://watson.brown.edu/events/2014/bruce-m-selya-view-inside-fisa-courts). See also Khin Su, "Federal Judge Speaks on Intelligence, Surveillance," *Brown Daily Herald*, February 11, 2014.

3. While the Foreign Intelligence Surveillance Court of Review released an unclassified version of its opinion in this case in January 2009, additional information, including the transcript of the oral argument, was released on *IC on the Record* in the fall of 2014 and again in 2016. "Release of Oral Argument Transcript from the Protect America Act Litigation," *IC on the Record*, November 17, 2014 (updated May 24, 2016) (https://icontherecord.tumblr.com/post/102 981813883/release-of-oral-argument-transcript-from-the).

4. Privacy and Civil Liberties Oversight Board, *Report on the Surveillance Program Operated Pursuant to Section 702 of the Foreign Intelligence Surveillance Act* (2014), pp. 18–19, 33–41. In a 2011 opinion of the FISA court, Judge Bates said that what became known as Prism collection accounted for "91% of the Internet communications acquired by NSA each year under Section 702." Memorandum Opinion (Foreign Intelligence Surveillance Court, October 3, 2011), p. 17. There is now some doubt about whether these widely cited figures are accurate. Upstream collection may account for a greater proportion than 9 percent. Charlie Savage, "Do the Upstream v. Prism Collection Numbers from Judge Bates' 2011 Opinion Add Up?," *Power Wars Blog*, May 9, 2016 (www. charliesavage.com/?p=1045).

5. See the Government's Motion for an Order of Civil Contempt (May 9), the FISA court's Order Denying Yahoo's Motion for a Stay (May 9) and Yahoo! Inc.'s Compliance Report (May 14), *In re Directives to Yahoo Inc.*, No. 105B(g) 07-01 (Foreign Intelligence Surveillance Court 2008), in "Statement by the Office of the Director of National Intelligence and the U.S. Department of Justice on the Declassification of Documents Related to the Protect America Act Litigation," *IC on the Record*, September 11, 2014 (https://icontherecord. tumblr.com/post/97251906083/statement-by-the-office-of-the-director-of).

6. Yahoo also had a separate argument against the Protect America Act because it permitted the NSA to designate Americans who were overseas as tar-

gets. The government argued this was constitutional because Executive Order 12,333 does not permit such direct targeting of a U.S. person without a finding by the attorney general that there is probable cause the target is an agent of a foreign power.

7. The total number of foreign targets under the successor to the Protect America Act grew from 89,138 in calendar year 2013 to 106,469 in calendar year 2016. As a result of additional reporting required by the Freedom Act, the report for calendar year 2016 also disclosed that there were 5,288 queries of the content of these data for information involving Americans and 30,355 queries for noncontent information, a number that excludes queries conducted by the FBI. ODNI Calendar Year 2016 Transparency Report, "Statistical Transparency Report Regarding Use of National Security Authorities," *IC on the Record*, April 2017 (https://icontherecord.tumblr.com/transparency/odni_transparency report_cy2016).

8. Transcript of Oral Argument, *In re Directives to Yahoo*, No. 08-01 (Foreign Intelligence Surveillance Court of Review, June 19, 2008), pp. 10–12, 23.

9. Ibid., p. 23.

10. Ibid., pp. 34–35. See also *Marbury v. Madison*, 5 U.S. 137, 177 (1803).

11. Watson Institute for International and Public Affairs, Brown University, "Bruce M. Selya."

12. This heavily redacted opinion is the version published in the *Federal Reporter*. *In re Directives [Name Redacted by the Court]*, 551 F.3d 1004, 1016 (Foreign Intelligence Surveillance Court of Review, August 22, 2008).

13. "Dear NSA, Let Me Take Care of Your Slides," social media post by Emil and De Cubber, June 11, 2013 (www.slideshare.net/EmilandDC/dear-nsa -let-me-take-care-ou).

14. Director of National Intelligence, "Facts on the Collection of Intelligence Pursuant to Section 702 of the Foreign Intelligence Surveillance Act," June 8, 2013 (www.dni.gov/files/documents/Facts on the Collection of Intelligence Pursuant to Section 702.pdf).

15. "Statement by the Office of the Director of National Intelligence," *IC on the Record*, September 11, 2014 (https://icontherecord.tumblr.com/post/972519 06083/statement-by-the-office-of-the-director-of).

16. Watson Institute for International and Public Affairs, Brown University, "Bruce M. Selya."

17. *Comments of the Judiciary on Proposals Regarding the Foreign Intelligence Surveillance Act* (January 10, 2014) (www.judiciary.senate.gov/down load/01-14-14-record-submission-grassley).

18. "Transcript: President Obama's August 9, 2013, News Conference at the White House," *Washington Post*, August 9, 2013.

19. *Liberty and Security in a Changing World: Report and Recommendations of the President's Review Group on Intelligence and Communications Technologies* (December 12, 2013), pp. 203–04.

20. USA FREEDOM Act of 2015, Pub. L. No. 114-23, 129 Stat. 268 at § 401, codified at 50 U.S.C. § 1803(i).

21. Cody M. Poplin, "Amici Curiae for FISC Announced," *Lawfare*, December 1, 2015 (www.lawfareblog.com/amici-curiae-fisc-announced). See also Laura Donohue, *The Future of Foreign Intelligence: Privacy and Surveillance in a Digital Age* (New York: Oxford University Press, 2016); David S. Kris and J. Douglas Wilson, *National Security Investigations and Prosecutions*, 2nd ed. (Eagan, Minn.: West, 2012).

22. See Shira A. Scheindlin and Jonathan M. Redgrave, "Special Masters and E-Discovery: The Intersection of Two Recent Revisions to the Federal Rules of Civil Procedure," *Cardozo Law Review* 30, no. 347 (2008), pp. 274–82.

23. *Peretz v. United States*, 501 U.S. 923, 928–29 n. 5 (1991).

24. Orin S. Kerr, "Ex Ante Regulation of Computer Search and Seizure," *Virginia Law Review* 96 (2010), pp. 1241, 1260–73 (exploring limits on the role of magistrates in the execution of search warrants); William G. Young, "The Expanding Role of Magistrate Judges in the Federal Courts, *Valparaiso University Law Review* 39 (2005), p. 661; James E. Pfander, "Article I Tribunals, Article III Courts, and the Judicial Power of the United States," *Harvard Law Review* 118 (2004), pp. 643, 765–66 (describing constitutional limits on the role of magistrate judges.)

ODNI Calendar Year 2016 Transparency Report, "Statistical Transparency Report Regarding Use of National Security Authorities," *IC on the Record*, April 2017. There were 1,559 traditional FISA orders in 2016. If judges had reviewed the 5,288 U.S. person queries of content collected under section 702 in that same year, and if each of these reviews was considered a separate case, the total number of cases would be 6,847, which is more than a fourfold increase.

25. While one of the eleven FISA court judges had been appointed by President Clinton in 2000, even she was actually a Republican selection, part of a deal between Bill Clinton and the Republican-controlled Senate allowing some of Clinton's preferred judges to be confirmed late in his term. Charlie Savage, *Power Wars: Inside Obama's Post-9/11 Presidency* (New York: Little, Brown, 2015), p. 594. See also Charlie Savage, "Roberts's Picks Reshaping Secret Surveillance Court," *New York Times,* July 25, 2013.

26. U.S. Senate, Committee on the Judiciary, *Confirmation Hearing on the Nomination of John G. Roberts, Jr. to be Chief Justice of the United States*, S. Hrg. 109-158, 109th Cong., 1st sess. (Government Printing Office, 2005), p. 212–13.

27. See FISA Judge Selection Reform Act, S. 1460, 113th Cong.

28. U.S. Senate, Committee on the Judiciary, *Confirmation Hearing on the Nomination of John G. Roberts, Jr.*

29. Jennifer Granick and Christopher Sprigman, "The Secret FISA Court Must Go," *Daily Beast,* July 24, 2013 (www.thedailybeast.com/articles/2013/07/24/the-secret-fisa-court-must-go.html).

30. Beverly Gage, "What an Uncensored Letter to M.L.K. Reveals," *New York Times Magazine,* November 11, 2014.

31. Comey's predecessor, Robert Mueller, also began his government career

as a federal prosecutor, but he did so in 1976, two years before Congress enacted FISA.

32. This is discussed further in chapter 11. The quotation is from an interview with Yahoo News. See chapter 1, note 21.

33. *United States v. United States District Court*, 407 U.S. 297 (1972).

34. In fact, the numbers are even more lopsided when one takes into account that the reported FBI statistics before 1968 also include criminal surveillance operations. Statistics for FBI warrantless wiretaps and bugging operations are taken from the Church Committee's final report. See *Final Report of the Senate Select Committee to Study Governmental Operations with Respect to Intelligence Activities*, Senate Report No. 94-755 (Government Printing Office, 1976), book 3, p. 301. Statistics for FISA court orders have been aggregated by the Electronic Privacy Information Center. See "Foreign Intelligence Surveillance Court Orders 1979–2014" (epic.org/privacy/wiretap/stats/fisa_stats.html). The annual FISA reports themselves have been collected by the Federation of American Scientists at "FISA Annual Reports to Congress" (fas.org/irp/agency/doj/fisa/#rept). See also ODNI Calendar Year 2015 Transparency Report, "Statistical Transparency Report Regarding the Use of National Security Authorities," *IC on the Record*, May 2, 2016 (icontherecord.tumblr.com/transparency/odni_transparencyreport_cy2015).

35. Carol D. Leonnig, "Secret Court Says It Is No Rubber Stamp; Led to Changes in U.S. Spying Requests," *Washington Post*, October 15, 2013.

36. *Riley v. California*, 134 S. Ct. 2473 (2014).

CHAPTER 8

1. Ellen Nakashima and Joby Warrick, "For NSA Chief, Terrorist Threat Drives Passion to 'Collect It All,'" *Washington Post*, July 14, 2013.

2. National Security Agency (NSA), "The National Security Agency: Missions, Authorities, Oversight and Partnerships," white paper, August 9, 2013 (www.nsa.gov/news-features/press-room/statements/2013-08-09-the-nsa-story.shtml), p. 6. Sean Gallagher, "NSA 'Touches' More of Internet Than Google," *Ars Technica*, August 13, 2013 (arstechnica.com/information-technology/2013/08/the-1-6-percent-of-the-internet-that-nsa-touches-is-bigger-than-it-seems/). The NSA points out that only a tiny fraction of the data it "touches" (0.025 percent of the 29.21 petabytes) is actually selected for review. Critics of the NSA point out that this seemingly small fraction may be misleading for a variety of reasons. For example, the denominator includes streaming movies along with other traffic in which privacy concerns may be minimal.

3. "The National Security Agency and Fourth Amendment Rights, October 29 and November 6, 1975," *Hearings before the Select Committee to Study Governmental Operations with Respect to Intelligence Activities of the United States Senate* (Government Printing Office, 1976), vol. 5,

4. White House, "Presidential Policy Directive—Signals Intelligence Activi-

ties (Presidential Policy Directive 28/PPD-28)," news release, January 17, 2014, (https://obamawhitehouse.archives.gov/the-press-office/2014/01/17/presiden tial-policy-directive-signals-intelligence-activities), p. 3 n. 5.

5. Siobhan Gorman, "Meltdowns Hobble NSA Data Center; Investigators Stumped by What's Causing Power Surges That Destroy Equipment," *Wall Street Journal,* October 7, 2013.

6. Glenn Greenwald, *No Place to Hide: Edward Snowden, the NSA, and the U.S. Surveillance State* (New York: Henry Holt, 2014), p. 195.

7. Donald Rumsfeld was secretary of defense from 2001 to 2006. In making the case for the Iraq War, the Bush administration argued that the government of Iraq under Saddam Hussein might give weapons of mass destruction to terrorists. At a press conference in 2002, Rumsfeld gave this answer to a reporter's question asking him about "reports" that there was "no evidence" of links between terrorist organizations and the government of Iraq:

> "Reports that say that something hasn't happened are always interesting to me, because as we know, there are known knowns; there are things we know we know. We also know there are known unknowns; that is to say we know there are some things we do not know. But there are also unknown unknowns—the ones we don't know we don't know. And if one looks throughout the history of our country and other free countries, it is the latter category that tend to be the difficult ones."

"DoD News Briefing—Secretary Rumsfeld and Gen. Myers," February 12, 2002 (http://archive.defense.gov/Transcripts/Transcript.aspx?TranscriptID= 2636).

8. National Research Council, *Bulk Collection of Signals Intelligence: Technical Options* (Washington: Government Publishing Office, 2015).

9. Ibid., p. 50.

10. Glenn Kessler, "Clapper's 'Least Untruthful' Statement to the Senate," *Washington Post,* June 12, 2013.

11. United States Signals Intelligence Directive 18 §§ 9.2, 9.14 (January 25, 2011) (declassified and approved for release November 13, 2013).

12. See "Department of Defense Releases Updated Procedures Governing the Conduct of DoD Intelligence Activities," *IC on the Record,* August 10, 2016 (icontherecord.tumblr.com/post/148743183768/department-of-defense-releases-updated-procedures). The new definition of collection is stressed in the fact sheet accompanying the release, available at the preceding link. The definition itself is on p. 46 of the revised procedures. See DoD Manual 5240.01, "Procedures Governing the Conduct of DoD Intelligence Activities," paragraph G.2. The original definition is contained on p. 15 of Department of Defense Regulation DoD 5240.1-R, "Procedures Governing the Activities of DoD Intelligence Components That Affect United States Persons" (December 1982), paragraph C2.2.1, available on the website of the Federation of American Scientists (https://fas.org/irp/doddir/dod/d5240_1_r.pdf).

13. If you wonder how two institutions in Cambridge, Massachusetts, ended up on opposite coasts although they are only a mile apart, Larry Lessig will tell you that MIT counts as a West Coast institution. Larry Lessig, *Code: Version 2.0* (New York: Basic Books, 2006), pp. 72–74.

14. *Olmstead v. United States*, 277 U.S. 438, 478 (1928) (Brandeis, J., dissenting). *Katz v. United States*, 389 U.S. 347 (1967).

15. Memorandum of Law in Support of Application for Certain Tangible Things for Investigations to Protect against International Terrorism, Docket No. BR 06-05 (F.I.S.C. May 23, 2006), p. 3. The FISC granted the government's motion to release this memorandum to the House and Senate Judiciary and Intelligence Committees, pursuant to the reporting requirements of §1871(c), leading up to the 2009 reauthorization; see "Order Granting the Motion to Unseal," [redacted], Docket No. BR 06-05 (F.I.S.C. July 22, 2009).

16. Ron Rivest, Adi Shamir, and Len Adleman, "A Method for Obtaining Digital Signatures and Public-Key Cryptosystems," *Communications of the ACM* 21, no. 2 (1978), pp. 120–21.

17. Tim Cook, "A Message to Our Customers," February 16, 2016 (www.apple.com/customer-letter/); "Transcript of Obama's remarks at SXSW," *Boston Globe*, March 12, 2016. An excellent summary of the debate is provided in Harold Abelson and others, "Keys under Doormats: Mandating Insecurity by Requiring Government Access to All Data and Communications," MIT, Computer Science and Artificial Intelligence Laboratory Technical Report, July 6, 2015 (http://dspace.mit.edu/bitstream/handle/1721.1/97690/MIT-CSAIL-TR-2015-026.pdf). A diverse group of security and policy experts from academia, civil society, and the U.S. intelligence community wrote a report in 2016 questioning the narrow focus of the "going dark" debate. Matt Olsen and others, "Don't Panic: Making Progress on the 'Going Dark' Debate," Berkman Center for Internet and Society at Harvard University, February 1, 2016 (https://cyber.law.harvard.edu/pubrelease/don't-panic/Dont_Panic_Making_Progress_on_Going_Dark_Debate.pdf).

18. National Research Council, *Bulk Collection of Signals Intelligence*, pp. 9-10.

19. Seny Kamara, "Are Compliance and Privacy Always at Odds?," *Outsourced Bits*, July 23, 2013 (http://outsourcedbits.org/2013/07/23/are-compliance-and-privacy-always-at-odds/)

20. Seny Kamara, "Restructuring the NSA Metadata Program," in *Financial Cryptography and Data Security* (Berlin: Springer, 2014), pp. 235–47.

21. Carl Landwehr, "Results of Workshops on Privacy Protection Technologies," in *Protecting Persons While Protecting the People* (Berlin: Springer, 2009), pp. 45–56.

22. The two most successful projects to emerge from the program are described in David Cash and others, "Dynamic Searchable Encryption in Very-Large Databases: Data Structures and Implementation," *IACR Cryptology ePrint Archive* (2014) (https://eprint.iacr.org/2014/853.pdf), and Vasilis Pappa-

set and others, "Blind Seer: A Scalable Private DBMS," in *2014 IEEE Symposium on Security and Privacy* (Berlin: Springer, 2014), pp. 359–74.

23. Compare National Security Presidential Memorandum 2 (NSPM-2), January 28, 2017 and National Security Presidential Memorandum 4 (NSPM-4), April 4, 2017, with Presidential Policy Directive 1 (PPD-1), February 13, 2009. See also Cory Doctorow, "Trustycon: How to Redesign NSA Surveillance to Catch More Criminals and Spy on a Lot Fewer People," *BoingBoing*, March 1, 2014 (http://boingboing.net/2014/03/01/trustycon-how-to-redesign-nsa.html).

24. Rafail Ostrovsky and William E. Skeith III, "Private Searching on Streaming Data," *Journal of Cryptography* 20, no. 4 (October 2007), pp. 397–430.

25. Craig Gentry, "Fully Homomorphic Encryption Using Ideal Lattices," in *Proceedings of the Forty-First Annual ACM Symposium on Theory of Computing (STOC 2009)* (New York: Association for Computing Machinery, 2009), pp. 169–78.

26. See ODNI, "Security and Privacy Assurance Research (SPAR)" (www.iarpa.gov/index.php/research-programs/spar). A link on the right-hand side of the program website will generate a Google Scholar search for research papers funded by this program.

27. Bruce Schneier, "NSA Surveillance: A Guide to Staying Secure," *The Guardian*, September 6, 2013.

28. The French diplomat and historian Alexis de Tocqueville wrote in 1835 that lawyers constituted the true aristocracy of the United States. Alexis de Tocqueville, *Democracy in America*, translated by Arthur Goldhammer (New York: Penguin Putnam, 2004), pp. 301–09.

CHAPTER 9

1. Tamlin Magee, "Obama's First Privacy Chief Backs NSA's Right To Spy—with Reform," *Forbes*, May 14, 2014 (www.forbes.com/sites/tamlinmagee/2014/05/14/obamas-first-privacy-chief-backs-nsas-right-to-spy-with-reform/#196ae199465b).

2. White House, "Presidential Policy Directive—Signals Intelligence Activities (Presidential Policy Directive 28/PPD-28)," news release, January 17, 2014 (obamawhitehouse.archives.gov/the-press-office/2014/01/17/presidential-policy-directive-signals-intelligence-activities).

3. See discussion in chapter 4. Lee Ferran, "Ex-NSA Chief: 'We Kill People Based on Metadata,'" *ABC News*, May 12, 2014 (http://abcnews.go.com/blogs/headlines/2014/05/ex-nsa-chief-we-kill-people-based-on-metadata/).

4. Huppert described this episode to journalist Ewen MacAskill in an earlier interview. As my notes from this meeting are incomplete, I am relying on that story for the quotations. See Ewen MacAskill, "British Intelligence Watchdog Is Like Yes Prime Minister, Says MP," *The Guardian*, March 18, 2014 (www.theguardian.com/politics/2014/mar/18/intelligence-watchdog-like-tv-sitcom).

The parallels to a scene in the episode "One of Us," involving oversight of the intelligence agencies, are really quite striking. *Yes, Prime Minister,* season 1, episode 8 (www.youtube.com/watch?v=mLD0YK6CdjE).

5. *Liberty & others v. Secretary of State,* No. UKIPTrib 13 77-H (February 6, 2015) (www.ipt-uk.com/docs/Liberty_Ors_Judgment_6Feb15.pdf). During the course of the case, the government said that GCHQ did not obtain information from the NSA about U.K. citizens unless it had obtained the "ministerial warrant" under British law that would have been required for direct surveillance. The tribunal decided that the government's failure to make this safeguard known publicly had violated the European Convention on Human Rights, but that because it had done so during the course of the litigation, the government was now in compliance.

6. Ewen MacAskill, "'Extreme Surveillance Becomes UK Law with Barely a Whimper," *The Guardian,* November 19, 2016.

7. *Investigatory Powers Act 2016,* chap. 25 (London: Stationery Office, 2016). See also "Investigatory Powers Factsheets," *Big Brother Watch* (undated) (www.bigbrotherwatch.org.uk/factsheets-category/investigatory-powers-factsheets/). Natasha Lomas, "UK Parliament Rubberstamps Mass Surveillance Law," *TechCrunch,* November 17, 2016 (https://techcrunch.com/2016/11/17/uk-parliament-rubberstamps-mass-surveillance-law/).

8. Statement of the UK Home Office, Rt. Hon. Amber Rudd MP, "Investigatory Powers Bill Receives Royal Assent," November 29, 2016 (www.gov.uk/government/news/investigatory-powers-bill-receives-royal-assent).

9. Stephen J. Schulhofer, "An International Right to Privacy? Be Careful What You Wish For," *International Journal of Constitutional Law* 14, no. 1 (2016), pp. 247–49.

10. MacAskill, "British Intelligence Watchdog."

11. *10 Human Rights Organizations and Others v. United Kingdom,* application no. 24960/15, lodged May 20, 2015, European Court of Human Rights (http://hudoc.echr.coe.int/eng?i=001-159526); *Bureau of Investigative Journalism and Alice Ross v. United Kingdom,* application no. 62322/14, lodged September 11, 2014, European Court of Human Rights (hudoc.echr.coe.int/eng?i=001-150946); *Big Brother Watch and Others v. United Kingdom,* application no. 58170/13, lodged September 4, 2013, European Court of Human Rights (http://hudoc.echr.coe.int/eng?i=001-140713).

12. "Report of the Special Rapporteur on the Right to Privacy, Joseph A. Cannataci," March 8, 2016, Human Rights Council, UN Doc. A/HRC/31/64 (www.ohchr.org/EN/Issues/Privacy/SR/Pages/SRPrivacyIndex.aspx).

13. *International Covenant on Civil and Political Rights,* adopted December 16, 1966, by UN General Assembly, Art. 17.

14. David Cole and Federico Fabbrini, "Bridging the Transatlantic Divide? The United States, the European Union, and the Protection of Privacy across Borders," *International Journal of Constitutional Law* 14, no. 1 (2016), pp. 223–28.

15. Carly Nyst, "European Human Rights Court Deals a Heavy Blow to the Lawfulness of Bulk Surveillance," *Just Security*, December 9, 2015 (www.just-security.org/28216/echr-deals-heavy-blow-lawfulness-bulk-surveillance).

16. William E. Pomeranz, "Uneasy Partners: Russia and the European Court of Human Rights," *Human Rights Brief* 19, no. 3 (2012), pp. 17–21.

17. Charlie Savage, "U.S. Seems Unlikely to Accept That Rights Treaty Applies to Its Actions Abroad," *New York Times*, March 6, 2014.

18. Robert Levine, "Behind the European Privacy Ruling That's Confounding Silicon Valley," *New York Times*, October 9, 2015.

19. Levine, "Behind the European Privacy Ruling"; Kashmir Hill, "Max Schrems: The Austrian Thorn in Facebook's Side," *Forbes*, February 7, 2012 (www.forbes.com/sites/kashmirhill/2012/02/07/the-austrian-thorn-in-facebooks-side/)

20. *Maximilian Schrems v. Data Protection Commissioner* (Court of Justice of the European Union, October 6, 2015), no. C-362/14, Judgement of the Court (Grand Chamber).

21. See Mark Scott, "Data Transfer Pact between U.S. and Europe Is Ruled Invalid," *New York Times*, October 6, 2015.

22. Jedidiah Bracy, "How Julie Brill Is Cultivating a Defense of the U.S. Privacy Framework," *Privacy Perspectives*, February 24, 2015 (iapp.org/news/a/how-julie-brill-is-cultivating-a-defense-of-the-u-s-privacy-framework).

23. *Schrems v. Data Protection Commissioner*, paragraph 94.

24. Peter Swire put forward his arguments in "Don't Strike Down the Safe Harbor Based on Inaccurate Views about U.S. Intelligence Law," *Privacy Perspectives,* October 5, 2015 (iapp.org/news/a/dont-strike-down-the-safe-harbor-based-on-inaccurate-views-on-u-s-intelligence-law/).

25. Cameron Kerry's law firm, Sidley Austin LLP, wrote an exhaustive, 188-page report making the case that U.S. law afforded similar protection to that provided by EU member states. See Jacques Bourgeois and others, "Essentially Equivalent: A Comparison of the Legal Orders for Privacy and Data Protection in the European Union and the United States," report prepared for the president of the European Commission and others (New York: Sidley Austin LLP, January 2016) (datamatters.sidley.com/essentially-equivalent-a-comparison-of-the-legal-orders-for-privacy-and-data-protection-in-the-european-union-and-united-states/). See also the discussion of national security surveillance standards in Center for Democracy and Technology, "Comparative Study of Standards for Government Access" (Washington, 2013) (govaccess.cdt.info./).

26. This figure is from the Office of the United States Trade Representative, "European Union" (https://ustr.gov/countries-regions/europe-middle-east/europe/european-union)

27. Christopher Wolf and Winston Maxwell, "Why the U.S. Is Held to a Higher Data Protection Standard Than France," *Privacy Perspectives*, November 2, 2015 (https://iapp.org/news/a/why-the-u-s-is-held-to-a-higher-data-pro

tection-standard-than-france/). See also Christopher Wolf and Winston Maxwell, *A Global Reality: Governmental Access to Data in the Cloud*, Hogan Lovells White Paper, May 23, 2012 (updated July 18, 2012) (www.hoganlovells.com/en/publications/hogan-lovells-white-paper-government-access-to-data-in-the-cloud).

28. *Treaty of Lisbon, amending the Treaty on European Union and the Treaty establishing the European Community*, Art. 1, sec. 3a (December 13, 2007).

29. Timothy Edgar, "To Preempt Far Right, Europe Should Review Counterterrorism Policies," *Lawfare*, March 23, 2016 (www.lawfareblog.com/preempt-far-right-europe-should-review-counterterrorism-policies); Nils Muiznieks, "Europe Is Spying on You," *New York Times*, October 27, 2015.

30. Privacy and Civil Liberties Oversight Board, *Report on the Surveillance Program Operated Pursuant to Section 702 of the Foreign Intelligence Surveillance Act*, July 2, 2014, p. 110.

31. Pew Research Center, "Global Opinions of U.S. Surveillance," July 14, 2014 (www.pewglobal.org/2014/07/14/nsa-opinion/).

32. White House, "Presidential Policy Directive—Signals Intelligence Activities," PPD-28 at § 2.

33. Peter Margulies, "Defining 'Foreign Affairs' in Section 702 of the FISA Amendments Act: The Virtues and Deficits of Post-Snowden Dialogue on U.S. Surveillance Policy," *Washington and Lee Law Review* 72 (Summer 2015), p. 1283.

34. Schulhofer, "An International Right to Privacy?," p. 239.

35. Alan Ehrenhalt, "Hypocrisy Has Its Virtues," *New York Times,* February 6, 2001.

36. Henry Farrell and Martha Finnemore, "The End of Hypocrisy: American Foreign Policy in the Age of Leaks," *Foreign Affairs* (November/December 2013) (www.foreignaffairs.com/articles/united-states/2013-10-15/end-hypocrisy).

CHAPTER 10

1. German Bundestag, 18th Electoral Term, *Draft Act on Enhanced Parliamentary Oversight of the Federal Intelligence Services*, Printed Paper 18/9040, July 5, 2016 ("Parliamentary Oversight Law") (official translation, on file with author); German Bundestag, 18th Electoral Term, *Draft Act on Communications Intelligence Gathering by the Federal Intelligence Service on Foreign Nationals Abroad*, Printed Paper 18/9041, July 5, 2016 ("BND Law") (official translation, on file with author).

2. "The NSA's Secret Spy Hub in Berlin," *Spiegel Online*, October 27, 2013 (www.spiegel.de/international/germany/cover-story-how-nsa-spied-on-merkel-cell-phone-from-berlin-embassy-a-930205.html).

3. Adam Entous and Danny Yadron, "Some Senior U.S. Officials Not Com-

fortable with Obama's Curbs on NSA Spying on Leaders," *Wall Street Journal*, December 30, 2015; David E. Sanger, "Obama Panel Said to Urge N.S.A. Curbs," *New York Times*, December 12, 2013.

4. In November 2016 the inquiry committee lost its case on the selectors issue, but the committee's minority succeeded in its court challenge on its request for Snowden to testify, forcing another vote. "German Constitutional Court Rules Out Access to NSA 'Selectors' List," *Deutsche Welle*, November 15, 2016 (www.dw.com/en/german-constitutional-court-rules-out-access-to-nsas-selectors-list/a-36396385); Marcel Fürstenau, "Opinion: Wonderful Snowden Verdict," *Deutsche Welle*, November 22, 2016 (www.dw.com/en/opinion-won derful-snowden-verdict/a-36483599).

5. Deutscher Bundestag, 1. Untersuchungsausschuss, "Surveillance Reform after Snowden," September 8, 2016 (statement of Timothy H. Edgar) (www. bundestag.de/blob/439638/48d024231c036c252cf853037d53b033/mat-a-sv-16-2a-data.pdf).

6. Hearing transcript, Deutscher Bundestag, 1. Untersuchungsausschuss, September 8, 2016 (on file with author), p. 24.

7. Russell A. Miller, "Intelligence Oversight: Made in Germany," in *Global Intelligence Oversight: Governing Security in the Twenty-First Century*, edited by Zachary K. Goldman and Samuel J. Roscoff (Oxford University Press, 2016), pp. 257–88. Thorsten Wetzling, "The Key to Intelligence Reform in Germany: Strengthening the G-10 Commission's Role to Authorise Strategic Surveillance," Policy Brief 02/2016, Stiftung Neue Verantwortung (www.stiftung-nv.de/sites/default/files/snv_g10.pdf).

8. Ibid., pp. 100–02. I am indebted to my former student Cassandra Carothers for her translation of von Notz's statement from the original German.

9. Hearing transcript, Deutscher Bundestag, 1. Untersuchungsausschuss, p. 24.

10. BND Law, p. 2.

11. Compare, for example, the BND Law, p. 8, amending the Federal Intelligence Service Act (BND-Gesetz) at § 6(5) ("It shall be prohibited to gather communications on foreign nationals abroad in order to obtain competitive advantages (economic espionage)") with PPD-28 § 1(d) ("It is not an authorized foreign intelligence or counterintelligence purpose to collect such information to afford a competitive advantage to U.S. companies and U.S. business sectors commercially").

12. Compare BND Law, p. 40 (describing how new § 7(2) "prohibits the 'circular exchange' of information") with Executive Order 12,333 at § 2.12 ("No element of the Intelligence Community shall participate in or request any person to undertake activities forbidden by this Order").

13. BND Law, p. 43 (explaining that new § 9(5) includes a requirement of notification for some EU selectors and a power to conduct "random checks" on all of them).

14. BND Law, pp. 36–37 (explaining new § 6(2)).

15. "Bundestag to Vote on Better Scrutiny of Intelligence Services," *Deutche*

Welle, October 21, 2016 (www.dw.com/en/bundestag-to-vote-on-better-scru tiny-of-intelligence-services/a-36108764).

16. Parliamentary Oversight Law, pp. 2, 4 (adding a new §10(3) to the Parliamentary Oversight Panel Act of 2009).

17. Hearing transcript, Deutscher Bundestag, p. 128.

18. Assange's statement is in "German BND-NSA Inquiry Exhibits," *WikiLeaks*, December 1, 2016 (www.wikileaks.org/bnd-inquiry/). For Patrick Sensburg, see "Ermittlungen wegen Leaks aus dem NSA-Ausschuss möglich," *Zeit Online*, December 2, 2016 (www.zeit.de/politik/deutschland/2016-12/ wikileaks-nsa-unterlagen-strafrechtliche-ermittlungen-norbert-lammert).

19. "German Spy Chief: Russia Trying to 'Destabilize' Germany Ahead of Elections," Radio Free Europe/Radio Liberty, December 8, 2016 (www.rferl. org/a/germany-maassen-russia-destabilize-elections/28164207.html).

20. Hearing transcript, Deutscher Bundestag, p. 96.

CHAPTER 11

1. Eli Rosenberg, Jennifer Medina, and John Eligon, "Protesters Take Anti-Trump Message to His Doorstep, and Plan Next Steps," *New York Times*, November 12, 2016.

2. Jack Goldsmith, "Libertarian Panic, Unlawful Action, and the Trump Presidency," *Lawfare,* November 22, 2016 (www.lawfareblog.com/libertarian-panic-unlawful-action-and-trump-presidency); Emily Bazelon, "How a Wonky National-Security Blog Hit the Big Time," *New York Times Magazine*, March 14, 2017.

3. "Letter from G.O.P. National Security Officials Opposing Donald Trump," *New York Times*, August 8, 2016.

4. Brett Max Kaufman, "A Word to a Newfound Ally," *Just Security*, December 2, 2016 (www.justsecurity.org/35107/word-newfound-ally/).

5. Christopher Woolf, "Ex-CIA Director to Trump: 'Bring Your Own Bucket' If You Want to Waterboard," *PRI's The World*, February 29, 2016 (www.pri.org/ stories/2016-02-29/ex-cia-director-trump-bring-your-own-bucket-if-you-want-waterboard); Jenna Johnson, "Donald Trump on Waterboarding: 'Torture Works,'" *Washington Post*, February 17, 2016; Sam Stein, "Trump Says He Never Pledged to Kill Family Members of Terrorists," *Huffington Post,* March 9, 2016 (www.huffingtonpost.com/entry/donald-trump-terrorists_us_56e0d7cde4b065e2e3d4d82d); Maggie Haberman, "Donald Trump Reverses Position on Torture and Killing Terrorists' Families," *New York Times,* March 4, 2016; Tom LoBianco, "Donald Trump on Terrorists: 'Take Out Their Families,'" *CNN Politics*, December 3, 2015 (www.cnn.com/2015/12/02/politics/donald-trump-terrorists-families/).

6. David Marks and Jeremy Diamond, "Trump: 'I Want Surveillance of Certain Mosques,'" *CNN Politics*, November 21, 2015 (www.cnn.com/2015/11/21/ politics/trump-muslims-surveillance/); Matt Apuzzo and Joseph Goldstein, "New York Drops Unit That Spied on Muslims," *New York Times*, April 15, 2014.

7. See chapter 1, note 21. See also Maggie Haberman and Richard Pérez-Peña, "Donald Trump Sets Off a Furor with Call to Register Muslims in U.S.," *New York Times*, November 20, 2015.

8. White House, " 'Islam Is Peace,' Says President," news release, September 17, 2001 (https://georgewbush-whitehouse.archives.gov/news/releases/2001/09/20010917-11.html).

9. Glenn Kessler, "Trump's Outrageous Claim That 'Thousands' of New Jersey Muslims Celebrated the 9/11 Attacks," *Washington Post*, November 22, 2015.

10. Salena Zito, "Taking Trump Seriously, Not Literally," *The Atlantic*, September 23, 2016.

11. Eliot A. Cohen, "To An Anxious Friend . . . ," *American Interest*, November 10, 2016 (www.the-american-interest.com/2016/11/10/to-an-anxious-friend/)

12. Eliot A. Cohen, "I Told Conservatives to Work for Trump. One Talk with His Team Changed My Mind," *Washington Post,* November 15, 2016.

13. Matthew Rosenberg, "Ex-General and Critic of Islam to Help Guide Trump in White House," *New York Times*, November 18, 2016.

14. Mark Landler and Eric Schmitt, "H. R. McMaster Breaks with Administration on Views of Islam," *New York Times*, February 24, 2017.

15. White House Press Office, "The Inaugural Address," news release, January 20, 2017 (www.whitehouse.gov/inaugural-address).

16. White House Press Office, "National Security Presidential Memorandum 2," news release, January 28, 2017 (www.whitehouse.gov/the-press-office/2017/01/28/presidential-memorandum-organization-national-security-council-and).

17. Katie Glueck, "Fear Rises That Bannon Could Bring the 'Alt-Right' into White House," *Politico*, November 14, 2016 (www.politico.com/story/2016/11/stephen-bannon-breitbart-backlash-231371).

18. Matea Gold, "Bannon Film Outline Warned U.S. Could Turn into 'Islamic States of America," *Washington Post*, February 3, 2017.

19. Sebastian Gorka, *Defeating Jihad: The Winnable War* (Washington: Regnery Publishing, 2016); Greg Jaffe, "For a Trump Adviser, an Odyssey from the Fringes of Washington to the Center of Power," *Washington Post*, February 20, 2017; "Gorka: The New Commander in Chief Sent a Powerful Message" (video), Fox News, January 20, 2017 (http://video.foxnews.com/v/5291476797001/?playlist_id=930909813001#sp=show-clips).

20. Samuel Walker, *Presidents and Civil Liberties from Wilson to Obama: A Story of Poor Custodians* (Cambridge University Press, 2012), pp. 266–67.

21. Intelligence Community Assessment, "Assessing Russian Activities and Intentions in Recent US Elections," *IC on the Record,* January 6, 2017 (https://icontherecord.tumblr.com/post/155494946443/odni-statement-on-declassified-intelligence).

22. Goldsmith, "Libertarian Panic."

23. Jack Goldsmith, *Power and Constraint: The Accountable Presidency after 9/11* (New York: W. W. Norton, 2012).

24. Shortly after the 2016 election, Bobby Chesney, a law professor and co-founder of *Lawfare*, made a list of Obama orders and directives he believed were certainly "doomed." Obama's surveillance reform directive, PPD-28, was high on his list. Bobby Chesney, "Annals of the Trump Administration #2: Which Executive Orders and Directives Are Doomed?," *Lawfare*, November 18, 2016 (www.lawfareblog.com/annals-trump-administration-2-which-executive-orders-and-directives-are-doomed). It was a reasonable prediction, but I was not so sure. As we have seen, Obama's signals intelligence reforms protecting the privacy of foreigners were crucial to negotiating the Privacy Shield, the data-sharing agreement with the European Union that was critical to American businesses. While Trump surely had little interest in protecting the privacy of foreigners, lobbyists would object to anything that might threaten the ability of American companies to do business in Europe. Fundamental changes to more established limits such as those of Executive Order 12,333 seemed even more unlikely.

25. "Legal Effectiveness of a Presidential Directive, as Compared to an Executive Order," *Opinions of the Office of Legal Counsel*, vol. 24 (Government Printing Office, 2000), p. 24.

26. "SSCI Additional Prehearing Questions for Daniel Coats upon His Nomination to Be Director of National Intelligence," February 28, 2017 (www.intelligence.senate.gov/hearings/open-hearing-nomination-daniel-coats-be-director-national-intelligence), p. 34. See also Matthew Rosenberg and James Risen, "Trump's Intelligence Nominee Gets Early Lesson in Managing White House," *New York Times*, March 9, 2017.

27. Eugene Scott, "Omarosa: Trump Campaign Keeping 'List' of Enemies," *CNN Politics*, November 9, 2016.

28. Glenn Kessler, "Does Huma Abedin Have 'Ties' to the Muslim Brotherhood?," *Washington Post*, August 25, 2016; Paul Sperry, "Huma Abedin Worked at Muslim Journal That Opposed Women's Rights," *New York Post*, August 21, 2016.

29. "The Attorney General's Guidelines for Domestic FBI Operations," September 29, 2008 (www.justice.gov/archive/opa/docs/guidelines.pdf), pp. 17, 19.

30. "E.O. 12333 Raw SIGINT Availability Procedures," *IC on the Record*, January 12, 2017 (https://icontherecord.tumblr.com/post/155766785323/eo-12333-raw-sigint-availability-procedures); Jane Chong, "E.O. 12333 Raw SIGINT Availability Procedures: A Quick and Dirty Summary," *Lawfare*, January 12, 2017 (www.lawfareblog.com/eo-12333-raw-sigint-availability-procedures-quick-and-dirty-summary). See also Robert Litt, "The New Intelligence Sharing Procedures Are Not about Law Enforcement," *Just Security*, March 30, 2016 (www.justsecurity.org/30327/intelligence-sharing-procedures-not-law-enforcement/).

31. "Joint IG Report of the PSP," *IC on the Record,* April 25, 2015 (https://

icontherecord.tumblr.com/post/117330907753/the-department-of-justice-releases-inspectors).

32. White House Press Office, "The Inaugural Address." For a fascinating discussion of the constitutional implications of whether President Trump's oath of office should be taken seriously, see Benjamin Wittes and Quinta Jurecic, "The Revolt of the Judges: What Happens When the Judiciary Doesn't Trust the President's Oath," *Lawfare*, March 16, 2017 (www.lawfareblog.com/revolt-judges-what-happens-when-judiciary-doesnt-trust-presidents-oath).

33. Jack Goldsmith, "The Real Constitutional Danger," *Lawfare*, February 14, 2017 (www.lawfareblog.com/real-constitutional-danger).

34. Michael S. Schmidt, Mark Mazzetti, and Matt Apuzzo, "Trump Campaign Aides Had Repeated Contacts with Russian Intelligence," *New York Times*, February 14, 2017; Julie Hirschfeld Davis, "Rumblings of a 'Deep State' Undermining Trump? It Was Once a Foreign Concept," *New York Times*, March 6, 2017.

35. Steven Swinford, "Donald Trump Fuels Diplomatic Row with Britain after Apology from US officials over GCHQ Wiretapping Claims," *The Telegraph*, March 18, 2017. White House Office of the Press Secretary, "Press Briefing by Press Secretary Sean Spicer, 3/16/2017, #25" (transcript) (www.whitehouse.gov/the-press-office/2017/03/16/press-briefing-press-secretary-sean-spicer-3162017-25); Jordan Fabian, "Trump: 'Wiretap Covers a Lot of Different Things,'" *The Hill*, March 15, 2017; Julie Hirschfeld Davis, "Using Air Quotes, White House Walks Back 'Wiretap' Talk," *New York Times*, March 13, 2017.

36. Matt Apuzzo, Matthew Rosenberg, and Emmarie Huetteman, "F.B.I. Is Investigating Trump's Russia Ties, Comey Confirms," *New York Times*, March 20, 2017.

37. Greg Miller, Karoun Demirjian, and Devlin Barrett, "House Intelligence Chair Says Trump Campaign Officials Were Ensnared in Surveillance Operations," *Washington Post*, March 22, 2017. Ryan Lizza, "The Continuing Fallout from Trump and Nunes's Fake Scandal," *New Yorker*, April 18, 2017.

38. Eli Lake, "The Resistance Cheers Tactics Trump Will Likely Use against Them," *Bloomberg View,* March 17, 2017 (www.bloomberg.com/view/articles/2017-03-17/the-resistance-cheers-tactics-trump-will-likely-use-against-them).

39. Callum Borchers, "Donald Trump's Policy on Leaks is Highly Hypocritical," *Washington Post*, March 21, 2017.

40. *The 9/11 Commission Report: Final Report of the National Commission on Terrorist Attacks Upon the United States* (New York: W. W. Norton, 2004), pp. 339–48.

41. "Intelligence under a Trump Administration," 2016 Cato Surveillance Conference, Cato Institute, Washington, D.C., December 14, 2016 (video) (www.c-span.org/video/?420109-1/cato-institute-hosts-forum-privacy-government-surveillance&start=2882).

CHAPTER 12

1. David Pollock, "How Edward Snowden Inspired a Musical Vision of the Future," *The Scotsman,* August 20, 2015 (www.scotsman.com/lifestyle/culture /music/how-edward-snowden-inspired-a-musical-vision-of-the-future-1-3863 946).

2. Laura Poitras and Glenn Greenwald, "NSA Whistleblower Edward Snowden: 'I Don't Want to Live in a Society That Does These Sort of Things,' " *The Guardian* (video), June 9, 2013.

3. James Warren, interview with Geoffrey Stone, "Snowden and the NSA: Behind the Scenes," *US News and World Report,* May 18, 2016.

4. Marcy Wheeler, "A Cosmopolitan Defense of Snowden," *EmptyWheel,* September 16, 2016 (www.emptywheel.net/2016/09/16/a-cosmopolitan-defense -of-snowden/).

5. White House, "Presidential Policy Directive—Signals Intelligence Activities (Presidential Policy Directive 28/PPD-28)," news release, January 17, 2014 (obamawhitehouse.archives.gov/the-press-office/2014/01/17/presidential-policy-directive-signals-intelligence-activities).

6. Nick Hopkins, "Former NSA Chief: Western Intelligence Agencies Must Be More Transparent," *The Guardian,* September 30, 2013 (www.theguardian. com/world/2013/sep/30/nsa-director-intelligence-public-support).

7. Charlie Savage, "Was Snowden a Russian Agent?," *New York Review of Books,* February 9, 2017.

8. Hearing transcript, Deutscher Bundestag, 1. Untersuchungsausschuss, September 8, 2016 (on file with author), pp. 28–29.

9. Glenn Greenwald, *No Place to Hide: Edward Snowden, the NSA, and the U.S. Surveillance State* (New York: Henry Holt, 2014), p. 94.

10. Jeremy Stahl, "What You Should Know about Trump's Anti-Snowden CIA Director Pick, Mike Pompeo," *Slate,* November 18, 2016 (www.slate.com/ blogs/the_slatest/2016/11/18/what_you_should_know_about_trump_s_cia_ director_pick_mike_pompeo.html).

11. Timothy Edgar, "Why Obama Should Pardon Edward Snowden," *Lawfare,* September 14, 2016 (www.lawfareblog.com/why-obama-should-pardon-edward-snowden)

12. Akhil Reed Amar, *America's Unwritten Constitution: The Precedents and Principles We Live By* (New York: Basic Books, 2012), p. 309.

13. Timothy Edgar, "Why Global Privacy Should Matter to Americans: A Reply to Jack Goldsmith," *Lawfare,* September 20, 2016 (www.lawfareblog. com/why-global-privacy-should-matter-americans-reply-jack-goldsmith).

INDEX